Alan E. Kazdin currently is Professor of Psychology at the Pennsylvania State University. He received his Ph.D. at Northwestern University (1970). He has been at Pennsylvania State University since 1971 except for a leave of absence as a Fellow at the Center for Advanced Study in the Behavioral Sciences, Stanford, California (1976-1977). Kazdin is President-Elect of the Association for Advancement of Behavior Therapy. He has been an Associate Editor of the *Journal of Applied Behavior Analysis* and presently is an Associate Editor of *Behavior Therapy*. He serves on the editorial boards of the *Journal of Consulting and Clinical Psychology, Behavior Modification, Journal of Behavior Therapy and Experimental Psychiatry,* and *Cognitive Research and Therapy*. He has authored *Behavior Modification in Applied Settings* and *The Token Economy: A Review and Evaluation* and has coauthored (with W.E. Craighead and M.J. Mahoney) *Behavior Modification: Principles, Issues, and Applications.*

G. Terence Wilson is Professor of Psychology at the Graduate School of Applied and Professional Psychology, Rutgers University. He holds graduate degrees from the University of Witwatersrand (Johannesburg) and the State University of New York at Stony Brook and was a Fellow at the Center for Advanced Study in the Behavioral Sciences, Stanford, California (1976-1977). He has served on the editorial boards of several journals including the *Journal of Consulting and Clinical Psychology, Behavior Therapy,* and *Cognitive Therapy and Research,* and is an Associate Editor of the *Journal of Applied Behavior Analysis*. He is co-author (with K.D. O'Leary) of *Behavior Therapy: Application and Outcome* and edits (with Cyril M. Franks) the *Annual Review of Behavior Therapy: Theory and Practice.*

Evaluation of Behavior Therapy: Issues, Evidence, and Research Strategies

Evaluation of Behavior Therapy:

Issues, Evidence, and Research Strategies

Alan E. Kazdin
G. Terence Wilson

Ballinger Publishing Company • Cambridge, Massachusetts
A Subsidiary of J. B. Lippincott Company

This book is printed on recycled paper.

International Standard Book Number: 0-88410-520-2

Library of Congress Catalog Card Number: 77-12006

Printed in the United States of America

Library of Congress Cataloging in Publication Data

Kazdin, Alan E
  Evaluation of behavior therapy.

  Includes bibliographical references.
    1.   Behavior therapy. 2.   Psychology, Pathological.
I. Wilson, G. Terence, 1944–   joint author.
II. Title.
RC489.B4K38   616.8'914   77-12006
ISBN 0-88410-520-2

✻

To Joann and Elaine

Contents

Chapter 1

Behavior Therapy: An Overview

Chapter 2

Comparative Clinical Outcome Studies

Chapter 3

Conceptual and Assessment Issues

Chapter 4

Research Strategies for Therapy Evaluation

Chapter 5

Summary and Conclusions

List of Tables

Foreword

Has behavior therapy after twenty years of productive exis-
tence reached a crisis? Some see the field as a passing fad while
others consider that the claims for therapeutic efficacy have
been overstated. Yet others view the various new splinter groups—from
applied behavior analysis to cognitive behavior modification—with jaun-
diced eye, or view the various new directions such as behavioral medicine
or applications to the community with some alarm. Are these new directions emerging because of failures in more traditional areas of concern? A
sense of hesitancy and uncertainty hangs over the field. Compounding this
malaise, reviews of the comparative psychotherapy literature by
Luborsky, Singer, and Luborsky (1975) and Smith and Glass (1977) conclude that everyone has won, that all psychotherapies work, and that
behavior therapy and psychodynamic psychotherapy are equally effective.

In this book, Kazdin and Wilson address this crisis in a particularly
admirable way bringing clarity out of confusion. From the beginning,
behavior therapy and psychoanalytic psychotherapy have been viewed by
many as participating in a race. Apparently the race is so close that
depending upon one's vantage point one, or other, or neither, has won.
Many of us hoped that the comparative outcome study of Sloane and his
colleagues (1975) would clarify the situation, but it did not.

Apparently no one had the temerity to challenge the question being
asked. For what, after all, is behavior therapy or psychotherapy? In this
form of the question neither procedure is well specified. Each is usually
applied to a diverse set of behavior problems, and the outcome is mea-

sured with global rating scales depending, for the most part, on patient self-report with very low correlation the observations made by different assessors. Apparently the race was being run in a fog. The question, "Is behavior therapy more or less effective than psychotherapy?" is as misguided as asking whether medicine is more effective than surgery. The more profitable question is, "What procedure is effective in which condition under what circumstances?" The more tightly each of these parameters is defined, the better will be the answer. Moreover, it turns out that we already have some answers to this more appropriate question. There are procedures that are better than others in specific circumstances. Thus the general conclusion that all are equal does not stand up to close scrutiny. Such conclusions are based on an oversimplification of the literature—a dangerous simplification which could easily mislead both therapists and researchers.

There are, however, broader issues that can easily become obscured in the question of comparative outcome. Behavior therapy is firmly linked conceptually and methodologically to the science of psychology and has brought new theory, new procedures, and, above all, new methods of evaluation to the field of psychotherapy research. These facets of behavior therapy, so often minimized, form the core of this book and should not be overlooked by the thoughtful reader. The research, inspired by systematic desensitization, is an excellent example of these aspects of behavior therapy. From the beginning Wolpe (1958) had specified the therapeutic procedure well enough to allow replication by others, and had provided a theoretical explanation of the mode of action buttressed by animal experiments. Moreover, phobia could be objectively measured along several parameters of which a behavioral avoidance task and physiologic arousal were the most used. Very quickly two interconnected lines of research developed, one pointed toward outcome, the other toward understanding mechanisms of action. The resulting ferment produced a diversity of theoretical speculation and empirical findings. Thus not only has the first procedure, systematic desensitization, been supplanted by demonstrably more effective direct exposure techniques such as flooding, shaping, and participant modelling, but also some of the parameters enhancing exposure have been identified. Indeed we can conclude that the therapy of choice for phobia is a direct exposure method. The fog has begun to lift!

One of the dangers of talking about phobia is that the old stereotype of behavior therapy only being applicable to a limited set of disorders is brought to mind. However, it will be clear to the readers of this volume that behavior therapy has potential or actual application to a wider range of problems than any other psychotherapy, and that the evidence for efficacy—however incomplete—is overwhelming when compared to that of psychoanalytic psychotherapy.

Considerations of efficacy and applicability become increasingly important as a National Health Service draws near. Should any form of psychotherapeutic service be paid for? If so, then what criteria should underlie such choices? Two seem self-evident. First, only procedures that have been demonstrated to be effective should be considered, and even then their use should be restricted (for these purposes) to the conditions in which effectiveness has been shown. Second, given a choice between two equally effective procedures, then the most cost-effective should be used. In addition, it would seem reasonable to demand that the therapeutic procedure in question be well enough specified to be replicable in the hands of a variety of therapists with different backgrounds. Similar considerations might guide therapists in choosing which procedure to use in a particular condition, and there is little doubt in my mind that the research findings over the next few years will be increasingly helpful to the practitioner.

The issues discussed in this book also have important implications for directions in research and research funding. The old-style comparative psychotherapy research project using relatively unspecified procedures and global measures will not yield useful information. Since such projects are also costly, it seems that they should no longer be funded. Instead we need investigations of the process and outcome of well-defined procedures applied to specific problems using objective measures of behavior (preferably in the natural environment), of physiologic arousal, and of self-report gathered in circumstances that minimize the demand characteristics of the usual interview. Projects in which a logical sequence of hypotheses can be tested in a series of interactive experiments would seem to be an excellent way to proceed, both in the organization of research and in research funding. A parallel but neglected issue has also been raised by the research activity of behavior therapy concerning the etiology of the various behavior problems. For while we can have effective therapy without an understanding of etiology, there seems no doubt that both our theories concerning therapeutic behavior change, and our therapeutic effectiveness would be enhanced by such knowledge. Small forays into this arena have been made but many more are needed if we are to have a useful experimental psychopathology.

As research grows and the range of behavior change procedures widens, a new view of behavior therapy is beginning to emerge, as an applied research endeavor with firm links to psychology. In this light the apparent splintering of the field becomes emphases of inquiry. It is the approach that matters. Differing theories and hypotheses should be welcomed and should be subject not only to informed debate but also to experimental scrutiny, always remembering that the desired end is to enhance the efficacy of behavior change procedures and our understanding of human behavior.

This book clarifies the view of the emergent field of behavior therapy and as such should be useful to those within and outside the field who are interested in the therapeutic applications of behavior change procedures.

Stewart Agras
Stanford, California

Preface

Although it is something of a custom to write a book while privileged to be a Fellow at the Center for Advanced Study in the Behavioral Sciences in Stanford, California, neither of us initially had any intentions of embarking on the present venture. Aside from other competing interests and obligations, the prospect of contributing still another book to the behavioral literature, which has far outdistanced substantive scientific and clinical accomplishments, was unexciting. Yet we were ultimately persuaded to pursue this project for three reasons.

First, during our many discussions with the other members of our behavior therapy group at the Center—Stewart Agras, Nate Azrin, Alex George, Walter Mischel, and Jack Rachman—it became clear that unresolved and often unidentified issues in the evaluation of outcome of behavioral methods needed to be made explicit. Although all of us had participated in numerous published evaluations of component parts of behavior therapy, no single volume existed that provided an overall appraisal. More important, a systematic analysis of the comparative clinical outcome literature and the critical research issues it raises had yet to be conducted by behaviorally-inclined investigators.

The second reason concerned a meeting with the Foundation Fund for Research in Psychiatry, an organization that provided funding for the presence of a behavioral group at the Center. Members of the Foundation—Peter Dews, Daniel X. Freedman, Frederick C. Redlich, Melvin Sabshin, and Robert S. Wallerstein—wished to know the status of behavior therapy in comparison with the traditional psychotherapies. Although receptive to our views about the merits of current behavioral research strategies, their prime interest lay in the question of the comparative clinical outcome literature. The consensus of our behavioral group was that comparative outcome research as traditionally conceived and executed was not the place to find answers to the question of therapeutic efficacy. However, members of the Foundation argued persuasively that comparative research would inevitably be relied upon in making important decisions with far-reaching consequences. For example, the inevitability of some sort of national health insurance system would require legislators to make judgments at some level about the relative merits of different approaches to mental-health services.

Finally, as we began researching the topic, it was clear that there was something of a resurgence of interest in the question of comparative outcome studies. The recent or imminent publication of several reviews of the outcome literature with which we found ourselves in disagreement provided the final impetus to conduct a critical appraisal of the evaluation of behavior therapy. Comparative outcome research warrants special evaluation in its own right. Whenever a comparative therapy investigation is published that contrasts techniques from divergent conceptual positions, it tends to receive a great deal of attention. The attention is not always commensurate with the information that can be drawn based upon sound conceptual and methodological grounds. Yet, in the end comparative research often is viewed as the bottom line for drawing conclusions about treatment efficacy. The snag is that comparative research, at least as currently conducted in the majority of behavior therapy and psychotherapy studies, has unique problems and limitations that need to be placed in perspective.

We had two major purposes in undertaking this volume. First, mindful of the concerns of the Foundation Fund for Research in Psychiatry, which we took to reflect the probably prevailing attitude among the broader community of mental-health professionals, we hoped to present a frankly realistic view of the efficacy of behavior therapy. Since we have participated for some time in behavioral research and have distinct positions on substantive issues, it is quite possible that our "realistic" view might reflect an all too favorable appraisal of the field. While we do not adhere to the "panacea view" of behavior therapy, we must acknowledge our own conceptual commitments in advance. The other purpose was to encourage needed new directions in outcome research strategies in behavior therapy in particular, but also in the field of therapy in general. This purpose helped cushion the biases that may have entered in fulfilling the other purpose of the volume. By elaborating the needs for improved research strategies, we have tried to convey commitment to the processes through which effective interventions are developed and the criteria for assessing efficacy rather than adherence to any particular technique or singular conceptual approach. It seemed especially fitting to undertake an overall evaluation of the strengths and weaknesses of behavioral methods while Fellows at the Center for Advanced Study in the Behavioral Sciences, where Wolpe had completed his pioneering book just twenty years earlier. Indeed, our sense of historical nicety was served well by planning much of the present volume in the very study in which Wolpe had worked

We are aware that many, including some of our behavioral colleagues, will not necessarily concur with our evaluation. Evaluating the outcome of contemporary behavior therapy is an imposing task. We are not un-aware of some of the shortcomings of the present attempt. However, we hope that we have achieved a reasonably balanced and objective ap-praisal, one more credible than the doctrinaire extremes of impassioned advocacy of behavior therapy as a panacea or its outright rejection as an ineffective or even dangerous source of mechanistic manipulation. We are especially appalled at crass commercial propaganda that in its hyperbolic selling of behavior therapy debases the whole endeavor by its unsubstan-tiated claims for success (e.g., *New York Times Book Review,* Sunday, 29, May 1977). To the extent that this volume provides a corrective to this damaging sort of oversell and also encourages improved research evalua-tion of behavioral methods, our efforts will have been amply rewarded.

The opportunity to complete this volume was made possible by our Fellowships at the Center for Advanced Study in the Behavioral Sciences through the financial support of the Foundation Fund for Research in Psychiatry, the National Institute for Mental Health (Grant number 1 T32 MH14581), and the Spencer Foundation. In addition, we are grateful to our respective universities—Pennsylvania State and Rutgers—for partly supporting our year at the Center.

It would be impossible to improve upon the appreciative comments that have been heaped upon the Center by previous Fellows at this most idyllic and stimulating of intellectual and social environments. We wish nonetheless to express our deep gratitude to the Center, its staff, and its director, Gardner Lindzey. It is with special pleasure and appreciation that we thank the members of our behavior therapy group at the Center, good friends and esteemed colleagues one and all. Albert Bandura de-serves our thanks for his generous assistance and feedback. While these fellows influenced our thinking in countless ways, the final responsibility for the views expressed here is ours and ours alone. This responsibility is shared, for we have contributed equally to this volume. The order of authorship is alphabetical.

Finally, we wish to express our gratitude to specific staff members at the Center whose constant kindness, congeniality, and camaraderie added immensely to this wonderful experience. Margaret Amara and Christine Hoth tracked down books, journal articles and the like with patience and persistence. Kay Jenks, Anna Tower, and Mary Tye typed the manuscript. Kay—a morale-boosting friend—also aided in other ways, cutting through our rougher drafts and sticking to her task despite competing responsibilities. And last, and certainly least, we thank our many Fellow volleyball players at the Center for their cooperation in allowing us to indulge ourselves in the philosophy of *Mens sana in corpore sano*—apparent, we hope, in the book, if not in our court performances.

Chapter 1

Behavior Therapy: An Overview

It is no longer possible to engage in a serious discussion of behavior therapy without specifying precisely one's conceptualization of the field.[a] The once simple definition of behavior therapy as the application of "modern learning theory" (conditioning principles) to clinical disorders is now part of its short, successful, and often stormy history. Contemporary behavior therapy is marked by a diversity of views, a broad range of heterogeneous procedures with different rationales, and open debate about conceptual bases, methodological requirements, and evidence of efficacy. In short, there is no clearly agreed upon or commonly accepted definition of behavior therapy.

Our own views about the historical development and present nature of behavior therapy have been spelled out in other publications (e.g., Kazdin, 1975a, 1977d, in press e; O'Leary & Wilson, 1975; Wilson, in press b, in press c). There is no need to repeat them here. However, it is useful to outline briefly the several major conceptual approaches within behavior modification. The approaches embrace various theoretical positions about the nature of human behavior, a particular therapeutic focus, a set of intervention techniques, and research evaluation strategies. The different approaches in contemporary behavior modification include applied behavior analysis, a neobehavioristic mediational model, social-learning theory, cognitive behavior modification, and multimodal behavior therapy. The purpose in delineating these different approaches is to identify the breadth of behavior modification. The schema for referring to the different

[a] The term "behavior therapy" is used synonymously with "behavior modification" throughout this volume. Although some writers have distinguished these two terms, there has been no consistent use, and little has been gained in the process (Wilson, in press c).

approaches is not necessarily exhaustive nor the only manner in which the subject matter can be divided. However, the present schema encompasses conceptual models and treatment approaches in current use.[b]

CONTEMPORARY CONCEPTUALIZATIONS OF BEHAVIOR THERAPY

Applied Behavior Analysis

Applied behavior analysis can be defined broadly as the application of interventions to alter behaviors of clinical and social importance (Baer, Wolf & Risley, 1968). The hallmark of applied behavior analysis is the focus upon overt behaviors in settings where clients normally function and the application of interventions that rely upon changes in the client's environment. Exemplified by the research in the *Journal of Applied Behavior Analysis,* the approach toward treatment is philosophically consistent with Skinner's (1953, 1971) doctrine of radical behaviorism. Applied behavior analysis typically relies upon techniques derived from operant conditioning. One of the most fundamental assumptions of operant conditioning is that behavior is a function of its consequences. As such, most treatment procedures are based upon altering the relationship between specific overt behaviors and their consequences. Consistent with operant conditioning, applied behavior analysis eschews the modification and analysis of cognitive processes and private events. Treatment techniques are based upon rearranging environmental events and consequences largely independently of considerations of the individual's perceptions, cognitions, and similar processes.[c]

A distinct characteristic of applied behavior analysis is its strategy for evaluating treatment interventions. Applied behavior analysis has focused on the intensive study of the individual subject similar to the approach of the experimental analysis of behavior derived from animal laboratory research. The behavior of the subject usually is examined under highly controlled and continuously monitored conditions. The effects of the interventions are evaluated in any of a number of single-case experimental

[b] Not treated in detail is Lazarus's (1976) multimodal behavior therapy which is severely criticized by some behavior therapists as a form of eclecticism that is inaccurately described as behavior therapy (Eysenck, 1970). Lazarus (1977) himself has essentially placed multimodal therapy beyond behavior therapy. Although there is some historical connection and considerable overlap in terms of therapeutic techniques, multimodal therapy departs from behavior therapy on both conceptual and methodological grounds.

[c] The techniques, intervention focus, and accomplishments of applied behavior analysis have been elaborated in several sources (e.g., Brigham & Catania, in press; Kazdin, 1975a; Ramp & Semb, 1975.).

designs where the subject serves as his or her own control (Hersen & Barlow, 1976; Kazdin, in press d; Leitenberg, 1973).

The general approach of applied behavior analysis is to search for environmental variables that will effect marked changes in behavior. The need for effecting clinically important changes dictates the search for extremely potent variables. In addition, the effects of the variables should be sufficiently clear and replicable to obviate the need for statistical evaluation. Hence, applied behavior analysis has relied heavily upon visual inspection rather than statistical analyses to evaluate the impact of treatment, although there are exceptions.

Interventions in applied behavior analysis include a wide range of techniques based upon reinforcement, punishment, extinction, stimulus control, and other principles, most of which have been derived from laboratory research (Kazdin, 1975a; Sulzer-Azaroff & Mayer, 1977). The techniques have been applied on an individual basis or across several subjects simultaneously, as, for example, in the case of a ward of psychiatric patients. Although operant techniques were originally extended to populations considered to have limited cognitive capacities, including chronic psychotic patients and the mental retarded, the range of treatment applications has extended well beyond any single population with common characteristics. Applied behavior analysis includes interventions in institutional, rehabilitation, and educational settings as well as the community at large, the home, and outpatient treatment (Kazdin, in press a).

The Neobehavioristic
Mediational S-R Model

This approach has been defined as the application of the principles of conditioning, especially classical conditioning and counterconditioning, to the treatment of abnormal behavior. It derives from the pioneering contributions of Eysenck (1960, 1964), Rachman (1963), and Wolpe (1958), who sought to base theory and practice in behavior therapy on the learning theories of such figures as Pavlov, Guthrie, Hull, Mowrer, and Miller. This has always been a "liberalized" S-R approach in which intervening variables and hypothetical constructs play a prominent part. The two-factor theory of avoidance learning (Mowrer, 1947, 1960) is a classic example. According to this mediational theory, escape-avoidance behavior was assumed to be acquired and maintained on the basis of the reduction of a classically conditioned fear response to the aversive stimulus.

The construct of fear or anxiety has been central to this conceptualization of behavior therapy because the concern with neurotic disorders has always been its major therapeutic concern. For example, the treatment techniques of systematic desensitization and flooding, which are most closely associated with this model, are both directed toward the extinction of the underlying anxiety that is assumed to maintain phobic disorders. Imaginal, and to a lesser extent, verbal mediational processes are inherent in the techniques that derive from this view. The rationale behind all these methods is that covert processes follow the same laws of learning that govern overt behaviors.

The neobehavioristic nature of this approach dictates that unobservable processes such as the imaginal representation of an anxiety-eliciting event are anchored to antecedent and consequent operational referents. Thus, psychophysiological studies have shown that symbolic representations of a feared stimulus produce autonomic arousal similar to that evoked by the stimulus itself. Moreover, these arousal responses have been shown to covary systematically with the introduction and repeated presentation of hierarchy items during systematic desensitization in a manner consistent with conditioning concepts (Lang, Melamed, & Hart, 1970).

It is important to note that although frequent use is made of symbolic processes such as imagery in behavioral techniques of this genre, covert activities have usually been strictly defined in terms of S and R (or rather, as a chain of s and r reactions). Cognitive formulations of these mediational constructs have found little favor in this approach. This emphasis on conditioning as opposed to cognitions as the conceptual basis of behavior therapy is not surprising in view of the early reliance on principles from the animal conditioning laboratory and the vehement reaction against seemingly mentalistic concepts that characterized early behaviorism (Koch, 1964).

Social-Learning Theory

The social-learning conceptualization of behavior therapy is a comprehensive approach to human functioning in which both deviant and prosocial behaviors are assumed to be developed and maintained on the basis of three distinct regulatory systems (Bandura, 1977c). Some response patterns are primarily influenced by external stimulus events and are affected largely by classical conditioning processes. External reinforcement constitutes a second form of influence. The third and most important system of regulatory influence is assumed to operate through cognitive mediational processes.

In terms of a social-learning analysis, the influence of environmental events on the acquisition and regulation of behavior is largely determined by cognitive processes. The latter determine what environmental influences are attended to, how they are perceived, and whether they might affect future action. Symbolic modeling is one of the best known and most widely used methods derived from the social-learning approach (Bandura, 1971; Rachman, 1976b; Rosenthal & Bandura, in press). In modeling, learning is assumed to occur through coding of representational processes based upon exposure to instructional, observational, or imagined material (Bandura, 1970). As usually conducted, modeling entails observation of the behavior to be developed. Learning occurs through observation alone without the need for direct reinforcement of the specific behavior that is acquired.

A second characteristic of social-learning theory is that psychological functioning is considered to involve a reciprocal interaction between a person's behavior and the environment. A person is both the agent as well as the object of environmental influence. A third characteristic of social-learning theory, related to the notion that the person is an agent of change, is that it highlights the human capacity of self-directed behavior change. Operant conditioning accounts of behavioral self-control ultimately reduce to analyses of situational, environmental control and fundamentally deny the notion of *self*-control (Rachlin, 1974). In addition to the acquisition and maintenance of behavior, activation and persistence of behavior is based mainly on cognitive mechanisms. The importance assigned to cognitive processes that explain how learning experiences have lasting effects and serve to activate future actions enables social-learning theory to explain the fact that humans initiate behavior that, at least in part, shapes their own destinies (Thoresen & Mahoney, 1974).

A fourth feature of the social-learning view of behavior therapy is the theoretical integration of the different sources of influence governing behavior that it provides. This is illustrated in Bandura's (1977b) conceptual analysis of the modification of phobic behavior. The key assumption in this analysis is that psychological treatment methods produce changes in a person's expectations of self-efficacy. Self-efficacy is considered to determine the activation and maintenance behavioral strategies for coping with anxiety-eliciting situations. Self-efficacy expectations are modified by different sources of psychological influence, including performance-based feedback (e.g., participant modeling), vicarious information (e.g., symbolic modeling), physiological changes (e.g., systematic desensitization), and verbal persuasion (e.g., traditional psychotherapy).

Cognitive Behavior Modification

The most recent development within behavior therapy is the emergence of what is referred to as cognitive behavior modification or cognitive behavior therapy (Meichenbaum, 1974, 1977; Mahoney, 1974a; Mahoney & Arnkoff, in press). Actually, this development incorporates a number of different views and therapy techniques, some of which have developed independently of behavior modification. Cognitively-based techniques merged with developments within behavior modification to constitute a new area.[d] The unifying characteristic of cognitive behavior modification techniques is the emphasis on the importance of cognitive processes and private events as mediators of behavior change. Implicit assumptions about the world, interpretations and attributions of one's own behavior, thoughts, images, self-statements, sets, strategies of responding, and similar processes are considered the source of a client's problem and the determinants of therapeutic change.[e]

The oldest and most prominent cognitive behavior therapy is Ellis's (1962) rational-emotive therapy, an approach that until the 1970s had been beyond the mainstream of behavior therapy. The therapy is based upon the notion that psychological disorders arise from faulty or irrational thought patterns. These thought patterns are evident in implicit self-defeating verbalizations that arise from assumptions that an individual makes about the world and events that happen to him (Ellis, 1962, 1970). Therapy seeks to make these assumptions explicit, to replace them with more adaptive interpretations of the world, and to have the individual act in situations in such a way as to bolster these adaptive assumptions.

Another cognitive behavior therapy technique is self-instructional training (Meichenbaum, 1977). This technique, based on a rationale similar to that of rational-emotive therapy, develops in clients the ability to provide covert self-instructions to guide behavior. Depending upon the therapeutic focus, the client is systematically trained to provide overt and ultimately covert statements to promote adaptive behaviors and responses that meet the demands of the problematic situation.

Another technique is referred to as cognitive therapy (Beck, 1976). As with the previous techniques, the goal of cognitive therapy is to develop rational, adaptive thought patterns. These patterns are developed through behavioral and cognitive tasks. The former include the prescription of an explicit activity schedule, graded tasks aimed at providing success experiences, and various homework assignments. The latter include techniques to help the client obtain a more rational and objective perspective regarding his or her thoughts in order to recognize counterproductive thought patterns. A number of other treatments can be included in cogni-

---

[d] The techniques and varied views of cognitive behavior modification have been reviewed elsewhere (Mahoney & Arnkoff, in press; Meichenbaum, 1974, 1977.)

[e] The domain of therapeutic techniques included under the rubric of cognitive behavior modification is not consistently defined, so a definitive list of procedures is difficult to provide. For example, some investigators include any procedures that rely upon internal states of the client, including imagery, thought patterns, and self-verbalizations (e.g., Mahoney, 1974a; Meichenbaum, 1974); others tend to restrict use to procedures that rely heavily upon thought processes (Beck, 1970). Only major techniques generally included in this category will be provided.

tive therapy techniques, including problem solving, stress inoculation, coping skills training, language behavior therapy, thought stopping, attribution therapy, and others. In many cases, these techniques represent procedures not addressed by other conceptualizations and approaches within behavior therapy; in other cases, the procedures merely emphasize components of a given technique whose interpretation has yet to be resolved (Wilson, in press b).

CHARACTERISTICS OF THE BEHAVIOR THERAPIES

Common Features

For the purposes of evaluation of the field in this volume, we have adopted the broad view of behavior therapy, including within our purview, for example, the "cognitive therapy" of Beck (1976). Although the preceding approaches often involve conceptual differences, there remains a common core of fundamental assumptions that behavior therapists hold. In the ultimate analysis, behavior therapy is defined in terms of two basic characteristics: one is a psychological model of human behavior that differs fundamentally from the traditional intrapsychic, psychodynamic, or quasi-disease model of mental illness; the other is a commitment to scientific method, measurement, and evaluation. The rejection of the quasi-disease or psychodynamic model of abnormal behavior has profound implications for assessment, treatment, and evaluation. In the behavioral model, abnormal behavior that is not a function of specific brain dysfunction or biochemical disturbance is assumed to be governed by the same principles that regulate normal behavior. Many types of abnormal behavior, formerly regarded as illnesses in themselves, or as signs and symptoms of illness, are better construed as nonpathological "problems of living" (key examples include the neuroses, various forms of sexual deviance, and conduct disorders). Most abnormal behavior is assumed to be acquired and maintained in the same manner as normal behavior; it can be treated directly through the application of behavioral procedures.

Based upon a social-learning analysis, behavioral assessment focuses on the *current* determinants of behavior rather than the post hoc analysis of possible historical antecedents. *Specificity* is the hallmark of behavioral assessment and treatment, and it is assumed that the person is best understood and described by what he or she does in particular situations. Treatment requires a fine-grain analysis of the problem into components or subparts and is targeted at these components specifically and systematically.

The scientific commitment in behavior therapy dictates that treatment is either derived from or consistent with both the substance and method of psychology as it is broadly conceived. Treatment methods must be described with sufficient precision to be measured objectively and replicated; the experimental evaluation of methods and concepts is essential.

Evaluation of Behavior Therapy

Evaluation of behavior therapy is closely tied to both the conceptual model and the scientific foundation on which it is based. The model influences the sort of questions about evaluation that should be asked as well as the methods used to answer them. As later chapters show, failure to recognize the conceptual context often has resulted in misguided and methodologically marred outcome research, particularly with respect to comparative outcome research. Scientific methodology provides the means to complete this research.

The extensive professional impact of behavior therapy in clinical psychology and psychiatry, medicine, education, and rehabilitation has been well documented (e.g., Bandura, 1969; Brady, 1973; Franks & Wilson, 1973–1977; Hoon & Lindsley, 1974; Kazdin, 1975c; Thoresen, 1973; Williams & Gentry, 1977). Possibly the most significant facet of the development of behavior therapy has been the dramatic increase in research studies on clinical behavior change. It is safe to say that in the field of psychotherapy, which has long been inimical towards attempts at experimentally controlled investigations of treatment outcome, behavior therapy has generated significantly more controlled outcome research than any other form of psychological treatment (Chesser, 1976).

Of course, debate abounds over the scientific adequacy and clinical relevance of much of this unprecedented outpouring of research. That the quality of much of the research is uneven is quite clear; that better controlled, improved research studies are still needed to identify mechanisms of behavior change and establish therapeutic efficacy is indisputable. Subjectivity, personal prejudice, and pet notions have not been vanquished in the field of psychotherapy—or in behavior therapy for that matter. Yet, the significant fact is that this experimentally-based investigation of the treatment process and outcome has been done and, even more important, will continue to be done in the future.

Aside from the inestimable importance of the mere subjecting of clinical theories and treatment methods to experimental testing, and the sheer quantity of research that has thus evolved, behavior therapy has given rise to several different forms of research strategies: laboratory analysis under rigorously controlled conditions of actual treatment methods with individuals with genuine problems, often misleadingly slighted as mere "analogue" studies; single-case experimental designs that enable cause-effect relationships to be demonstrated in the treatment of the individual client; dismantling and constructive research strategies; more sophisticated control groups and more discriminating measurement criteria. These are among the many methodological innovations and refinements that have developed directly as a function of the growth of behavior therapy. Whatever else, this has been a signal contribution. It provides the means for accomplishing what is still a distant goal: a clinical psychology of experimentally validated treatment techniques and applications that supplants the doctrinaire divisions that contemporary schools of therapy display.

Estimates of the efficacy of behavior therapy have varied widely. In contrast to its initial hostile reception at the hands of the orthodox psychotherapists, behavior therapy is now generally regarded as at least of some value as a treatment modality, even among nonbehavioral therapists (e.g., American Psychiatric Association, 1973; Bergin & Strupp, 1970; Strupp, 1976). Often overlooked is the fact that there is no consensus among its proponents on the outcome efficacy of behavior therapy. The first significant estimate of behavior therapy success was Wolpe's (1958) controversial claim that 90 percent of the 210 adult neurotic clients he treated were either "cured" or "much improved." Sampling bias and the lack of appropriate controls and objective measures make it difficult if not impossible to infer much from these well-publicized results. In his analysis of his results, for example, Wolpe (1958) excluded some clients who had received less than fifteen sessions of therapy. Evidence from other studies has repeatedly shown that clients who drop out of therapy are those least likely to improve (Franks & Wilson, 1976). In this instance, therefore, the effects of behavior therapy were confounded with client-selection factors. Similar problems of insufficient control and, hence, of difficulty of interpretation attach to Lazarus's (1963) estimate of 78 percent overall success in the treatment of 408 adult neurotic clients. Treatment of 126 particularly severe cases, Lazarus reported, yielded a success rate of 62 percent. Other clinical estimates of efficacy have been frequently reported.

Historically, the pioneering claims of Wolpe (1958) and Lazarus (1963) for the apparently dramatic efficacy of behavior therapy were undoubtedly important in generating interest in an alternative approach to psychodynamic therapy and in prompting subsequent investigators to conduct controlled evaluations. In this sense, their value was immense. However, global and subjective judgments of this sort are not in themselves useful in the systematic evaluation of outcome. Indeed, such claims today serve more to distract from serious analysis than to further it. In the absence of suitable controls and objective outcome measures, global estimates of success based upon heterogeneous samples treated with diverse techniques often only fan the flames of controversy between different therapeutic approaches and lend themselves to internecine disputes between rival authorities within behavior therapy. Thus, Lazarus (1969) questioned the long-term success of the clients Wolpe (1958) had originally treated and asserted the superiority of a "broad-spectrum" approach as opposed to "narrow-band" behavior therapy. Specifically, Lazarus (1971) cited 122 clients treated with his broad-spectrum, or multimodal, approach whose long-term improvement he reported to be superior to that achieved with other behavioral methods. In turn, Wolpe (1976) rejected Lazarus's (1971) claim of greater durability of his multimodal approach. Citing Lazarus's (1971) statement that forty-one of his clients (36 percent) relapsed "anywhere from one week to 6 years after therapy," Wolpe (1976) concludes that this is "at least 10 times the relapse rate that behavior therapists have found (e.g., Wolpe, 1958)." Conflicting claims of this sort appear as inevitable as they are divisive and inconclusive as long as subjective claims derived from uncontrolled clinical practice of any nature are put forward as evaluations of outcome. The virtue of the behavioral outcome research studies has been the attempt to replace such clinical judgments with experimental evidence.

The Applicability of Behavior Therapy

Just as behavior therapy is still often viewed as a naive form of behaviorism that is limited to simplistic, nonmediational stimulus-response theory, so the misconception persists that its applicability is restricted to monosymptomatic phobias and simple habits. In this sense behavior therapy is seen as a useful but limited adjunct to other more traditional therapeutic approaches. However, this view reflects a basic misunderstanding of the conceptual basis, empirical foundations, and clinical utility of behavior therapy.

The position that behavior therapy is of limited applicability to psychiatric behavior disorders is expressed by Marks (1976b). In his estimation, behavior therapy "can help perhaps 10% of all *adult* psychiatric patients when used as the chief instrument of change. This means that 90% of all adult cases require other approaches as the main form of treatment" (p. 254). For phobic disorders and compulsive rituals, Marks (1976b) considers behavior therapy the "treatment of choice." It is regarded as "helpful" in the case of sexual dysfunction and deviance, social skills deficits, habit disorders, and some personality disorders. Behavior therapy is "*not of value*," concludes Marks (1976b), in cases of acute schizophrenia, severe depression, hypomania, and "in adult neurotic patients for whom clearly definable goals cannot be worked out" (p. 254).

Arriving at a quantitative estimate of applicability across the often bewilderingly complex range of behavior disorders that confront the practicing therapist is arbitrary at best, pointless at worst. A more accurate perspective from the vantage point of the psychiatric specialist is provided by Chesser (1976), who comments that

> if one considers behaviour therapy as a broad approach which informs and influences the total management of the patient not only in hospital, then the range of applicability can be extended to crisis intervention in families . . . social work . . . group therapy . . . marital problems . . . family therapy . . . interpersonal problems, chronic neurotic depression, weight disorders, alcohol and drug abuse, some organic disorders, and the rehabilitation of patients with organic deficits or chronic schizophrenia (p. 302).

It is not without irony that discussion has tended to center on the breadth of applicability of behavior therapy when conventional psychodynamic psychotherapy has long since been limited predominantly to certain neurotic and personality disorders in adults. Applications of psychodynamic psychotherapy to the addictive disorders, severe forms of sexual dysfunction and deviance, and the full range of childhood problems, among others, have not been extensive. Evaluation of the efficacy of behavior therapy—or of any form of psychological treatment—must include this wider range of problems, which are more representative of the psychological problems in the community at large than the overemphasized, intensively treated and studied adult neurotic reactions of largely middle-class society. A summary overview of some of the diverse applications of behavioral methods to different problems of personal and social significance is presented in the next section.

THE EMPIRICAL BASIS OF BEHAVIOR THERAPY

A total accounting of the empirical evidence for the efficacy of behavior therapy would require a systematic analysis of the results of all behavioral techniques that have been applied to the exceptionally wide range of diverse psychological, medical, and educational problems represented in the burgeoning behavioral treatment literature. The magnitude of such a task would call to mind the trials of Sisyphus, let alone the labors of Hercules, and is obviously beyond the scope of this or any other single volume. The present section is therefore *illustrative* rather than exhaustive in the presentation of outcome evidence on the more commonly used behavioral methods with respect to the more frequent or publicized disorders. Our intent is to provide some idea—albeit incomplete—of the scope and diversity of behavioral interventions, to point out some of the different research strategies employed in behavior research and therapy, and to summarize the nature of much of the evidence indicating the efficacy of behavior therapy. The studies discussed below are restricted to research designs in which a behavioral method was compared to one or more of the following treatment conditions: another behavioral method, a placebo control group, or no treatment. Comparative outcome studies in which behavioral methods are evaluated against specific nonbehavioral alternative treatments are discussed in detail in Chapter 2.

Neurotic Disorders

The pioneers of the clinical practice of behavior therapy with adults, such as Wolpe (1958) and Lazarus (1958, 1961), treated predominantly neurotic outpatients. Applications of different behavioral methods to neurotic disorders continues to be especially common. As a result, behavior therapy is often identified with neurotic disorders. Indeed, many of the best known and most widely used behavioral techniques were developed within the context of treating anxiety reactions and avoidance behavior. Systematic desensitization, relaxation training, flooding, modeling and its variants, assertion training, and thought stopping are all cases in point.

Anxiety and Phobic Reactions. Anxiety, operationally defined in terms of a conditioned autonomic response and/or overt avoidance behavior, has been a favorite focus of behavior therapy. Of the multitude of methods used to treat anxiety-related disorders, systematic desensitization must rank as the most intensively researched on record. In this regard many impressive statistics can be bandied around. Suffice it to note that a cursory count by Kazdin and Wilcoxon (1976) of controlled group outcome studies in only five journals between the years 1970 and 1974 revealed seventy-four such studies.[f] In part, the attraction of systematic desensitization for experimentally-minded clinical researchers lay in the procedural precision with which it had been described (a relative rarity in the history of psychological treatment methods). In part, the early claims for its dramatic success encouraged further experimental investigation.

Several of the comparative outcome studies that bear directly on the evaluation of the efficacy of systematic desensitization are discussed in the following chapter. An annual accounting of outcome research on systematic desensitization, flooding, assertion training, modeling and its variants is available in Franks and Wilson (1973-1977). For the present purposes, reference need only be made to the conclusions of several exhaustive and methodologically searching reviews of the desensitization research literature. In his appraisal, Paul (1969b) arrived at the following

[f] The journals included the *Journal of Abnormal Psychology, Journal of Consulting and Clinical Psychology, Behavior Therapy, Behaviour Research and Therapy,* and the *Journal of Behavior Therapy and Experimental Psychiatry.*

verdict: "The findings were overwhelmingly positive, and for the first time in the history of psychological treatments, a specific treatment package reliably produced measurable benefits for clients across a broad range of distressing problems in which anxiety was of fundamental importance" (p. 159). Developments over the succeeding years, including such well-controlled demonstrations of efficacy as Gelder, Bancroft, Gath, Johnston, Mathews, and Shaw's (1973) study, have done little to modify this conclusion. Systematic desensitization has proved effective not only in the treatment of simple animal phobias, but also for more complex social anxieties and agoraphobic disorders (e.g., Gelder et al., 1973), as well as asthma (Moore, 1965), insomnia (e.g., Steinmark & Borkovec, 1974), and sexual dysfunction (see below). Leitenberg (1976a), for example, has concluded: "Systematic desensitization is demonstrably more effective than both no treatment and every psychotherapy variant with which it has so far been compared" (p. 131). And while there is considerable controversy over the therapeutic mechanisms of systematic desensitization, few psychodynamicists seem to dispute the efficacy of the overall treatment package (e.g., Weitzman, 1967).

Aside from its applied utility as an effective treatment technique, systematic desensitization has been invaluable in two other ways. First, it has provided a treatment prototype for the laboratory investigation of the maintenance, measurement, and modification of fear (e.g., Borkovec & O'Brien, 1976; Lang, 1969). Second, as an effective, easily replicable treatment method it can serve as a standard of comparison against which newer behavioral techniques can be evaluated and as a testing ground for conflicting theoretical positions (e.g., Bandura, 1977b).

Reinforced practice is a treatment technique that includes repeated graded practice in approaching the phobic situation, consistent feedback of improvement, social reinforcement for progress, and instructions designed to inculcate expectancies of therapeutic gain (Leitenberg, 1976a). Compared to no-treatment control subjects, reinforced practice has been shown to be effective in the treatment of a wide variety of different fears (Leitenberg & Callahan, 1973). Moreover, both Barlow, Agras, Leitenberg, and Wincze (1970) and Crowe, Marks, Agras, and Leitenberg (1972) have demonstrated its superiority relative to systematic desensitization in the treatment of snake-fearful subjects and phobic outpatients, respectively.

Participant modeling is a technique that resembles reinforced practice. In contrast to systematic desensitization, which is directed toward extinguishing underlying conditioned autonomic responses that purportedly mediate overt avoidance behavior, reinforced practice and participant modeling effect change by modifying avoidance behavior directly. In the latter procedure the therapist first models the appropriate behavior, assists the individual in the task of approaching the feared situation or object, and then gradually withdraws this supportive function as the individual develops independence. Well-controlled comparative outcome studies have clearly shown that participant modeling is more effective that both systematic desensitization and symbolic modeling (e.g., Bandura, Blanchard, & Ritter, 1969; Thase & Moss, 1976).

Flooding is a method in which the client is exposed to the maximum-intensity fear-producing situation directly without any graduated approach. This exposure might be symbolic or in vivo. Real-life exposure has been shown to be more effective than imaginal presentation of fearful stimuli (e.g., Stern & Marks, 1973), unless the client engages in self-directed in vivo exposure between therapy sessions. In this case, the superiority of flooding treatment sessions in vivo appears to be reduced (Mathews, Johnston, Lancashire, Munby, Shaw, & Gelder, 1976). Marks, Boulougouris, and Marset (1971) showed that flooding (combining both imaginal and in vivo exposure) was consistently superior to systematic desensitization in the treatment of simple phobias and severe agoraphobia. Similarly, Crowe et al. (1972) found that flooding in imagination produced greater improvement than systematic desensitization, although this difference was not statistically significant. Finally, Gelder et al. (1973) failed to demonstrate any significant difference between flooding and systematic desensitization, although both treatments were superior to a placebo control treatment.

Obsessive-Compulsive Disorders. Obsessive-compulsive disorders have remained refractory to modification by the full panoply of psychiatric treatments, ranging from psychotherapy to chemotherapy and lobotomy (e.g., Goodwin, Guze, & Robins, 1969; Kringlen, 1965). Systematic desensitization has similarly proven ineffective. However, performance-based methods such as in vivo flooding and participant modeling have shown considerable success (see Rachman & Hodgson, in press). A two-year follow-up of compulsive clients treated with these methods by Marks, Rachman, and Hodgson (1975) showed that fourteen were much improved, one improved, and five unchanged. In contrast to the rapid success of the participant modeling method, a control treatment of progressive muscular relaxation had no significant effect on compulsive behavior. Similar results were obtained by Röper, Rachman, and Marks (1975).

An important procedural element of the behavioral treatment employed by Marks et al. (1975) was client-directed response prevention. Meyer (1966) and Levy and Meyer (1971) had originally shown the efficacy of staff-supervised prevention of compulsive rituals after inpatients had been exposed to stimuli that triggered the compulsive. A well-controlled outcome study by Mills, Agras, Barlow, and Mills (1973) showed that response prevention produced substantial and lasting reduction in compulsive behavior in all five patients treated. The use of single-case experimental methodology identified response prevention as the agent of therapeutic change. Booster treatments and procedures designed to facilitate generalization of improvement to the client's home environment are often necessary for long-term success. However, it can be concluded that participant modeling with response prevention is effective and is the treatment of first choice in the treatment of compulsive rituals (Chesser, 1976; Rachman & Hodgson, in press). Few controlled studies on the modification of obsessional states unaccompanied by compulsive behaviors have been conducted. While promising, behavioral methods have yet to be shown to be effective in these cases (Leitenberg, 1976a; Rachman, 1976).

Other Neurotic Disorders. Behavioral treatment of hysterical reactions have been confined largely to uncontrolled clinical reports. Impressive evidence on the highly effective treatment of depression has been reported by Rush, Beck, Kovacs, and Hollon (1977) (see Chapter 2). The extensive applications of behavior therapy to psychophysiological disorders are summarized below in the section on medical and psychophysiological applications.

Sexual Dysfunction and Deviance

Behavioral methods for the treatment of sexual dysfunction have been accepted more readily by nonbehavioral practitioners than almost any other form of behavior therapy (Kaplan, 1974). Many of the techniques described in the previous section on neurotic disorders have been used in the treatment of sexual disorders in addition to a number of procedures designed specifically for these problems. Perhaps the most dramatic demonstration of the efficacy of the direct behavioral treatment of sexual dysfunction has been Masters and Johnson's (1970) two-week rapid therapy program. Of 790 individuals treated, only 142 (18.9 percent) were treatment failures at the end of therapy. A five-year follow-up based upon 313 of all clients treated yielded only a slightly lower success rate: 74.5 percent. These figures represent a relatively conservative estimate of outcome. Thus, three couples who returned to the program for additional treatment which proved to be successful, as well as many individuals who voluntarily reported achieving fully effective sexual functioning anywhere from seventy-two hours to six months following the program without receiving any intervening therapy, were all counted as program failures.

Of course, the Masters and Johnson report was not a controlled outcome study. Their clients were select and selected, with a disproportionate number of highly motivated physicians and behavioral scientists. Yet previous psychotherapy had been unsuccessful for over 50 percent of these presumably good prognosis clients, a fact that argues against an interpretation of the results in terms of nonspecific treatment factors. Also compelling in this respect is the unprecedented success rate; with the exception of some behavioral programs (Wolpe & Lazarus, 1966), nothing like it had been recorded even with selected clients in uncontrolled clinical reports. Furthermore, although they omitted to provide a detailed analysis of the findings, both Hartman and Fithian (1972) and Kaplan (1974) have reported consistently comparable clinical success with several hundreds of clients.

A multifaceted behavioral program was shown to be significantly more effective than a waiting-list control group in the treatment of women with primary and secondary orgasmic dysfunction (Munjack, Cristol, Goldstein, Phillips, Goldberg, Whipple, Staples, & Kanno, 1976). These results, consistent across several different outcome measures, were maintained at an average follow-up of nine months. Mathews, Bancroft, Whitehead, Hackmann, Julier, Bancroft, Gath, and Shaw (1976) conducted a more analytical study in order to identify the mechanisms of change in the behavioral treatment of sexual dysfunction. A modified version of the Masters and Johnson program proved to be superior—though the difference was not statistically significant—to imaginal systematic desensitization in the treatment of couples with sexual problems.

Behavior therapy has shown considerable promise in the treatment of several forms of sexual deviance, including homosexuality,[g] transvestism, exhibitionism, fetishism, and even transsexualism (e.g., Bancroft, 1974; Brownell & Barlow, in press; Franks & Wilson, 1975, 1977; Marks, 1976a). Conclusive evidence of efficacy, however, must await adequately controlled outcome studies, of which there have been notably few. Of the systematic outcome studies that have been conducted, McConaghy and Barr (1973) compared three forms of electrical aversion conditioning in the modification of homosexuals' sexual preferences. A one-year follow-up showed no significant differences between either of the two conditioning groups (classical and avoidance conditioning, respectively) and a backward conditioning group. Since backward conditioning would not be predicted to alter behavior according to learning principles,[h] and can

---

[g] The inclusion of homosexuality within the category of sexual deviance does not imply that it is a form of "mental illness" qualitatively different from heterosexuality. Similarly, that homosexual behavior has been a target of some behavioral outcome studies should not be interpreted to suggest that heterosexuality is necessarily the appropriate therapeutic goal of treatment (Bancroft, 1974; Davison & Wilson, 1973a; Wilson & Davison, 1974).

[h] In contrast to the prevailing consensus on backward conditioning (e.g., Kimble, 1961), Eysenck (1975) has argued that under certain circumstances conditioned responses can be developed in this manner.

therefore be viewed as an attention-placebo control group, these findings do not indicate the efficacy of electrical aversion conditioning with homosexuals. In other group outcome studies, electrical aversion conditioning was as effective as systematic desensitization in significantly reducing homosexual behavior (Bancroft, 1970), and superior to a self-regulation and placebo control treatment with persistent exhibitionists (Rooth & Marks, 1974).

Single-case experimental designs have shown the efficacy of specific behavioral techniques such as electrical aversion conditioning and covert sensitization in eliminating unwanted sexual behavior in homosexuals, transvestites, and fetishists (e.g., Brownell & Barlow, in press; Marks & Gelder, 1967). Long-term effects of these techniques, however, have yet to be demonstrated in controlled studies. Finally, Barlow, Reynolds, and Agras (1973) demonstrated the successful modification of gender-role identity in a transsexual. This is the only carefully documented instance—subsequently replicated (Brownell & Barlow, in press)—of the efficacy of a psychological as opposed to a surgical procedure in the treatment of a transsexual.

Marital Discord

A large number of demonstrations of behavior therapy techniques have been reported to reduce marital conflict and to increase specific positive interactions in individual couples (see Gurman & Kniskern, in press; Jacobson & Martin, 1976). Outcome studies have evaluated the effects of altering multiple facets of spouse interaction to improve marital satisfaction. Although several different specific procedures have been used to alter marital interaction, they are similar in focus and technique. The goal of treatment is to increase positive communication and problem-solving skills. Partners are trained to identify specific problem areas, to provide feedback to their spouses, to negotiate constructively in conflict situations, to express positive statements, and in general to develop a positive reciprocal relationship (e.g., Azrin, Naster, & Jones, 1973; Jacobson, 1977; Patterson & Hops, 1972; Weiss, Birchler, & Vincent, 1974).

The treatment package to improve marital interaction typically involves feedback and instructions from the therapist, modeling of appropriate communications, and behavioral rehearsal. To ensure that spouses engage in specific target behaviors, a contractual arrangement is devised in which the incentives for performing the desired behaviors are written into a formal agreement. The contract may specify the way that changes in the behavior of one spouse are contingent upon related changes in the behavior of the other. The purpose of the contract is to ensure the reciprocity of the demands and the agreement in advance of the consequences associated with specific patterns of performance (e.g., Weiss, Hops, & Patterson, 1973; Weiss et al., 1974).

Although a number of studies have been reported in the literature, a large proportion have been conducted with a single group of couples, have studied couples whose marriages are not seriously disturbed (even not disturbed at all), or have assessed outcome on measures that do not reflect improvements of marital interaction in specific problem areas. More controlled investigations of behavioral marital therapy are needed before clear conclusions about the treatment of marital discord can be drawn (Gurman & Kniskern, in press; Jacobson & Martin, 1976).

Addictive Behaviors

Alcoholism. The behavioral treatment of problem drinking has developed from the early, somewhat simplistic use of aversion conditioning to complex and sophisticated multifaceted treatment programs that take account of many controlling variables (e.g., Franks & Wilson, 1975–1977; Litman, 1976; Marlatt & Nathan, in press; Nathan & Briddell, in press). Numerous treatment methods have been applied in the modification of problem drinking. Electrical aversion conditioning has been clearly shown to be ineffective; uncontrolled clinical evidence suggests that chemical aversion conditioning using emetine may be effective, but controlled outcome studies have yet to be completed (Nathan & Briddell, in press; Wilson, in press a). Treatment procedures based on manipulating the operant consequences of drinking within institutional settings have been particularly successful in modifying patterns of excessive alcohol consumption. Both positive reinforcement of decreased intake (Cohen, Liebson, Faillace, & Allen, 1971) and punishment of alcohol abuse (Wilson, Leaf, & Nathan, 1975) have demonstrated that drinking is, at least in part, a function of its environmental consequences. These procedures have been used successfully in the treatment of alcoholics in the community (Hunt & Azrin, 1973).

Other behavioral treatment methods have included behavioral family counseling (including assertion training and contingency contracting) and blood alcohol discrimination training combined with discriminated aversion conditioning or differential reinforcement. The former has been shown to be superior to systematic desensitization, covert sensitization, and electrical aversion conditioning (Hedberg & Campbell, 1974). The latter, while promising, has yet to be demonstrated to be effective in well-controlled clinical studies.

Alcoholism is a complex disorder requiring multifaceted intervention programs. Indeed, the efficacy of the behavioral treatment of alcoholism has been most convincingly shown in the multifaceted therapy programs of Hunt and Azrin (1973), Azrin (1976), and Sobell and Sobell (1976), studies discussed in detail in Chapter 2.

Obesity. The behavioral treatment of obesity has emphasized the development of self-control skills, featuring techniques such as self-monitoring, self-reinforcement, stimulus control, and contingency contracting. The lively research activity in this area can be summarized as follows. At least in the short-term, behavioral treatment has been shown to be superior to alternative approaches. However, the amount of weight lost has rarely been clinically significant, outcome has been marked by considerable and unaccounted for interindividual variability, and long-term evaluations of treatment efficacy have been conspicuously lacking (e.g., Franks & Wilson, 1975–1977; Stunkard, 1976a; Stunkard & Mahoney, 1976).

The relative absence of long-term evaluations of weight loss is a major problem, especially in view of findings that short-term weight loss is not maintained over time (e.g., Ashby & Wilson, replication 1, in press; Hall, Hall, Hanson, & Borden, 1974; Hanson, Borden, Hall, & Hall, 1976). On the positive side, however, long-term maintenance of treatment-produced weight loss has been demonstrated in other studies (e.g., Ashby & Wilson, replication 2, in press; Jeffery, Wing & Stunkard, in press; Mahoney, 1974b; McReynolds & Paulsen, 1976). (See also Kingsley & Wilson, 1977; Levitz & Stunkard, 1974; and Stunkard & Mahoney, 1976, as discussed in Chapter 2.) These latter findings, allied to the impressive short-term results of behavior therapy, strongly suggest that behavioral methods might be extremely useful in the management of obesity. Yates's (1975) conclusion that the treatment of obesity is an instance "where behavior therapy fails" is distinctly premature, if not inaccurate.

Cigarette Smoking.   A wide variety of different behavioral techniques have been employed in the treatment of cigarette smoking, frequently in well-designed outcome studies (e.g., Bernstein, 1969; Lichtenstein, 1971). The methods have included systematic desensitization, role playing, stimulus control, contingency contracting, and different aversion conditioning procedures. The results, however, have in general shown few treatment-specific effects. Control treatments emphasizing nonspecific factors have usually equalled the success of specific behavioral techniques. This success has been limited largely to dramatic reductions in cigarette smoking during treatment followed by a progressive return to smoking to near pretreatment levels over the course of a one-year post-treatment follow-up (e.g., Bernstein & McAlister, 1976; Hunt & Matarazzo, 1973).

A promising exception to this otherwise discouraging state of affairs has been the outcome obtained with the rapid-smoking method. Impressive reductions in smoking rates have been demonstrated at a six-month follow-up (Lichtenstein, Harris, Birchler, Wahl, & Schmahl, 1973), a finding of significance, since most of the return to orginal smoking rates occurs during the first three months after treatment. The efficacy of the rapid-smoking method appears attributable to as yet unidentified nonspecific treatment factors aside from the specific rapid-smoking procedure itself. Moreover, its usefulness has been questioned on the grounds that the procedure might have adverse physical consequences for the client (e.g., Horan, Hackett, Nicholas, Linberg, Stone, & Lukaski, 1977).

Drug Addiction.   Several behavioral methods, including aversion conditioning, desensitization, and contingency contracting, have been applied to the problems of drug addiction. Relative to behavioral research on alcoholism, obesity, and cigarette smoking, studies on drug addiction have been sparse. Controlled outcome studies of the efficacy of behavioral treatment methods for drug addiction are completely lacking. In a comprehensive review of behavioral techniques in the treatment of drug abuse, Götestam, Melin, and Öst (1976) found that only 14 percent of all studies used any type of control design. Moreover, most of these were single-case experimental designs that are difficult to interpret. Several other major deficiencies in the behavioral literature have been discussed in detailed reviews by Callner (1975) and Götestam et al. (1976). Among them are the use of subjects or clients who are unrepresentative of the general population of drug addicts; the sole use of self-report data and the failure to obtain multiple, reliable measures of outcome; and the absence of acceptable follow-up evaluations.

Psychotic Disorders

Psychoses include several subcategories of disorders involving diverse problems in thought, beliefs, affect, and perception. Behavior modification programs for psychotic patients have focused upon circumscribed behaviors that may have contributed to the diagnoses rather than on psychosis as such. Many of the diagnostic signs associated with psychoses can be tied to specific problems such as delusions, hallucinations, social withdrawal, and similar areas that can be altered individually.

Typically programs with psychiatric patients have utilized techniques based upon operant conditioning methods. Patients may receive reinforcing or, less commonly, punishing consequences for their behaviors on the ward. The bulk of the applications have focused upon chronic schizophrenic patients usually in state institutions when custodial ward care is the common form of treatment. However, programs have been effective with adult patients diagnosed as suffering organic psychoses or acute psychoses and with adolescent or child psychotic patients (Kazdin, 1977d). The application of behavior modification techniques to psychiatric patients is vast and has been reviewed extensively in several other sources (e.g., Alevizos & Callahan, 1977; Hersen & Bellack, in press; Kazdin, 1976b;

Stahl & Leitenberg, 1976; Wallace, 1976). The present section highlights applications that focus upon self-care and adaptive behaviors on the ward, symptomatic behaviors, and communication and social interaction.

Self-Care and Ward Behaviors. By far the greatest emphasis of behavior modification programs has been in developing adaptive behavior in the hospital environment. Behaviors focused upon include completing self-care tasks, performing jobs on and off the ward, attending and participating in activities, taking medication, cleaning one's room, and so on. A vast amount of evidence reveals that these behaviors can be readily altered (see Carlson, Hersen, & Eisler, 1972; Gripp & Magaro, 1974; Kazdin, 1977d). Typically, wardwide reinforcement programs are implemented in which patients earn tokens (points, tickets, or some other medium of exchange) for engaging in several different behaviors. The tokens can be exchanged for various privileges, activities, and canteen items.

Altering routine ward behaviors has been considered useful in overcoming maladaptive and dependent behaviors and apathy associated with institutionalization. Interestingly, developing such behaviors as self-care, participation in activities, and similar adaptive responses on the ward not only increases general activity, but also reduces symptomatic and bizarre behaviors such as screaming, depression, and ritualistic behaviors associated with hallucinations (Kazdin, 1977d). Many other improvements in behavior are evident when adaptive ward behaviors are altered, including increases in cooperativeness on the ward, communication skills, social interactions, and mood states, and decreases in psychoticism and reliance upon medication (e.g., Maley, Feldman, & Ruskin, 1973; Shean & Zeidberg, 1971).

Perhaps the most global measure of improvement, and consequently the one most amenable to the influence of nontreatment variables, is discharge and subsequent readmission. Programs focusing on general ward behaviors frequently show increased patient discharge and lower readmission rates relative to custodial care (e.g., Hollingsworth & Foreyt, 1975; Rybolt, 1975). The extent to which changes in these measures can be unambiguously attributed to the specific treatment program rather than to a change on overall hospital philosophy with respect to discharge is not easily discerned (Gripp & Magaro, 1974; Kazdin & Bootzin, 1972).

Symptomatic Behaviors. A large number of programs have focused upon behaviors that would ordinarily be viewed as symptomatic of psychoses. These programs usually are designed for one or a few patients, in contrast to the wardwide programs that develop adaptive behaviors for large numbers of patients simultaneously. The most common focus is on delusional or incoherent speech (e.g., Ayllon & Haughton, 1964; Rickard, Dignam, & Horner, 1960). For example, Wincze, Leitenberg, and Agras (1972) altered the delusional speech of ten paranoid schizophrenics. Feedback provided to the patients for delusional talk (by the therapist saying "that was incorrect") produced only transitory effects. However, token reinforcement was provided in specific therapy sessions in which nondelusional talk was reinforced directly. This resulted in a decrease in delusional speech. Several other investigators have shown that delusional speech can be altered by terminating conversation with patients or withdrawing tokens contingent upon delusional speech and by providing special privileges, attention, or consumable rewards contingent upon coherent or rational speech (e.g., Kazdin, 1971; Liberman, Teigen, Patterson, & Baker, 1973; Meichenbaum, 1969; Patterson & Teigen, 1973).

Hallucinations have been focused upon less often than has delusional speech. For example, Anderson and Alpert (1974) reported a case in which hallucinations were associated with overt ritualistic and compulsive mannerisms that interferred with the patient's completion of routine self-care and ward activities. Tokens were provided for decreases in latency in performing routine behaviors considered incompatible with the intrusive hallucinations. Improvements and performance in routine behaviors were associated with decreases in behavioral manifestations and self-report of hallucinations.

In many applications, self-report has served as the primary measure of hallucinations and consequences have been provided on the basis of the patient's report of their frequency (e.g., Rutner & Bugle, 1969; Bucher & Fabricatore, 1970). Although operant techniques appear to be the most frequent source of techniques for altering hallucinations or hallucinatory behaviors, other techniques have been applied, such as systematic desensitization, assertion training, and imagery-based punishment (e.g., Moser, 1974; Nydegger, 1972; Slade, 1972). Aside from delusions and hallucinations, a large variety of bizarre or acting-out behaviors have been altered, including aggressive acts, screaming, violating ward rules, excessive noise, excessive crying, setting fires, not eating, hoarding, compulsive handwashing, and others. These behaviors have been markedly reduced or eliminated entirely by altering consequences associated with behavior and by developing prosocial behaviors (see Alevizos & Callahan, 1977; Kazdin, 1976b; Stahl & Leitenberg, 1976; Wallace, 1976).

Social and Communicative Behaviors.   Psychiatric patients commonly evince severe deficits in social interaction and communication skills. Numerous reports have addressed communication behaviors ranging from rudimentary skills to complex forms of social interaction. Speech has been reinstated in mute chronic psychiatric patients (e.g., Isaacs,

Thomas, & Goldiamond, 1960; Sherman, 1965). For individuals who already speak, reinforcement techniques have been effective in increasing behaviors ranging from simple greeting responses on the ward (e.g., Kale, Kaye, Whelan, & Hopkins, 1968) to conversation with staff or fellow patients (e.g., Bennett & Maley, 1973; Leitenberg, Wincze, Butz, Callahan, & Agras, 1970; Wallace & Davis, 1974). Occasionally, contingencies are devised to increase communication in the context of group therapy or group activities (e.g., Liberman, 1972; Tracey, Briddell, & Wilson, 1974).

Developing social interaction has extended beyond verbal skills. For example, Doty (1975) provided psychiatric patients with money contingent upon interpersonal skills involving such behaviors as speaking up, describing one's own feelings, having eye contact with others, asking questions of others to stimulate their reactions, and so on. Social behaviors increased between patients on the ward as a function of incentives provided for interaction. Several studies have used modeling, incentives, role-playing, feedback, and instructions to systematically develop social skills in psychiatric patients (see Hersen & Bellack, 1976b, for a review). In these studies, select behaviors such as eye contact with another person, number of requests made of others, speech duration, number of smiles, words spoken within a specified time period, and appropriate affect associated with speech have been increased (e.g., Hersen & Bellack, 1976b; Williams, Turner, Watts & Bellack, & Hersen, in press).

Other Behaviors. A wide range of other behaviors of psychotic patients has been altered in institutional settings, including assisting staff, adhering to ward rules, losing weight, overcoming phobias, and so on. A few areas seem particularly worth noting in passing. In one application, the use of PRN (pro re nata) medication (those pills delivered "as needed") were decreased (Parrino, George, & Daniels, 1971). Charging patients tokens, exchangeable for ward reinforcers on the ward, decreased consumption of medication. Another area that affects the hospital stay of psychiatric patients is the plans made for their own treatment. Select programs have increasingly fostered patient participation in their own treatment by developing suggestions for ward practices and management, planning individual goals with a therapist, group decision-making, and developing treatment and discharge proposals (e.g., Greenberg, Scott, Pisa, & Friesen, 1975; Liberman, Fearn, DeRisi, Roberts, & Carmona, 1977; O'Brien, Azrin, & Henson, 1969; Olson & Greenberg, 1972). Hence, patients are given greater control over their own fate in the hospital.

Not all programs for psychiatric patients are conducted in traditional hospital settings. Programs have successfully developed community relevant behaviors (e.g., seeking job interviews, procuring employment, attending social functions) while patients live in facilities such as halfway houses, community mental health centers, and day treatment programs enmeshed in the community (Fairweather, Sanders, Cressler, & Maynard, 1969; Henderson & Scoles, 1970; Kelley & Henderson, 1971; Liberman, 1973).

Child Disorders

Children varying in problems and severity of impairment have been included in behavioral treatment. The focus of programs has ranged from very circumscribed habit disorders in children whose behaviors are otherwise "normal" to multiple responses of children who suffer all encompassing excesses, deficits, or bizarre behavior patterns (e.g., autistic children). Major areas of focus have included deportment, conduct problems and delinquency, autism and childhood schizophrenia, specific role- or age-inappropriate behaviors, and behavioral deficits or excesses. Many child-treatment programs are for retarded or neurotic children and hence have been considered in previous sections.

Deportment, Conduct Problems, and Delinquency. Conduct problems include such behaviors as aggressive acts, truancy, theft, noncompliance with adults, and several others. The severity of the problem treated varies tremendously. Children included as conduct problems may vary from individuals whose behaviors are mildly disruptive to those referred for treatment as an alternative to adjudication. The distinction is a matter of degree from the standpoint of behaviors focused upon rather than a class or qualitative designation of a particular type of disorder. It is useful to sample different levels of severity of conduct problems to convey the breadth of the applications.

The least severe behaviors are relatively mild problems of deportment: failing to perform chores at home, not complying with parental instructions, failing to cooperate with siblings or peers at home or at school, mild tantrums, and neglecting a task or an assignment at school—in short, the problems that frequently arise in everyday interactions with parents and teachers. An extremely large number of behaviors of this sort have been altered (e.g., see Drabman, 1976; Kazdin, 1975a; Patterson, 1971). While the ultimate goal of these programs is to alter the problem child's behavior, the immediate focus is in training parents or teachers to conduct behavior-change techniques to effect these changes. Hence, considerable attention has been devoted to training individuals who are in contact with the clients (e.g., Tharp & Wetzel, 1969; Yen & McIntire, 1976).

More severe problems than deportment in everyday situations are conduct problems of children and adolescents who have been referred to treatment by various community agencies such as mental-health centers or juvenile courts. For example, Patterson and his colleagues (Patterson, 1974; Patterson, Cobb, & Ray, 1973; Patterson & Reid, 1973) have altered such behaviors as stealing, running away from home, setting fires, fighting, and similar behaviors of children referred for treatment. Behavioral programs usually alter environmental contingencies at home and at school to reduce these behaviors. Interestingly, deviant behaviors of the treated children have been reduced to acceptable levels, as defined by the performance of children at home and at school who are functioning adequately (Patterson, 1974). The behavior of children and adolescents with rather severe conduct problems has been effectively altered by using individuals in the natural environment to conduct treatment (e.g., Fo & O'Donnell, 1974; Kent & O'Leary, 1976).

One type of conduct problem viewed by many as distinct from simple deportment problems is labeled hyperactivity. Hyperactivity has been used to denote such behaviors as constant activity, aggressive behavior, running around, failure to sit still or to attend to a task, and gross motor activity. Hyperactive behaviors in such settings as classrooms or institutions have been controlled by reinforcing activity incompatible with constant movement (e.g., Ayllon, Layman, & Kandel, 1975; Christensen, 1975). The success of behavioral treatments of hyperactivity has made them a viable alternative to drug treatment, a point elaborated in the next chapter.

The final level of conduct problems that can be distinguished refers to those whose behavior is sufficiently severe for criminal agencies to intervene. Programs with adjudicated youths have been frequently conducted within institutions (see Braukmann & Fixsen, 1975; Davidson & Seidman, 1974; Stumphauzer, 1973 for reviews). One of the most elaborate and well investigated program has been at Achievement Place, a home-style facility in Kansas. Adjudicated children (separate facilities for boys and girls) participate in a family-style facility with a few other delinquent youths and a highly trained couple who administer a behavioral program that encompasses virtually all aspects of their everyday life. Diverse behaviors have been altered, including room cleaning, social interaction and communication patterns, academic performance at school, chores, saving money, aggressive behavior, decision making, and others (Burchard & Harig, 1976, Kazdin, 1977d; for reviews). Evidence suggests that recidivism and school performance after treatment may be enhanced through intensive behavioral treatment relative to traditional institutional care or probation (Fixsen, Phillips, Phillips, & Wolf, 1976). Many programs for delinquents have been conducted in traditional institutional facilities, including reform schools and correctional centers. In such settings, programs have focused upon altering academic behaviors and social interaction, vocational tasks, and self-care (e.g., Cohen & Filipczak, 1971; Jesness & DeRisi, 1973;

Karacki & Levinson, 1970). Programs often are conducted to influence diverse aspects of institutional life.

Autism and Childhood Schizophrenia. Autism and childhood schizophrenia refer to two related disorders characterized by such symptoms as lack of affect, performance of repetitive and self-stimulatory behavior, severe withdrawal, muteness or echolalia, and other problems.[1] Usually such children are institutionalized where intensive treatment programs can be conducted to overcome bizarre behaviors as well as to develop specific skills in place of massive response deficits. The focus of many programs has been on self-stimulatory and self-destructive behavior such as head banging and biting, where aversive events may be used to suppress or eliminate behavior (e.g., Bucher & Lovaas, 1968). Positive behaviors have been developed to improve language and speech, play and social interaction, and basic academic skills (e.g., Lovaas, Berberich, Perloff & Schaeffer, 1966). Many programs have increased the social responsiveness of these children. Responses frequently developed include imitating others, responding to instructions, and seeking out peers or adults (e.g., Lovaas, Schaeffer, & Simmons, 1965). The behaviors developed in these children may be trained very gradually to shape increasingly complex response repertoires. For example, language training may begin by developing single speech sounds, then words. After words are developed, emphasis shifts to comprehension of the words and to word meaning, and finally to generative speech (Lovaas & Newsom, 1976).

Although several investigators have altered the behavior of autistic children, the work of Lovaas and his colleagues has programmatically evaluated several interventions across a wide range of behaviors (Lovaas & Bucher, 1974; Lovaas & Newsom, 1976). In Lovaas' program, children receive an intensive behavioral training program for several hours daily. The program is based upon operant conditioning principles and develops language and social behaviors and eliminates self-destructive behavior. While only a small number of individuals have been treated, the reports have demonstrated that significant changes in specific behaviors can be developed. However, these gains are only maintained if the children are placed in situations where the programs are continued, at least on a partial basis (Lovaas, Koegel, Simmons, & Long, 1972).

---

[1] A distinction frequently is made between autism and childhood schizophrenia. Behavior modifiers have not adhered to this distinction in designing treatment programs and, instead, have focused directly upon the behaviors of interest independently of the diagnosis. Although the disorders can be distinguished along several dimensions, there are great similarities in the specific treatment programs designed for each disorder (O'Leary & Wilson, 1975). Hence, the differences of autism and childhood schizophrenia will not be elaborated here.

Other Behaviors. A wide range of behaviors other than those reviewed above have been focused upon with children. The behaviors fall in such global categories as avoidance reactions, age-inappropriate or role-inappropriate behaviors, and behavioral excesses and deficits.

Age-inappropriate responses might include such behaviors as enuresis, thumbsucking, and baby talk beyond the ages appropriate for such behaviors. A frequently studied age-inappropriate behavior is bedwetting. The widely used bell-and-pad method has been very effective in reducing nocturnal bedwetting. The procedure requires a child to sleep on a moisture sensitive pad that activates an alarm during bedwetting. Repeated exposure to the apparatus results in a high improvement rate, upwards of 80 percent in many reports (e.g., DeLeon & Mandell, 1966; DeLeon & Sacks, 1972; Doleys, 1976). Toileting accidents have been effectively altered with other procedures as well (Azrin & Foxx, 1974; Foxx & Azrin, 1973).

One interesting *role*-inappropriate behavior to receive attention is sex-role behaviors. For example, Rekers and Lovaas (1974) developed male-role behaviors in a male child who preferred female clothes, used cosmetics, evinced female mannerisms and vocal characteristics, and in general identified as a female. Reinforcement techniques implemented at the clinic and at home developed appropriate role behaviors.

Behavioral deficits refer to behaviors that are absent or relatively infrequent in the response repertoires. Programs have developed such behaviors as social interaction, play, language, academic responses, responsiveness to instructions, and self-care skills such as feeding or performing chores. Behavioral excesses refer to behaviors performed at inappropriately high rates, with great intensity, or under inappropriate circumstances. Many of the programs that focus on deportment and conduct problems, mentioned earlier, focus upon excesses. Whether programs are conceptualized as overcoming deficits or reducing excesses, similar procedures are applied. In each case, the focus is upon developing prosocial behavior to replace the deficit or excess. Procedures based upon operant techniques and modeling are often used.

Mental Retardation

Behavior modification with the mentally retarded has focused upon a wide range of behaviors (Birnbrauer, 1976; Gardner, 1971; Kazdin, in press c; Thompson & Grabowski, 1977). The range of behaviors reflects the diversity of age groups, levels of retardation, and treatment settings in which the retarded reside. The greatest attention has been devoted to developing behaviors to overcome the severe deficits, frequently encountered with the retarded, in skills such as self-care, language, and social behavior. Behavioral techniques used with the mentally retarded are multifaceted. Techniques based upon operant conditioning principles have been relied upon very heavily to shape specific responses or to suppress deviant behavior. Yet, a variety of other techniques such as modeling, role-playing, and rehearsal have been used as well, either alone or in conjunction with operant techniques.

Ward and Self-Care Behaviors. Self-care behaviors represent a particularly important focus in programs with the retarded because fundamental care skills frequently are unlearned or performed very inconsistently. Self-care responses include toileting, feeding, dressing, grooming, exercising, personal hygiene, and similar responses. Many institutional programs include responses in each of these categories in a general ward program (Thompson & Grabowski, 1977), although frequently only one area is focused upon at any one time (Kazdin, in press c).

The applications of behavioral techniques to self-care skills are extensive and are not easily enumerated here. Toilet training, the area that has received the greatest attention and notoriety, well illustrates the approach and overall goal of developing self-care skills. Although several investigators have effectively trained toileting skills, Azrin and Foxx (1974; Foxx & Azrin, 1973) have developed a particularly effective treatment "package" comprised of several techniques including frequent and immediate reinforcement of dry pants and for urinating correctly, a large number of trials to practice appropriate toileting, imitation and manual guidance to help initiate behaviors, symbolic rehearsal of the desired behavior, and other techniques. The procedure has effectively eliminated toileting accidents both with institutionalized retarded as well as "normal" children in a relatively brief period of time, for instance, in less than a day (Azrin & Foxx, 1974). Follow-up data suggest that the gains are maintained several months after treatment (Foxx & Azrin, 1973).

Self-Stimulatory and Bizarre Behaviors. Self-stimulatory behaviors such as rocking, head weaving, and hand gestures or self-destructive acts such as head banging, face slapping, and biting frequently are performed by the retarded. An extensive literature is available showing that operant conditioning techniques significantly reduce self-stimulatory behaviors (Forehand & Baumeister, 1976; Frankel & Simmons, 1976; Smolev, 1971). Electric shock has been especially effective in reducing these behaviors, although alternative procedures have been successful as well. Providing reinforcing consequences for not engaging in self-stimulation or especially requiring individuals to perform specific effortful behaviors contingent upon self-stimulation (i.e., positive practice) have been effective. For example, Azrin, Kaplan, and Foxx (1973) reduced self-stimulatory behaviors (e.g., rocking, head weaving) in severely and profoundly retarded adults with positive practice (requiring and manually guiding extensive rehearsal of behaviors incompatible with self-stimulation contingent upon the response) and reinforcement for incompatible behaviors. The combined practice and reinforcement procedures rapidly reduced self-stimulation to almost zero.

In addition to self-stimulatory behaviors, various bizarre behaviors have been suppressed. These include public disrobing (stripping) (Foxx, 1976), exhibitionism (Lutzker, 1974), sprawling on the floor (Azrin & Wesolowski, 1975), agitated behaviors such as screaming and crying (Webster & Azrin, 1973), and eating trash and excrement (Foxx & Martin, 1975), among others. In many reports, follow-up data indicate that the suppressed behaviors do not return.

Verbal Behavior and Language Acquisition. Diverse forms of verbal behavior have been altered, including receptive and productive language, topographical features of speech, speech content, and inappropriate speech. The behavior focused upon depends upon the age and initial skill level of the client. For example, with the severely retarded, language behaviors may consist of verbally identifying various stimuli such as letters and numbers and asking simple questions (e.g., Twardosz & Baer, 1973). With moderately retarded clients, the focus may be on developing correct subject-verb agreement in speech (e.g., Lutzker & Sherman, 1974). With borderline retardates, the focus may be upon verbalizations about specific topics such as current events (e.g., Keilitz, Tucker, & Horner, 1973). In many studies, idiosyncratic aspects of speech are altered. For example, Jackson and Wallace (1974) reinforced increases in voice volume with tokens in a mildly retarded child who spoke almost inaudibly. Wheeler and Sulzer (1970) developed appropriate sentences in a boy who omitted articles and auxiliary verbs when speaking.

An important focus that has received attention is the responsiveness of retardates to the language of others. Various studies have developed responsiveness to instructions or instruction-following behavior (e.g., Frisch & Schumaker, 1974; Gladstone & Sherman, 1975; Whitman, Zakaras, & Chardos, 1971). For example, Kazdin and Erickson (1975) used food and physical prompts (guidance) with severely and profoundly retarded adolescents and adults to develop instruction following. Developing responsiveness to instructions is an important focus with individuals who have severe response deficits. Once verbal control over behavior is established, it may facilitate the acquisition of other behaviors.

Social Behaviors. Relatively few operant programs have focused upon social behaviors with the retarded. Some studies have altered greeting responses in severely retarded children (e.g., Stokes, Baer, & Jackson, 1974). In other reports, with higher-level retardates, peer interaction has been altered (e.g., Kazdin & Polster, 1973). Knapczyk and Yoppi (1975) increased play behaviors of five institutionalized, educably retarded children who received praise and token reinforcement for initiating either cooperative or competitive play.

Work-Related Behaviors.　Programs frequently focus on aspects of work in an attempt to develop community job placements. In many programs, trainable retardates receive praise, or more commonly tokens, for increasing productivity and accuracy of task completion (see Kazdin, 1977d). Many studies have shown that behavioral techniques improve work behaviors in the rehabilitation settings (e.g., Bateman, 1975; Karen, Eisner, & Endres, 1974). Although change is demonstrated in the treatment setting, often an end in itself, whether clients achieve subsequent employment in light of such training is rarely addressed. In comprehensive behavioral programs that carefully train job performance, subsequent placement into the community cannot readily be attributed to the specific interventions (Welch & Gist, 1974).

Test Performance.　A major determinant of child placement into educational and rehabilitation settings is performance on standardized psychological tests. Interestingly, some studies have shown that the incentive conditions during test administration influence performance. For example, trainable retardates as well as children of "average" intelligence improved on readiness or intelligence tests under conditions of token or food reinforcement (Ayllon & Kelly, 1972, Exp. 1 & 2; Edlund, 1972). Altering the conditions of test administration, of course, alters the interpretation that can be made of the test results. Thus, perhaps of greater interest is the use of tests administered under standard conditions. Ayllon and Kelly (1972, Exp. 3) showed that trainable retardates who participated in a reinforcement program for academic responses showed superior performance on the Metropolitan Readiness Test to control subjects who were not exposed to the special program.

Additional Applications

The applications of behavior modification reviewed above address populations and clinical disorders that have been included in psychiatry and clinical psychology. These problems traditionally have been included under the rubric of "mental health." Interestingly, behavior modification has contributed to several other areas as well. The broad scope of behavior modification can be conveyed by highlighting applications in such areas as medical treatment, education, social and community problems, prison rehabilitation, and geriatrics.

Medical and Psychophysiological Applications. Behavior modification techniques have been applied to a wide range of medical and psychophysiological disorders, an area referred to as "behavioral medicine" (Birk, 1973; Blanchard, 1977). Behavioral medicine consists of the systematic application of principles and technology of behavior modification to areas of medicine, health, and illness (Katz & Zlutnick, 1974; Knapp & Peterson, 1976; Williams & Gentry, 1977). There is some overlap in the areas of interest in behavioral medicine and psychosomatic disorders. For example, behavioral techniques are applied to many problems where both psychological and physical concomitants are relevant and where mediating factors such as stress may be operative, as in some forms of asthma or hypertension (Alexander, 1977; Jacob, Kraemer, & Agras, in press). Yet, behavioral medicine is much broader and addresses a wide range of applications outside of the realm of psychosomatic medicine.

The greatest attention has been given to biofeedback, which has been used to alter diverse physiological responses. Biofeedback encompasses a set of procedures in which the client is provided with a means (e.g., auditory stimuli, visual display) to monitor a particular response (e.g., brain wave activity, heart rate). Biofeedback training attempts to produce either a semipermanent change in a particular response system or to provide the client with a means to regulate the response in the natural environment when external feedback cannot be provided (Blanchard & Epstein, 1977). The main focus of biofeedback has been with cardiovascular responses, especially heart rate and blood pressure. Several reports, mostly with normal subjects, have shown that cardiovascular functions can be controlled, although the magnitude of the changes in these functions is small and of unclear clinical relevance (Blanchard & Young, 1973). A few applications have shown changes with patients who have cardiovascular disabilities such as arrhythmias (e.g., Blanchard, Young, & Haynes, 1975; Engel & Bleecker, 1974; Scott, Blanchard, Edmundson, & Young, 1973). Although the specific role of feedback cannot be determined. Additional reports have suggested the clinical utility of biofeedback in altering epileptic seizures, tension and migraine headaches, partial loss of muscle control, tics, functional diarrhea, incontinence, sexual arousal, vaginismus, and others (see Blanchard & Epstein, 1977; Shapiro & Surwit, 1976, for reviews). A few of the demonstrations have been dramatic, although the lack of controlled investigations showing the specific role of biofeedback for clinical problems limits the conclusions that can be drawn.

Other behavioral interventions, such as contingency management, relaxation training, and desensitization, have been used for medical or physiological problems. For example, contingency management has been used for the treatment of chronic pain. Pain-related behaviors such as spending time out of one's bed, grimacing, moaning, verbal complaints, walking in a guarded or protective manner, reclining or sitting to ease pain, or relying upon medication have been altered by reinforcing activity and physical exercise and by decreasing attention and delivery of medication for complaints (e.g., Fordyce, Fowler, Lehmann, DeLateur, Sand, & Trieschmann, 1973). Relaxation training, hypnosis, and desensitization have been used to control a number of problems, including insomnia, headaches, and hypertension. For example, diverse relaxation techniques including progressive relaxation, autogenic training, yoga, and meditation have been used to control hypertension (Byassee, 1977; Jacob et al., in press).

Behavior modification also has been used to treat asthmatic attacks, epileptic seizures, spasmodic torticollis, ruminations, diarrhea and constipation, dermatitis, drooling, posture, anorexia nervosa, persistent coughing, sneezing, and vomiting and others. The area goes beyond treatment of specific disorders. For example, an important area of behavioral medicine that transcends any particular disorder is adherence to or compliance with medical regimens. Adhering to medication schedules, increasing fluid intake, using prosthetic devices (e.g., crutches), and exercising would be included in the area of adherence (see Gentry, 1977; Knapp & Peterson, 1976; Zifferblatt, 1975). Actually, the boundaries of the domain of behavioral medicine are not clear at this point. Some authors include such areas as cigarette smoking, obesity, alcoholism, and behavioral patterns associated with medical conditions (e.g., Type A behavior) (Brady, 1977).

Adult Offenders. Behavior modification programs have been implemented for adult criminal offenders in various settings ranging from minimal security facilities to maximum security prisons (Kennedy, 1976; Milan & McKee, 1974, for reviews). Programs have emphasized different goals. Initially, some programs have been designed explicitly to manage prisoners whose behavior is not otherwise easily controlled. Alternatively, many programs have been designed not only to manage behavior in prison but to decrease subsequent inmate recidivism after release. Each of these goals has been focused upon by developing reinforcement programs for inmates. Typically, the behaviors that are developed include self-care, getting up on time, attending activities, performing academic tasks or maintenance jobs in prison, or acquiring vocational skills (e.g., Bassett, Blanchard, & Koshland, 1975; Milan, Wood, Williams, Rogers, Hampton, & McKee, 1974). Programs have consistently demonstrated the marked effects of reinforcement on inmate behaviors. Hence, from the standpoint of inmate management, behavior modification has offered important new techniques that seem to be more effective than traditional practices. However, the results following inmate release have not been particularly encouraging. At best, only a slight or temporary decrease in recidivism is associated with inmate programs (e.g., Jenkins, Witherspoon, DeVine, de Valera, Muller, Barton, & McKee, 1974).

The Aged. A few inroads have been made with behavior modification of the aged in such settings as nursing homes and geriatric wards in hospitals. The general focus of such programs is to increase activity, particularly physical activity and social interaction. In institutional settings, physical activity has been developed by providing incentives such as tokens or special activities for physical exertion. For example, Libb and Clements (1969) developed exercise in geriatric patients by providing reinforcement for use of an exercycle. Other more readily available forms of exercise such as walking have been increased as well (e.g., MacDonald & Butler, 1974).

Social interaction has been increased in a few programs. Attention and praise have increased such behaviors as initiating conversation or responding verbally to others in nursing home residents and geriatric hospital patients (e.g., MacDonald, in press; Sachs, 1975). Some programs have focused upon increasing purposeful activity in general, such as reading, writing, using recreational materials and so on (e.g., Quilitch, 1974). Increases in activity can be accomplished by simply providing opportunities for reinforcing activities such as shopping (e.g., McClannahan & Risley, 1973).

Educational Applications. Behavior modification techniques have been widely applied in educational settings for diverse age groups and student populations. Populations included in the educational applications are "normal," conduct problem, mentally retarded, delinquents, and emotionally disturbed children and adolescents as well as "normal" college students (see Klein, Hapkiewicz, & Roden, 1973; O'Leary & O'Leary, 1976; Ulrich, Stachnik, & Mabry, 1974). The bulk of the applications in education have been with children, particularly at the preschool and elementary levels. Programs have emphasized deportment so that students are trained to work quietly, to attend to the teacher or task, to not disrupt class or argue, to comply with instructions, and in general to adhere to classroom rules designed to facilitate work. Typically, students receive reinforcing consequences in the form of approval, tokens, feedback, or special privileges contingent upon their classroom behavior. For example, Hall, Lund, and Jackson (1968) demonstrated that attentive behavior of elementary school students could be increased markedly by having teachers administer praise and approval for working.

In addition to deportment, academic performance has been altered as well in a large number of classroom applications. Behaviors such as accuracy in reading, arithmetic, handwriting, and spelling are included in many programs. Students may receive consequences for completing home or class assignments, creative writing, and developing vocabulary. For example, several investigations have reinforced use of novel sentences and words, different sentence beginnings, and similar responses to develop more creative compositions (e.g., Brigham, Graubard, & Stans, 1972; Maloney & Hopkins, 1973). In general, research has consistently shown that academic performance is readily altered as a function of incentives for assignment completion in the classroom. Interestingly, the gains in academic skills are not only reflected on specific assignments in class but can be seen on achievement and intelligent test performance as well (Bushell, 1974; Dickinson, 1974; Kaufman & O'Leary, 1972; Wolf, Giles, & Hall, 1968).

At the college level, behavioral techniques have been extended by providing students with self-paced or personalized instruction (e.g., Keller, 1968; Ryan, 1972). Course materials are structured so that students can receive constant feedback for performance and proceed at their own rate through the material as they master individual units towards completion of the course. The area of personalized instruction has developed on its own, although it has direct roots in behavioral interventions.

Social and Community Extensions of Behavior Modification.   Behavior modification has been extended to a wide range of social and community problems, an area referred to generally as "behavioral community psychology" (Briscoe, Hoffman & Bailey, 1975; Nietzel, Winett, MacDonald, & Davidson, 1977). Diverse problems have been attacked with behavioral techniques, including pollution control and energy conservation, job performance and unemployment, community self-government, racial integration, and others (see Kazdin, 1977b; Nietzel et al., 1977; Tuso & Geller, 1976).

In the area of pollution control, several different problems have been addressed. Extensive research has been devoted to decreasing littering in public places because of the unattractiveness of litter as well as the tremendous cost of litter cleanup. Applications based upon positive reinforcement have reduced littering and enhanced litter pickup in national parks and campgrounds, zoos, urban housing areas, schools, movie theaters, athletic stadiums, and other places (Clark, Burgess & Hendee, 1972; Kohlenberg & Phillips, 1973). Typically, small incentives are relied upon to increase deposits of waste material in designated areas. Similarly, to avoid accumulation of waste materials in the environment, reinforcement techniques have been used to stimulate recycling of waste products (metal cans, paper) and purchase of materials (returnable bottles) that can be recycled (Tuso & Geller, 1976). Diverse procedures, from small monetary incentives to raffles and contests, have encouraged antilittering and recycling of waste materials (e.g., Geller, Farris, & Post, 1973; Geller, Wylie, & Farris, 1971).

Behavioral techniques have been used to foster energy conservation in several areas of community life. Incentives and social recognition have been used to reward reductions of home consumption of energy (gas, oil, or electricity). Programs in apartment units, individual homes, or entire communities have effectively reduced energy consumption (e.g., Kohlenberg, Phillips, & Proctor, 1976; Seaver & Patterson, 1976). In addition, programs have been reduced for the use of automobiles to conserve gasoline. Individuals have received incentives for using mass transportation or for simply driving their cars less (e.g., Foxx & Hake, 1977; Everett, Hayward, & Meyers, 1974).

Behavior modification techniques have only recently been applied to the problems of unemployment. A large treatment package has been used to train individuals successfully to obtain and pursue job leads, to rehearse and role-play behaviors likely to enhance success at job interviews (e.g., dress and grooming, preparing a résumé), to expand job interests, and other behaviors (Azrin, Flores, & Kaplan, 1975). The package has been shown to enhance job procurement. Considerable attention has been directed toward enhancing on-the-job performance. Incentives ranging from feedback and social approval to small monetary rewards have increased efficiency at work, the amount of jobs completed, and have reduced absenteeism, tardiness, and cash shortages (e.g., Marholin & Gray, 1976; Pedalino & Gamboa, 1974).

Although less well investigated, behavioral techniques have been applied to several other social and community problems. Select investigations have increased participation of lower socioeconomic status individuals in community self-help groups and local government (e.g., Briscoe et al., 1975). Some reports have increased interracial interaction in applied settings such as the school classroon (Hauserman, Walen, & Behling, 1973) or have altered the tendency of children to view Afro-American people negatively (Best, Smith, Graves, & Williams, 1975). The military also has used behavioral techniques to develop basic training skills (Datel & Legters, 1970).

LIMITATIONS OF BEHAVIOR THERAPY

This review only highlighted substantive advances in behavior therapy and was not exhaustive. For example, applications in areas such as specific habit disorders (e.g., tics, nail biting, stuttering) were omitted. Because of the breadth of applications and extensiveness of research within specific areas, an incisive review of specific studies was not possible. Moreover, such a review would duplicate the many books and reviews available for problem areas and treatment techniques, as cited throughout our overview. A failure to criticize the studies within content areas should not be construed as unqualified acceptance of findings of individual studies or a belief that the definitive treatment techniques have been discovered. Although we believe that the evidence in support of behavior therapy is unrivaled by alternative approaches—in breadth of applications alone—this is not tantamount to saying that behavior therapy is free from limitations. Fundamental questions remain to be answered, and significant issues need to be resolved in behavior therapy before strong endorsements of substantive findings can be made. Four issues seem particularly important to raise given the current status of research: the conceptual basis of behavior therapy techniques, the etiology or development of behavior disorders, the clinical relevance of treatment effects, and follow-up and maintenance of behavior.

Conceptual Basis of Behavior Therapy Techniques

A significant issue in behavior therapy is the interrelationship between therapy techniques and theories from which the techniques were derived. Behavior therapy techniques have emerged from, or are allied with, a particular theory or, more narrowly, a specific experimental phenomenon established in laboratory research. Minimally, the theory provides an account for how behavior change comes about via the technique. In addition, the theory may make assumptions about how the behaviors have developed originally, although this is not necessary in a theory of behavior change. The underlying conceptual bases of diverse behavior therapy techniques vary in scope from specific aspects of Hullian theory or operant conditioning to more recent concepts of experimental cognitive psychology.

Contemporary research has established the efficacy of several techniques, but has raised serious questions about the conceptual basis for many techniques. As an example, consider the current status of systematic desensitization, one of the more widely used and well established behavior therapy techniques for the treatment of anxiety. The original conceptualization of systematic desensitization was based upon the notion of reciprocal inhibition, specific neurological hypotheses, and Hullian learning theory to explain the mechanism for eliminating anxiety. The theory assumed that anxiety could be suppressed by simultaneously evoking a response physiologically antagonistic to anxiety in the presence of anxiety-provoking stimuli (Wolpe, 1958). Three components were considered to be essential in treatment: a response (e.g., relaxation) considered to be incompatible with anxiety; a graded series of anxiety-provoking stimuli; and the pairing of the anxiety-competing response with the anxiety-provoking stimuli either in imagination or in vivo. To its credit, the conceptual basis and procedural requirements of systematic desensitization were well specified. The specificity permitted investigators to readily test the role of ingredients considered essential for behavior change. This stimulated a burst of research, much of which demonstrated that none of the ingredients considered crucial were in fact necessary for anxiety reduction (Davison & Wilson, 1973b; Kazdin & Wilcoxon, 1976; Wilkins, 1971).

Alternative interpretations of desensitization have been advanced. A major competitor is counterconditioning, which merely emphasizes the importance of pairing anxiety-provoking stimuli with nonanxiety responses (Bandura, 1969). Pairing anxiety-provoking stimuli with relaxation may be facilitory but not essential on a counterconditioning view. Another candidate has been extinction, or exposure, which stresses the importance of presenting anxiety-provoking stimuli that are not followed by actual aversive consequences (Marks, in press; Wilson & Davison, 1971). Anxiety responses resulting from repeated exposure to the aversive stimuli will eventually dissipate or habituate. A wide range of other theories or mechanisms have been advanced to account for desensitization, including development of coping skills (Goldfried, 1971), expectancies for change (Marcia, Rubin, & Efran, 1969), attribution (Valins & Ray, 1967) operant shaping (Leitenberg, Agras, Barlow, & Oliveau, 1969), symbolic or covert modeling (Kazdin, 1974b; Rachman, 1972), self-instructional training (Meichenbaum, 1972), and others. While some interpretations of desensitization are more plausible than others, there still is no single well-supported position that explains the effects of desensitization and the mechanisms responsible for change, and predicts parameters important in treatment.

Recently, Bandura (1977b) has posed a theoretical explanation to account for a wide range of therapy techniques, including desensitization and other techniques used for the treatment of avoidance behaviors. Bandura has suggested that diverse therapy techniques are effective because they increase an individual's expectations for personal effectiveness, or "self-efficacy." An expectancy for personal effectiveness refers to the conviction that one can successfully perform the requisite behaviors to produce a given outcome. The strength of an individual's self-efficacy expectations are presumed to affect the effort and persistance with which an individual will try to cope with a problematic situation. Higher levels of self-efficacy will lead the individual to engage in the behaviors in the natural environment which will provide corrective feedback experience. The reciprocal relationship between expectancies for personal effectiveness and increased competence sustains performance (Bandura, 1977b, 1977c).

Bandura has proposed different mechanisms through which self-efficacy may be increased, including overt performance accomplishment, vicarious symbolic experiences, verbal persuasion, and recognition of one's own physiological states. Different therapy techniques such as behavioral rehearsal, modeling, verbal psychotherapy, and attribution reflect these different mechanisms. Thus, self-efficacy has been posed as the final common pathway through which diverse techniques may accomplish change. Self-efficacy as an interpretation of therapeutic change has received support in experiments treating snake-phobic subjects with systematic desensitization, live modeling, or modeling with guided participation (Bandura & Adams, 1977; Bandura, Adams & Beyer, 1977). With each technique the strength and level of self-reported expectations of competence (self-efficacy) predict the amount of change achieved with treatment.

For present purposes, the importance of self-efficacy theory is that it provides a unifying theoretical framework to account for different therapy techniques. Self-efficacy theory illustrates the type of conceptual framework needed in behavior therapy. Although the discussion has emphasized systematic desensitization and the treatment of avoidance responses, the conceptual bases of many other techniques are ambiguous. For example, the conceptual basis of covert conditioning techniques, aversion therapy, bell-and-pad treatment of enuresis, and others are unclear at this point. Part of the ambiguity stems from much greater complexity in the behaviors treated than in those studied in laboratory research in learning, from which many techniques were drawn (Hunt, 1975). In addition, many of the experimental concepts themselves have undergone reevaluation in light of increasing complexities in their own right (e.g., Hinde & Stevenson-Hinde, 1973; Miller, Galanter, & Pribram, 1960). Some behavior modification techniques have not experienced the same degree of strain in the leap from experimental laboratory research to clinical applications. For example, many applications of operant conditioning adhere relatively closely to the processes and procedures established in laboratory research.

An important feature of behavior therapy has been its reliance both upon theory and findings of psychological research. When a technique is shown not to adhere to the theory from which it was derived, this is a positive sign of a research advance. Traditionally, the conceptual bases for treatment techniques such as psychoanalysis or psychoanalytically-oriented therapy have been invulnerable to falsification. This is not the case in contemporary behavioral research. As the theoretical basis of techniques are examined empirically, the mechanisms responsible for behavior change are likely to be uncovered. In the long run, understanding of these mechanisms will permit the development of increasingly effective techniques.

The Etiology or Development of Behavior Disorders

Numerous well-controlled studies have clearly shown that behavior can be modified effectively without a full understanding of its developmental history. This does not imply that a client's past is totally ignored by the behavior therapist. Current problems are inevitably influenced by one's social learning history. However, earlier learning experiences are usually no longer the functional variables that govern current difficulties. Behavioral assessment and therapy focus on those factors that are *currently* maintaining behavior, and historical learning events are emphasized only to the extent that they are presently controlling the behavior in question.

Although behavior disorders can be treated successfully without a firm understanding of their etiologies, the procedures used to modify psychological functioning cannot be fully understood independently of the theory of development and maintenance of behavior on which they are based. It follows that a better theoretical understanding of the factors that determine the development and maintenance of abnormal behavior will in all probability result in more effective methods of treatment. Yet behavioral theories of the development of behavior disorders are often inchoate and conflicting. Consider the behavioral approach to the schizophrenic disorders. On the one hand, Ullmann and Krasner (1975) have proposed that they are developed, maintained, and modified in the same manner as any normal behavior. On the other hand, Davison and Neale (in press) and Eysenck and Rachman (1965), among others, have criticized this formulation, arguing that many psychotic reactions are fundamentally biochemical or physical abnormalities related to brain dysfunction. Behavioral theories such as that put forward by Ullmann and Krasner (1975) are often predicated mainly on the basis of the successful modification of behavior disorders. However, therapeutic success is not tantamount to evidence pertaining to the development of behavior (e.g., Davison, 1969; Rimland, 1964).

Behavioral formulations of neurotic reactions are similarly inconsistent (Marks, 1969). The classical conditioning model, based on the over publicized case of little Albert (Watson & Rayner, 1920), has been abandoned as simplistic and inaccurate. One of the major problems with this and other learning accounts, such as Mowrer's (1947, 1960) two-factor theory of avoidance behavior, has been the apparent inability to explain why neurotic behavior persists in the face of what ostensibly are extinction conditions—the so-called "neurotic paradox." Seligman (1971) has sketched out a speculative theory in terms of the concept of biological preparedness for fear acquisition, and Eysenck (1976a) has proposed a new model of neurosis based on the incubation of anxiety. In this latter model, Eysenck (1976a) rejects an operant conditioning as nonfalsifiable and hence useless. Cognitive theories, Eysenck (1967b) suggests, have few differential experimental or clinical consequences other than conditioning theories of the sort he has outlined. However, Bandura (1969, 1977b, 1977c) has presented a social-learning account of the development of anxiety-related disorders which he claims accounts for phenomena such as the apparent neurotic paradox and which has been shown to be a superior predictor of behavior change than tradition S-R learning theory. Behavioral conceptualizations of the development of other disorders, such as sexual dysfunction and deviance (Bancroft, 1974; O'Leary & Wilson, 1975), depression (Eastman, 1976; Seligman, Klein, & Miller, 1976), obsessive-compulsive disorders (Rachman & Hodgson, in press), and various childhood problems (Patterson, in press; Wahler, 1976) are similarly plausible in view of the available evidence, but less than firmly established. As is the case with the conceptual bases of treatment techniques, better behavioral formulations of the development and maintenance of behavior are needed.

Clinical Relevance of Treatment Effects

The overview of behavior therapy conveys the breadth of changes that have been demonstrated across problem areas. While the predominant focus has been upon traditional problem areas, behavior modification has entered new areas where psychological interventions have made few inroads or which they have ignored entirely. Although enthusiasm seems warranted because of the breadth of applications and available evidence for the effectiveness of techniques in specific areas, questions can be raised about the importance of the changes that have been achieved.

Different dimensions are relevant for evaluating the importance of changes made in treatment. The magnitude of change effected with behavioral treatments is an important dimension. Although consistent changes may be obtained for a given target problem or therapy technique, sufficient attention has not always been given to the importance of these changes. Of course, the issue of the magnitude of change is only meaningfully raised after there is empirical evidence that a procedure demonstrates change. After change is shown, further attention is needed to refine the technique and to achieve the magnitude of change deemed clinically relevant.

The question of the clinical importance of behavior change is by no means a new issue for treatment evaluation. And the vast majority of behavior therapy studies included in the problem areas reviewed earlier failed to determine whether the changes resulting from treatment make any difference in overt performance in the life of the client. Quite recently, research in behavior therapy has begun to look at the importance of changes effected with treatment (Kazdin, in press b; Wolf, 1976). As such work is extended, questions about the importance of therapeutic changes can be answered directly. Meanwhile, claims made about the benefits of behavior therapy will have to be tempered accordingly.

The importance of behavior changes demonstrated in behavior therapy can be examined from another perspective. Researchers in behavior modification have been innovative in developing measures of overt behavior that are directly related to the focus of treatment. These measures have included samples of avoidance behaviors as subjects are required to approach anxiety-provoking stimuli, laboratory simulation of parent-child interaction, role-play measures of assertive behavior, physiological assessment of sexual arousal in response to audio, visual, or imagined stimuli, and others. These measures that rely upon samples of actual psychological functioning, as opposed to signs of underlying intrapsychic conflicts or personality traits, are consistent with recent developments in personality and assessment (Mischel, 1973, 1977).

Behavioral measures often sample the responses of ultimate interest in situations devised to evoke the relevant behaviors. However, the behaviors assessed may differ significantly from the behavior outside of the treatment setting. The high face validity of behavior measures may be very deceptive. Given the situational specificity of responding, measures of overt behavior in the clinic or laboratory situation may have little relation to the "same" behavior under natural conditions. For example, investigations have shown that the location of treatment (e.g., clinic versus nonclinic setting) and the set of the subject (e.g., assessment of a "problem" behavior versus assessment under some other guise) are factors that may influence the severity of behaviors that subjects evince in overt behavioral assessments (Bernstein, 1973; Bernstein & Nietzel, 1973, 1974).

Also, performance in situations that require simulation of the problem behavior may lead to different responses from those in the acutal everyday situations. The relatively simple response demands made of subjects on behavioral tests in simulated circumstances may yield different results from situations more closely resembling the much more complex cues encountered in the natural environment (Galassi & Galassi, 1976). Whether the effects of treatment on laboratory or clinical measures extend to the natural environment is not always assessed. Including laboratory measures, for example, that provide for assessment of behavior in response to varied and novel situations not directly targeted in treatment will enhance the validity of outcome assessment. However, the equivalents of concurrent and predictive validities of most behavior-measures used to evaluate treatment have not been established.

There are areas in behavior therapy where the behavior that is altered is assessed directly in the problematic situation. For example, interventions in the home to alter family interaction, in classrooms to improve academic performance of school children, in institutions to develop eating skills of retardates, and so on consist of direct assessment of the behavior of interest. However, direct assessment of the problematic behaviors in ordinary situations where they are performed is the exception rather than the rule. More direct tests of treatment efficacy need to be made to ensure that the marked gains with behavioral treatment are not restricted to laboratory measures.

Follow-up and Maintenance of Behavior

A major limitation of behavior therapy research is the general lack of follow-up data. The severity of the problem was noted by Keeley, Shemberg, and Carbonell (1976), who sampled two years of research (1972-1973) in three behavior modification journals to assess how frequently follow-up data were gathered. Although their data were restricted to applications of operant conditioning techniques, the results are instructive. Only about 12 percent of the articles examined long-term follow-up (defined as assessment at least six months after treatment was terminated). Also, many of the studies included in that percentage merely relied upon self-report assessment at follow-up. Thus, questions could be raised about the evidence for actual changes in target behaviors not observed directly.

Although the studies sampled by Keeley et al. (1976) are now over five years old, there is little reason to suspect the picture has changed. Still only a few studies have assessed long-term effects of treatment on behavioral measures outside of the treatment setting. Collecting follow-up data is beset with a host of problems that need not be described here (see Meltzoff & Kornreich, 1970; Paul, 1967b). The single problem of subject attrition alone is enough to discourage most investigators from asking questions about maintenance of therapeutic gains. However, follow-up data are of such importance that they need to be routinely collected.

The need for follow-up data is a perennial problem applicable to any therapeutic or treatment technique. Thus, one can question the need to raise the topic here. However, a few reasons make the topic of follow-up especially important in behavior therapy. The need for follow-up data in therapy is a function of the degree to which any therapeutic changes can be achieved during treatment. Obviously, it is premature to raise questions of follow-up in areas where the ability of treatments to make initial changes in target behaviors has not been demonstrated. Yet, in several areas of behavior modification across specific problems (e.g., phobias) or intervention techniques (e.g., applications of reinforcement techniques), sufficient research is available showing that therapeutic changes can be effected. The prospect of effective treatments in many areas does not seem as distant as was the case years ago when basic questions about the efficacy of therapy were first posed. Demonstrations that changes can be achieved in treatment makes salient the issue of durability of these changes.

A related reason for stressing follow-up is the pattern of results in areas where such data are available. Observation of durability of changes often has shown that changes during treatment may have little or no relation to follow-up performance. This has been a problem in some treatment areas more than others. For example, with addictive behaviors such as overeating and cigarette smoking, treatment effects have been demonstrated in several studies. Yet follow-up data have suggested that the effects of treatment are transient or nonexistent or of such a small magnitude as to be of little consequence. Similarly, interventions with conduct problem children in such settings as the classroom or home frequently show loss of therapeutic gains as soon as treatment is terminated. The loss of gains is not only painfully apparent but sometimes depended upon in experimental demonstrations where the effect of treatment is ascertained by showing that changes in behavior systematically covary with presentation and withdrawal of a specific intervention (Hartmann & Atkinson, 1973). As soon as the intervention is withdrawn, pretreatment levels or approximations of these levels often are quickly restored.

Even with the sparse evidence available, it is clear that treatment effects are not likely to be automatically maintained after the intervention is terminated and the client leaves the treatment setting. Specific provisions may be needed to ensure that the gains achieved during treatment are sustained. Behavior therapy has concentrated heavily upon the technology of behavior change, yet the technology of change may differ from the technology of maintenance of these changes. In different areas of behavioral treatment, investigators have developed specific interventions that can be added to the basic treatment approach to extend the durability of therapeutic change (e.g., Bandura, 1969; Fairweather et al., 1969; Jones & Kazdin, 1975; Kingsley & Wilson, 1977; Stokes & Baer, 1977; O'Leary, Turkewitz, & Ironsmith, 1975; Walker, Hops & Johnson, 1975). Further development and refinement of effective strategies for the maintenance of treatment-produced behavior change warrant concerted research efforts in the immediate future.

※ *Chapter 2*

Comparative Clinical Outcome Studies

The publication of Eysenck's (1952) now epic paper that called into question the efficacy of psychotherapy initiated a controversy that is still with us. The debate has not infrequently been marked by extremist views and professional rancor. Despite more than two decades of clinical research, the answers to two basic outcome questions continue to be the subject of lively dispute. The first is whether therapy is superior to no therapy. Comprehensive reviews of the pertinent literature by experts from different theoretical positions have produced conflicting interpretations (e.g., Bergin, 1971; Rachman, 1971). The second question is whether some forms of therapy are superior to others. Claims for the superiority of a particular approach are commonplace, the erstwhile adversaries of psychoanalysis and behavior therapy being joined by other contenders for the distinction of most effectively meeting the challenge of psychological disturbances.

Several recent publications have helped to focus renewed attention on the treatment outcome problem. These include a widely publicized comparative outcome study by Sloane, Staples, Cristol, Yorkston, and Whipple (1975), and two potentially influential reviews of the treatment outcome literature by Luborsky, Singer, and Luborsky (1975) and Smith and Glass (1977). These three groups of investigators arrived at similar conclusions in their evaluations of comparative treatment outcome research: therapy *is* more effective than no treatment, and different treatment approaches, including behavior therapy, are equally effective.[a] Ac-

[a] Two recent reviews of psychologically oriented treatment methods for alcoholism reached similar conclusions (Armor, Polich, & Stambul, 1976; Emrick, 1975).

45

ceptance of this position would have profound consequences for the future of psychologically-based treatment methods. The purpose of the present chapter is to conduct a searching appraisal of these views within the context of a comprehensive review of clinical comparative outcome studies.

For present purposes, behavior therapy was broadly defined as the application of principles derived from experimental psychology for the alleviation of human suffering and the enhancement of human functioning (e.g., Mahoney, Kazdin, & Lesswing, 1976; Wilson, in press c). All studies were reviewed in which a behavioral treatment or treatment package was compared either to a specific alternative form of treatment or to what is typically described as routine hospital treatment. Specific alternative treatments included commonly recognized formal treatment approaches (e.g., psychotherapy and pharmacotherapy) and active treatment methods as identified by the authors of these studies. Only studies in which prospective as opposed to retrospective comparisons were reported were reviewed. Finally, only published studies were evaluated; unpublished doctoral dissertations were excluded.

In their review, Luborsky et al. (1975) claimed to have included studies on "the general run of patient samples who seek psychotherapy." However, they deliberately excluded "the huge literature specifically on habit disorders (e.g., addiction and bed wetting)" (p. 1006). As a result, the studies they reviewed consisted of young adults and adults who were nonpsychotic and almost exclusively neurotic. This limited focus on an advantaged population of adult neurotic outpatients is characteristic of the traditional treatment-outcome literature. Similarly, Sloane et al. (1975) described the treatment of moderately disturbed individuals with neurotic and personality disorders. Smith and Glass (1977), however, extended their survey of the treatment literature to both neurotic and psychotic populations. The present chapter covers the full gamut of psychiatric problems. Luborsky et al. (1975) excluded studies that used "student volunteers" as opposed to "bona fide *patients*" in *"bona fide treatment"* (p. 1000). The present review makes no such distinction and includes all clinical comparative outcome treatment studies. Smith and Glass (1977) followed a similar policy.

Although we have attempted to undertake a thorough and comprehensive review of published comparative outcome studies, the possibility exists that some studies have escaped our attention. We console ourselves with the knowledge that it is highly improbable that the results of any single study that we have possibly overlooked could significantly alter the general pattern of the results of those studies reviewed here. Nor would any one study likely be cause for modifying the conclusions reached on the basis of our analysis of these data.

By way of preview, the present chapter evaluates the comparative therapy literature to determine precisely what claims can be made for the relative efficacy of different techniques for various clinical problems. Comparative research will be examined according to psychiatric disorders or therapeutic problems. Although the categorization of disorders closely approximates the traditional psychiatric nosological system, this does not imply endorsement of that system or a failure to recognize the criticisms that continue to be levied against it. While behavior therapists are interested in the effects of treatment on specific clinical problems, traditional diagnostic categories still constitute the most widely adhered to reference system and were selected for that reason.

This chapter reviews comparative research in the following areas: neurotic disorders, sexual dysfunction and deviance, addictive behaviors, psychotic disorders, delinquency, childhood disorders and mental retardation, and other problems. For each area, comparative research will be presented in tabular form followed by an overview of the findings. Specific studies will be critically evaluated on methodological grounds. Analysis of each area will indicate that the bulk of the comparative clinical research has been premature and usually methodologically misguided. The evaluation strategy that is exemplified in these studies has been ill-suited for identifying the mechanisms of therapeutic change or comparing the relative merits of alternative treatment methods. The implications of these conceptual and methodological analyses extend beyond the specific comparative studies that are the focus of the present chapter and, hence, are elaborated upon in the subsequent chapters.

AREAS OF COMPARATIVE RESEARCH

Neurotic Disorders
Overview of the Findings.   Table 2–1 summarizes the comparative outcome studies for neurotic disorders.[b] Since this category of problems was the primary focus of the Luborsky et al. (1975) review, a statement is in order about which studies included in that review overlap with the studies presented here. Seven of the twelve studies reviewed by

[b] In this and subsequent tables, the major comparisons are illustrated in summary form. These comparisons refer to direct contrasts of behavior therapy with an alternative procedure. For lack of space, comparisons among groups that are not directly germane to the overall question (e.g., comparison of alternate control groups) are not presented. The direction and significance of the comparison will be indicated by symbols showing that one technique for a given measure was more effective (>), less effective (<), not significantly different from (=) the other technique(s). In virtually all cases, statistical analyses and conventional levels of confidence employed in the original article were used to reach conclusions about the relative efficacy of different techniques. In the few cases where statistical analyses were not made, the conclusions in the tables are consistent with the interpretation of the original author(s) of the article.

Table 2-1.   Neurotic Disorders: Summary Tabulation of Comparative Treatment Studies

Study	Population and Problem	Treatment Methods	Measures	Results
Lazarus (1961)	Clients with diverse phobias	1. Group desensitization 2. Interpretive psychotherapy	Behavioral tests of previously phobic behavior; self-report	1 > 2
Gelder & Marks (1966)	Agoraphobic clients with related neurotic complaints (e.g., obsessions)	1. Behavior therapy = desensitization & other behavioral techniques plus drugs 2. Psychotherapy plus drugs	Clinical ratings of specific symptoms & general social adjustment; by therapist, patient, & assessor; psychometric tests	1 = 2 at post-treatment & one-year follow-up
Lazarus (1966)	Clients with specific social difficulties	1. Behavioral rehearsal 2. Direct advice 3. Nondirective reflection-interpretation	Self-report of behavior change for target problems	1 > 2 & 3
Paul (1966, 1967)	Undergraduates enrolled in a public speaking course	1. Desensitization 2. Psychotherapy 3. Attention-placebo 4. No treatment	Behavioral observations; psychophysiological measures; self-report & questionnaire measures of anxiety	1 > 2 & 3 > 4 at post-treatment & at two-year follow-up
Gelder, Marks, Wolff, & Clarke (1967); Marks (1971)	Clients with diverse phobias (e.g., agoraphobia, social phobias)	1. Behavior therapy = desensitization & other techniques (e.g., assertion training, graded homework assignments, & rational discussion) 2. Group psychotherapy 3. Individual psychotherapy (All groups received anti-anxiety drugs.)	Clinical ratings of specific symptoms & general social adjustment by therapist, patient, & assessor; psychometric tests	1 > 2 & 3 at six months into treatment; no difference at eighteen months. These results maintained at four-year follow-up

Study	Subjects	Treatments	Measures	Results
Levis & Carrera (1967)	Outpatients showing neurotic or psychotic type profiles on the MMPI	1. Implosion therapy 2. Psychotherapy 3. Waiting-list control	MMPI scales	1 > 2 & 3 in reduction of pathology on MMPI; no follow-up
Crighton & Jehu (1969)	Self-referred university students	1. Desensitization 2. Reeducative psychotherapy	Self-report questionnaires, grades, & medication	No differences; 1 = 2; no follow-up
DiLoreto (1971)	Undergraduates with interpersonal anxiety	1. Desensitization 2. Rational-emotive therapy 3. Client-centered therapy 4. No-treatment control 5. No-contact control	Behavioral observations; self-report & questionnaire measures of anxiety	1 > 2 & 3 > 4 & 5 on self-report of anxiety & behavioral observations at post-treatment and three-month follow-up; 2 > 1 > 3, 4 & 5 on increase on interpersonal activity beyond the treatment setting
Patterson, Levene, & Breger (1971)	Outpatients; majority diagnosed as personality or neurotic disorders	1. Behavior therapy = techniques (unspecified) drawn from Wolpe & Lazarus (1966) 2. Psychoanalytically oriented psychotherapy	Global ratings by therapists & patients; assessors' ratings based on case records	1 > 2 on patient ratings; no significant difference on assessor & therapist ratings; no differences at three-month follow-up
Boudewyns & Wilson (1972); Boudewyns (1975)	Psychiatric in-patients with elevated D or Pt scales on the MMPI; 50% were diagnosed as neurotic, 25% as psychotic	1. Implosion therapy 2. Modified desensitization 3. Hospital milieu treatment	MMPI, Mooney problem checklist; patient self-ratings; hospital readmissions & months of gainful employment	1 > 3 at post-treatment, six-month, one- & five-year follow-up

Table 2-1. continued

Study	Population and Problem	Treatment Methods	Measures	Results
Miller, Barrett, Hampe, & Noble (1972); Hampe, Noble, Miller, & Barrett (1973)	Mainly middle- & upper-middle-class children; most with school phobias	1. Behavior therapy = desensitization plus adjunctive techniques like assertion training, contingency management, & others 2. Psychoanalytically oriented psychotherapy 3. Waiting-list control	Global ratings by parents & an assessor; a behavior checklist & fear survey	1 = 2 = 3 on assessors' ratings at post-treatment six-week, one- & two-year follow-ups; 1 & 2 > 3 at six week follow-up on parents' ratings
Argyle, Bryant, & Trower (1974)	Patients diagnosed as personality disorders; severe interpersonal inadequacies, particularly with members of the opposite sex	1. Social skills training 2. Psychoanalytically oriented therapy 3. No treatment	Social-skills ratings of interpersonal behavior in a standardized situation; psychometric measures	1 & 2 > 3 in improving interpersonal behavior; 1 = 2 at post-treatment but 1 > 2 at six-week follow-up
Gillan & Rachman (1974)	Multiphobic outpatients	1. Desensitization 2. Modified desensitization without relaxation training 3. Relaxation training with discussion of neutral life events 4. Psychotherapy	Behavioral avoidance tests; clinical ratings by patient, therapist, & a blind assessor	1 & 2 > 3 & 4 on patient's therapists' & assessor's ratings at post-treatment & three-month follow-up
Sloane, Staples, Cristol, Yorkston, & Whipple (1975)	Outpatients suffering from moderately severe neurotic or personality disorders	1. Behavior therapy 2. Psychoanalytically oriented psychotherapy 3. Waiting-list control	Ratings of primary symptoms, general adjustment, & overall improvement by therapist, patient, assessor, & informant	1 & 2 > 3 at post-treatment on target symptoms; 1 > 2 on rating of overall improvement; 1 > 3 on target symptoms at one-year follow-up

Townsend, House & Addario (1975)	Psychiatric inpatients with chronic anxiety	1. EMG biofeedback 2. Group psychotherapy	EMG; mood disturbance; self-ratings of anxiety	1 > 2; no follow-up
Zitrin, Klein, & Woerner (1976)	Outpatient adult phobics; categorized as agoraphobics, simple phobics, or mixed phobics	1. Behavior therapy plus imipramine (Behavior therapy incompassed supportive therapy plus desensitization, assertion training, modeling, behavior rehearsal, & in vivo homework assignments.) 2. Behavior therapy plus placebo 3. Dynamically oriented supportive therapy plus imipramine	Global clinical ratings of primary phobia & overall improvement by therapists, independent assessor, & patients	1 > 2 and 1 = 3 on most ratings among agoraphobics and mixed phobics at post-treatment. With simple phobias, 1 = 2 = 3; incomplete one-year follow-up indicating no differences among treatments or diagnostic groups

Luborsky et al. (1975) are included in table 2–1. Three of the studies included by Luborsky et al. (1975) were excluded because they were retrospective in nature (Cooper, 1963; Cooper, Gelder, & Marks, 1965; Marks & Gelder, 1965); one is reviewed in the section on psychotic patients (King, Armitage, & Tilton, 1960); and one was an unpublished doctoral dissertation (McReynolds, 1969).

Of the sixteen studies in table 2–1, nine indicated some superiority of behavioral treatments over alternative methods, and seven showed no significant differences between behavioral and alternative treatments. Superficially, this might seem to argue for the greater efficacy of behavioral methods (predominantly imaginal systematic desensitization). However, caution has to be exercised in interpreting these data because of major methodological inadequacies in most of the studies. Even in the two well-controlled studies by DiLoreto (1971) and Paul (1966), interpretive problems exist.

Evaluation

Many of the conceptual and methodological difficulties inherent in the traditional model of comparative research in which something called "behavior therapy" is compared with something called "psychotherapy" can be illustrated by reference to the Sloane et al. (1975) study (Franks & Wilson, 1976). There are three main reasons for focusing on this study. First, it epitomizes the traditional approach to comparative outcome research. Second, it is the best controlled study of its kind yet conducted. Third, in addition to being credited with high methodological marks by psychotherapists (e.g., Bergin & Suinn, 1975; Garfield, 1976; Luborsky et al., 1975), no less a critic of traditional psychotherapy than Wolpe (1975) has endorsed it: "In the perceptiveness of its planning, the variety and vigor of its comparisons, and the care of its execution, it is unmatched by any other clinical study in the history of psychotherapy" (p. xix). Since many of the deficits of the other studies in table 2–1 are encompassed by the critical analysis that follows, they will be commented upon only briefly.

Several commendable methodological features distinguish this study:

1. the use of clinically experienced therapists;
2. the treatment of a large number of treatment-motivated clients;
3. successful random assignment of clients to groups;
4. the inclusion of a no-treatment control group;
5. a one-year follow-up; and
6. virtually no subject attrition, which often impedes interpretation of outcome studies.

Nonetheless, a number of questions can be raised about the study itself and, even more important, about the value of this type of treatment evaluation model in general.

Measurement Problems. Outcome evaluation consisted of ratings of three specific symptoms—global estimates of work, social, and sexual adjustment—and judgments of overall improvement.[c] These ratings were obtained from four different sources: therapist, client, an independent assessor (a psychiatrist), and an informant (a close friend or relative). Therapist and client ratings are useful, but they are particularly vulnerable to a variety of influences that may, as Sloane et al. (1975) themselves point out, distort or obscure outcome. For example, since both have invested time, effort, and money in a commitment to the treatment process, they might be reluctant to admit failure. Or they might have different ideas and expectancies about therapy and disagree about outcome.

The assessors' and informants' ratings might appear to provide greater objectivity, but there are major problems here as well. An important limitation on the value of the assessors' ratings is the fact that these ratings were based on the clients' own descriptions during the assessment interview and, aside from the interview itself, never on actual observations of the clients' behavior in real-life problem situations. Ideally, outcome measures should reflect the clients' functioning in the naturalistic environment. These clinical ratings must be distinguished from systematic observations of actual behavior. The therapist's or, by extension, an independent assessor's ratings of client functioning on the basis of a clinical interview has long been uncritically accepted as an appropriate means of measurement. As such, it is consistent with the traditional psychotherapy model that is predicated on the assumption that the relationship between therapist and client is the primary vehicle through which change takes place and is to be evaluated. The behavioral approach, based upon the rejection of internalized personality traits, and on the recognition of situation-specific effects of behavior (Mischel, 1968), has emphasized that clients' behavior in the clinical interview (a relatively contrived situation) does not necessarily provide a satisfactory sample of their behavior in the natural environment. Nor do changes that occur in the therapist-patient relationship necessarily generalize to other situations (Wilson & Evans, 1977). From a behavioral viewpoint, the assessor's ratings would have been more informative had they been based on samples of clinically-relevant behavior.

The assessor was deliberately uninformed about the nature of the treatment clients received, and Sloane et al. (1975) concluded that there

[c] Similar clinical ratings comprised the evaluations in the Gelder and Marks (1966), Gelder, Marks, Wolff and Clarke (1967), Miller, Barrett, Hampe, and Noble (1972), Patterson, Levene, and Breger (1971), and Zitrin, Klein, and Woerner (1976).

"was no evidence of bias in favor of one therapy by any of the assessors" (p. 142). Yet it is difficult to see how bias could have been evaluated given their procedures. They also stated that the assessors were "surprisingly successful in remaining blind to the type of treatment a patient received" (p. 108). The manner in which this was determined was not specified, although greater detail on this issue would seem appropriate, since one of the major measures at the one-year follow-up was a "description of the kind and amount of therapy received since the four-month assessment" (p. 118).

Gelder et al. (1967) noted that it was impossible to keep their assessor "blind" because of repeated contacts with patients over the course of treatment. However, they suggested that the therapist's knowledge of an independent assessor's ratings would encourage greater objectivity. Whether this is so remains undetermined. Similarly, Miller, Barrett, Hampe, and Noble (1972), concluding that it was impossible to sustain blind evaluation, deliberately informed their assessor of the therapist's name and type of treatment for all children. They speculated that "the gains made in acquiring uniform information and in freeing the primary evaluator from constraints in the inquiring process offset the loss attributable to an unknown bias" (p. 272). However, there was no significant disagreement between their assessor and another independent rater who was blind to the therapist and type of treatment on a sample of follow-up evaluation interviews. Finally, Patterson et al. (1971) could not keep their assessors blind and "relied upon their asserted lack of bias toward either therapy as the basis for participation" (p. 162).

The correlations among the four types of raters further indicate the problems involved in determining treatment outcome on the basis of the sort of ratings gathered by Sloane et al. (1975). Correlations of therapists' ratings with those made by assessors, clients, and informants were .13, .21, and −.04 respectively.[d] A significant correlation between assessors and clients (.65) is not surprising, given that assessors based their ratings on the information provided them by clients in interviews. Sloane et al. (1975) concluded that these "relatively low correlations support the hypothesis that different raters may have different goals for treatment or use different criteria for improvement" (p. 112). Gillan and Rachman (1974) found a significant discrepancy between their psychotherapists' ratings of client improvement and those provided by the external assessor or the clients themselves, the psychotherapists' ratings being consistently more favorable. Additional problems involved in the use of clinical rating

---

[d] Gelder et al. (1967) obtained much higher correlations among their raters on measures of clients' main phobia (e.g., .82 and .74 between therapist and assessor and therapist and client respectively). These correlations decreased on other less specific ratings.

scales as an outcome measure are highlighted by Teasdale, Walsh, Lancashire, and Mathews' (1977) finding of nonequivalence between the rating scales used by Gelder and Marks (1966) and a modified version of these rating scales with a similar client population. Clinical rating scales do not provide a uniform measure of outcome.

These findings on the unreliability of clinical ratings are summarized by Bandura (1969):

> Conflicting data of this sort are not at all surprising as long as they are not erroneously considered as measures of behavior outcome but are understood instead as differences between therapists' judgmental responses (which rarely correlate perfectly with clients' actual behavior functioning). Indeed, one would expect diminishing correspondence between actual behavior and subjective ratings as one moves from objective measures of clients' behavior to their own self-assessments, from clients' verbal reports of performance changes to therapists' judgments of improvement, [to] therapists' inferences based on clients' self-reports to information that happens to get recorded in case notes,[e] and from case notes of undetermined reliability to retrospective global ratings made by still another set of judges who never had any contact with the client (p. 458).

Other outcome measures included the Minnesota Multiphasic Personality Inventory (MMPI) (Levis & Carrera, 1967) and behavior checklists (Miller et al., 1972). Although it is empirically based, the MMPI does not reflect the specificity and accuracy of behavior change that is the ultimate focus of treatment outcome (Mischel, 1968). Behavior checklists are useful but share some of the problems inherent in clinical ratings. Lazarus (1961), Miller et al. (1972), and Gillan and Rachman (1974) included specific behavioral measures of phobic reactions where this was possible. The Lazarus (1961, 1966) studies can be criticized because the therapist conducted all outcome measures. However, all clinical ratings in the other studies, with the apparent exception of the Sloane et al. (1975) study, were made by assessors who were not blind to the nature and purpose of the study; specific behavioral avoidance tasks such as asking an acrophobic to climb a fire escape would appear to be less susceptible to extraneous assessor bias than subjective ratings.

Multiple measures of behavior change, including both subjective and objective indices (e.g., DiLoreto, 1971; Paul, 1966), are vital to adequate treatment evaluation. Specifically, where anxiety is of central concern, explicit measures of three response systems—overt behavior, physiological reactions, and self-report—appear warranted. The necessity for this broader yet more specific evaluative framework is underlined by evidence

---

[e] Patterson et al.'s (1971) assessors worked from case records.

showing that changes may occur in one of these systems but not the others; that changes may occur at different rates in these systems; that changes in one system are not necessarily correlated with changes in another; and that different systems may be differentially responsive to different treatment techniques (Borkovec, 1977; Kazdin, in press f; Lang, 1969, Rachman & Hodgson, 1974).

Omnibus versus Specific Behavioral Treatments.   Even if objective measures of behavior had been obtained, another problem with the Sloane et al. (1975) study from a behavioral point of view was the use of an omnibus treatment package that makes it impossible to identify the critical change-producing variables. A more appropriate question that emphasizes *specificity* of evaluation is "*What* treatment, by *whom,* is most effective for *this* individual with *that* specific problem, and under *which* set of circumstances" (Paul, 1967, p. 111). Sloane et al. (1975) drew up a list of stipulative definitions of both psychotherapy and behavior therapy, and commendably gathered process data to show that the treatments as implemented adhered to these definitions. However, the behavior therapy treatment still encompassed a wide range of procedures, including relaxation training, systematic desensitization, specific advice and direct intervention in problems, assertion training, role-playing, and aversion conditioning, let alone the possibly unspecified treatment and environmental factors that might have influenced outcome.

Only the Argyle, Bryant, and Trower (1974), Crighton and Jehu (1969), DiLoreto (1971), Lazarus (1961), Levis and Carrera (1967), and Paul (1966) studies tested a single, well-defined technique. All the other reports focused on systematic desensitization, but behavior therapy included several behavioral techniques (often unspecified) and even nonbehavioral treatments, for instance, Gelder & Marks (1966) and Gelder et al.'s (1967) concomitant use of drugs. Zitrin et al. (1976) noted that "many of the patients in supportive psychotherapy, on their own initiative, proceeded with in vivo desensitization," and that "the differences between the two therapeutic modalities may become blurred . . ." (p. 15).

Client Population and Problems.   Bergin and Suinn (1975) predicted that the Sloane et al. (1975) study would be compared to Paul's (1966) study, and stated that it "is clearly superior in the sense of involving clinical cases representing a number of syndromes and treatment by experts in a natural setting" (p. 511). The claim that the treatment of diverse clinical cases confers any superiority is debatable. Rather, the inclusion of different types of problems treated by widely differing techniques compounds the difficulties involved in answering the outcome question, namely, determining the specific effect of a specific treatment on a specific problem.

Moreover, the nature of the clients' and their problems bears close analysis. Well-educated, young, predominantly white, and not too severely disturbed, the clients typified the YAVIS type (*Y*oung, *A*ttractive, *V*erbal, *I*ntelligent, and *S*uccessful) that tend to have a favorable prognosis regardless of treatment (Goldstein, 1973). Selection criteria resulted in the exclusion of extremely disturbed clients (including sexual deviants and alcoholics); clients who did not request "talking therapy"; and clients, the assessor—himself a psychotherapist—would not have normally considered appropriate for psychotherapy. It can be argued that the clients selected for therapy were those who showed greater responsiveness to virtually any form of social influence procedure (Bandura, 1969). This responsiveness to the general social influence process that is a common denominator in virtually all forms of therapy may well have accounted for most of the observed improvement, creating a ceiling effect that minimized treatment differences. Consistent with this line of reasoning is the fact that a remarkable 77 percent of both psychotherapy *and* waiting-list clients were rated as either improved or recovered on a scale of overall improvement at post-treatment. Further support for this analysis derives from the finding that psychotherapy was significantly less effective with clients who were severely disturbed, as reflected in target behavior ratings and MMPI scores. Behavior therapy was equally effective with clients showing low and high initial disturbance. This pattern of results is in line with findings from laboratory treatment studies on fear reduction (Borkovec, 1973).

The DiLoreto (1971) and Paul (1966) studies are often criticized on the grounds that they involved "student volunteers" who were not "real patients." Although many "analogue" studies have methodological weaknesses, arbitrarily dismissing what has come to be called "analogue research" as irrelevant to clinical practice is a throwback to the quasi-disease model of mental illness in terms of which a person is either healthy or sick, normal or abnormal, a subject or a patient (Bandura, 1977a). Rather than implying a qualitative difference between the subjects treated by Paul (1966) and Sloane et al. (1975), for example, quantitative analyses can be made of the influence of variables such as severity of disturbance and subjects' motivation on treatment outcome.[f] There are numerous continua along which the generalizability of all treatment studies to spe-

---

[f] The arbitrariness of categorizing one study as "analogue" and another as "the real thing" is evident in Luborsky et al.'s (1975) exclusion of DiLoreto (1971) and Paul (1966) despite their inclusion of Crighton and Jehu's (1969) brief report of twenty-three students who sought counseling for test anxiety.

cific target situations can be ordered (Chapter 4). For instance, the Paul (1966) study included experienced therapists who administered well-defined treatments the effects of which were assessed using clinically important measures. It makes little sense to dismiss the significance of this study by faulting the generalizability of its subject sample when other "clinical" studies that are of questionable relevance (generalizability) on one or more other dimensions, such as unreliable and inadequate outcome measures, are uncritically accepted (Luborsky et al., 1975). From a behavioral, as distinct from the quasi-disease, model of psychological functioning, behavior change is behavior change, and the fact remains that behavioral treatment has been shown to be superior to alternative methods, at least under certain specifiable circumstances.

Client Attrition.   In contrast to the Sloane et al. (1975) study, the interpretability of some of the others is complicated by client attrition. For example, in the Zitrin et al. (1976) study, 42 percent of the psychotherapy group dropped out, in comparison to 29 percent and 10 percent in the behavior therapy plus imipramine and behavior therapy plus placebo groups, respectively. This differential attrition rate was not statistically significant, but the authors themselves observe that the remaining clients were probably the most highly motivated, a client self-selection process favoring psychotherapy. Four clients dropped out of the behavior therapy condition in the Gelder et al. (1967) study, all of whom were among the most severely disturbed clients. Gelder et al. (1967) stated that this probably did not bias the outcome in favor of behavior therapy, since they replaced these clients with four others with equally severe problems. Yet client severity may not have been the only treatment-relevant dimension along which the original and replacement patients may have differed. Finally, in the first Patterson et al. (1971) comparison, more clients dropped out than completed treatment, although the attrition did not differ significantly across treatments. The effects of this unusually high attrition rate can only be surmised.

Design Confounds.   There are at least two different types of confounds in the comparative studies with neurotic disorders. The first is that conduct of different treatments by two different groups of therapists technically constitutes a therapist× treatment confound.[g] It may be argued that it is both impractical and undesirable to try to avoid this sort of confound in applied clinical studies. Demonstrating the efficacy of particular behavior change methods over and above the influence of the therapist who

---

[g] Gelder and Marks (1966), Gelder et al. (1967), Patterson et al. (1971), Argyle et al. (1974), and Gillan and Rachman (1974) similarly had different therapists administer different treatments.

administers them may more properly be the purpose of well-controlled laboratory research, as in the case of DiLoreto (1971) and Paul (1966) studies. According to Bandura (1977a), the object of applied research in the naturalistic setting would be to find the optimal combination of proven techniques needed to maximize changes in particular types of conditions. Presumably, as in the Sloane et al. (1975) study, this would require that therapists experienced in each of the respective methods administer those methods. This conceptualization of the applied clinical research being directed toward the demonstration of the maximization of therapeutic benefits—as evidenced in a homogeneous sample of clients using objective outcome measures—is consistent with Azrin's (1977) outcome-oriented philosophy of applied research.

Nonetheless, the effects of specific treatments may be disentangled from the contributions of the therapist to the change process even in applied clinical research. One defining characteristic of behavioral methods is that they can be specified with sufficient precision so that other therapists can be trained in their use. It should be possible to do the same with specific psychotherapy techniques. The Paul (1966) study is a case in point, where experienced psychotherapists administered not only their own form of treatment but were trained to do desensitization as well. Similarly, the same therapists conducted both behavior therapy and psychotherapy in the Miller et al. (1972) and Zitrin et al. (1976) studies. Lazarus (1961, 1966) conducted all treatments himself, as a result of which therapist bias cannot be ruled out as a determinant of outcome. An alternative strategy that tends to rule out therapist factors is illustrated in the Rush, Beck, Kovacs, and Hollon (1977) study described below.

A second confound results from unequal procedural parameters among alternative treatments. In Gelder et al.'s (1967) study, for example, the different treatments were of significantly different durations. At six months, desensitization was significantly superior to individual and group psychotherapy. At the end of treatment the difference in favor of desensitization was not statistically significant. However, this assessment was made at the end of the treatment of longest duration, group psychotherapy after eighteen months. Systematic desensitization had been terminated after nine months. Thus, what was post-treatment assessment for group psychotherapy represented a nine-month follow-up for the behavioral treatment. This comparison was bound to put desensitization at a disadvantage.

In a variation of the same problem, clients in the social skills training condition in the Argyle et al. (1974) study received one session of treatment a week for six weeks, whereas clients in the psychotherapy condition received three sessions a week over six weeks. The rationale was that the additional time in therapy that the psychotherapy clients received would, if anything, bias the results against the greater efficacy of the behavioral method. Any superiority of the behavioral method therefore represents a very conservative, stringent evaluation. Paul (1966) used a similar strategy in having experienced psychotherapists administer both psychotherapy and systematic desensitization. The latter was more effective despite the fact that this choice of therapists presumably favored the psychotherapy treatment.

It may be impractical, however, and even undesirable to attempt to equate procedural parameters of alternative methods in applied clinical research of this nature. The reason is that in the process different treatments might not be fairly represented. Psychoanalytically-oriented psychotherapy, for instance, is said to require lengthy treatment, far longer than the usual duration of behavior therapy. To reduce such psychotherapy in duration to equal time spent in behavior therapy, as in the Paul (1966) and Sloane et al. (1975) studies, is to run the risk of undermining the adequacy of the experimental test. Marmor (1975), for example, anticipated this point in attributing the slightly less favorable showing of psychotherapy in the Sloane et al. (1975) study to the failure to conduct the treatment for a sufficient period of time. Procedural parameters can be equated in well-controlled laboratory research. In more naturalistic clinical research, Gelder et al.'s (1967) approach may be appropriate, provided that the confound is recognized and the results interpreted with this in mind. Specifically, a cost-benefit analysis of the outcome of this study should be emphasized, indicating the greater efficiency of systematic desensitization (Kazdin & Wilson, in press).

Adequacy of Control Groups.   One of the most striking features of Sloane et al.'s (1975) results is the improvement shown by the waiting-list control group. As compared to 93 percent of the behavior therapy group, 77 percent of these subjects were judged by the assessors to have improved on overall adjustment at the end of the four-month treatment phase. The improvement rate on target symptoms of the control group was less (48 percent), but still substantial. Sloane et al. (1975) attribute this improvement in the control group to therapeutic properties such as an active and public commitment to improvement, the diagnostic interview, and the intermittent telephone contacts with the clinic. However, their conclusion that the superiority of the two forms of treatment over the waiting-list control group demonstrates that success in therapy "is not entirely due . . . to the placebo effect of the nonspecific aspects of therapy, such as arousal of hope, expectation of help, and an initial carthartic interview" (p. 224) is questionable.

Recent research has called into question the adequacy of various control groups in controlling for the placebo effects noted by Sloane et al.

(1975), and it has emphasized that the success with which control groups do equate for factors such as therapeutic expectancy should be documented in outcome studies (Borkovec & Nau, 1972; Kazdin & Wilcoxon, 1976). It could be argued that a more stringent control group, possibly equating amount of contact with a therapist, might have resulted in even greater improvement, perhaps even equal to that of the two forms of treatment. However, the inclusion of an attention-placebo control group that meets the exacting criteria spelled out by Borkovec (1977) and Kazdin and Wilcoxon (1976) for laboratory research may, as O'Leary and Borkovec (1977) point out, be impractical because of compelling ethical considerations and methodological complexities. As we describe in Chapter 4, the applied clinical arena may be less the place to isolate specific mechanisms of behavior change than the place for demonstrating the efficacy of laboratory-tested methods.

There is only one study that compares behavior therapy with routine treatment (Boudewyns & Wilson, 1972). The clients were a heterogeneous group with diverse psychotic, neurotic, and personality disorders. In addition to measurement problems, such as a limited reliance on tests such as the MMPI and Mooney Problem Checklist, there is a major design difficulty in this study. Clients treated with implosion and modified desensitization were discharged before clients assigned to routine milieu therapy were even admitted. Follow-up was not uniform across treatment groups.

To summarize the foregoing analysis, it is argued that insufficiently discriminating and inadequate methodology has characterized traditional outcome research and has obscured possible differences between treatments. More definitive evaluation of the relative efficacy of specific behavioral methods over the more general social influence process inherent in most forms of therapy will be possible to the extent that outcome studies focus on more specific multiple measurements of the effects of well-defined treatment techniques applied to homogeneous groups of clients. The conceptual and methodological considerations that dictate this shift in strategy are discussed in the following chapters.

Sexual Dysfunction and Deviance

Overview of the Findings. Table 2–2 summarizes comparative outcome studies in this area. Only four comparative studies could be located.[h] All four studies reported some degree of superiority of behavioral treatment. However, the paucity of data and a number of methodological flaws make it impossible to draw firm conclusions about the relative

[h] In the Lazarus (1961) study reviewed in the previous section, both cases of impotence treated with systematic desensitization showed long-term improvement, whereas the three impotent men who received psychotherapy were treatment failures.

Table 2-2. Sexual Dysfunction and Deviation: Summary Tabulation of Comparative Treatment Studies

Study	Population and Problem	Treatment Methods	Measures	Results
Birk, Huddleston, Miller, & Cohler (1971)	Outpatient male homosexuals	1. A modification of the anticipatory avoidance conditioning procedure plus concomitant group psychotherapy 2. Placebo conditioning plus ongoing psychotherapy	Blind clinical ratings by an independent assessor; questionnaire measures of frequency of sexual behavior; MMPI & projective tests	1 > 2 in decreasing specific homosexual behaviors at post-treatment and one-year follow-up; global clinical ratings in the same direction but not significant
Feldman & MacCulloch (1971)	Outpatient male homosexuals	1. Anticipatory avoidance conditioning 2. Classical aversive conditioning 3. Psychotherapy	A sexual attitude scale & interview-based clinical judgments of therapists	At follow-up (mean = 44 weeks) 1 = 2 > 3 with respect to homosexuals with prior pleasurable heterosexual behavior; 1 = 2 = 3 with homosexuals with no prior heterosexual experience

| Obler (1973) | Adult outpatients with sexual dysfunction | 1. Desensitization and adjunctive techniques (e.g., instructions to abstain from intercourse, assertion training)
2. Neo-Freudian group psychotherapy plus matched exposure to films & slides of sexual encounters used in therapy
3. No treatment | Patient self-recordings of sexual experiences; psychometric measures of anxiety, & autonomic responses to filmed sexual stimuli | 1 > 2 on patient self-recordings, on physiological measures of arousal, & psychometric tests at post-treatment; results maintained at eighteen-month follow-up |
| Kockott, Dittmar & Nusselt (1975) | Impotent heterosexual males with cooperative partners | 1. Desensitization
2. Conventional medication & advice given by general practitioners & psychiatrists
3. Waiting-list control | Penile tumescence in response to a tape recording of a sexually stimulating scene; subjective responses to the same scene; ratings of sexual behavior based on semistructured interview | 1 > 2 & 3 in reducing self-reports of sexual anxiety; no differences in ratings of sexual behavior; no follow-up |

efficacy of behavioral treatment as compared to a specific alternative form of therapy.

Evaluation

Measurement. Direct behavioral measures of sexual behavior under nonlaboratory conditions are not feasible, but there are alternative objective measures of outcome. Obler (1973) obtained multiple measures of treatment efficacy, including self-monitoring of successful and unsuccessful performance (corroborated by the client's partner);[1] autonomic arousal (GSR and heart rate) in response to filmed material of anxiety-eliciting sexual scenes; and standardized tests that assess sexual behavior.

In contrast to this commendable multiple-response measurement, Feldman and MacCulloch's (1971) outcome measures were inadequate. Their only quantifiable measure of improvement was the Sexual Orientation Method (SOM), an attitude scale with questionable validity (Bancroft, 1974; MacDonough, 1972). Since there were no between-group differences on simple change scores on this scale, Feldman and MacCulloch (1971) selected an arbitrary criterion of success (a reduction of twelve units on the homosexual scale) in order to analyze the results further. In terms of this criterion only secondary homosexuals (those with prior pleasurable heterosexual experience) responded favorably to treatment (six out of eight in the anticipatory avoidance group; five out of seven in the classical aversive conditioning group; and two out of six in the psychotherapy group). These differences were not statistically significant; nor were there any differences on the heterosexual scale of the SOM. The only other outcome measure was an estimate of success derived from follow-up interviews with either one (or both) of the investigators. As a result, the possibility of observational bias cannot be excluded in interpreting these results.

Birk, Huddleston, Miller, and Cohler's (1971) evaluation methods were more satisfactory, including blind clinical ratings by an independent assessor with reliability checks; sexual behavior questionnaires that provided estimates of the frequencies of specific sexual acts; the MMPI and projective tests.

Other Methodological Considerations. Obler's (1973) study indicates the efficacy of a combination of behavioral methods for a range of sexual disorders, but it does not demonstrate the efficacy of a specific technique applied to a well-defined problem. Different therapists conducted different treatments; moreover, there was no follow-up. Marks (1976a) has suggested that Obler's clients were "student volunteers" who might have

---

[1] Obler (1973) did not report any information on these corroborative records, e.g., how many were obtained, or how consistent they were with client's self-recordings.

been biased in favor of desensitization as opposed to traditional group therapy. While two clients did refuse group treatment, Marks's inference is highly speculative. The assumption that the clients were students is Marks's, for Obler states that direct referrals were made from community-based clinics as well as counseling centers in local universities. Moreover, the implication that "volunteer students" sexual problems are less relevant in the evaluation of treatment efficacy can be challenged (Chapter 4).

Feldman and MacCulloch's (1971) study has been severely criticized by Bancroft (1974), who points out that the assignment of clients was such that the psychotherapy group was at a disadvantage relative to the conditioning group before treatment. Since psychotherapy was administered by one of the investigators, therapist bias provides an alternative explanation of the results. Bancroft (1974) has also criticized the Birk et al. (1971) study on the grounds that the patients randomly assigned to the conditioning treatment showed higher levels of homosexual behavior prior to treatment. He notes that the levels of homosexual behavior at post treatment were similar between the two groups and attributes the greater change in the conditioning group to a "floor effect," i.e., that it is easier to reduce a high-frequency behavior to a moderate frequency than a behavior of moderate frequency to one of low frequency. (Statistical regression toward the mean could account for this effect, depending upon the correlations of repeated assessment.) An alternative view might stress that a higher frequency of homosexual behavior might indicate greater severity of the problem, hence less likelihood of success, and putting the conditioning group at a disadvantage. Finally, psychotherapy was compared to behavior therapy plus psychotherapy. Given the total ineffectiveness of the placebo plus psychotherapy group, the differential effect can be attributed to the conditioning procedure, unless a specific interaction between group psychotherapy and conditioning is postulated.

In addition to ratings of specific sexual behaviors derived from a semistructured interview, Kockott, Dittmar, and Nusselt (1975) also obtained subjective and physiological measures. This was the only study that used penile plethysmographic measures of sexual arousal, the inclusion of which would have improved all of the foregoing studies (Barlow, 1977). Unfortunately, technical problems resulted in incomplete recordings that are uninterpretable.

Discussion. A recurrent problem in the comparative research reviewed here is the adequacy with which both the behavioral and psychotherapeutic approaches are tested. Both the Obler (1973) and Kockott et al. (1975) studies relied primarily or exclusively on systematic desensitization. Yet other behavioral methods, such as the Masters and

Johnson type of program, have been shown to be more effective than systematic desensitization (Mathews et al., 1976). Consistent with this fact is Kockott et al.'s report that eight of twelve of their clients who had shown no improvement in the initial study subsequently showed marked improvement when treated with this alternative behavioral approach.

It can be claimed that the nonbehavioral comparison treatments were not tested fairly, especially in the Feldman and MacCulloch (1971) study. With respect to the treatment of sexual dysfunction, however, there are to our knowledge no data—not even uncontrolled clinical trials—that suggest that traditional psychotherapy is particularly effective. The success of the behavioral treatments reviewed in the previous chapter is unprecedented (O'Leary & Wilson, 1975).

Addictive Behaviors
Obesity: Overview of the Findings.   Table 2–3 summarizes the comparative outcome studies in this category. Weight loss provides one of the rare, easily obtained, yet objective measures of treatment outcome that would seem to lend itself well to comparative outcome research. Therefore, it is surprising to note the relatively few studies of this nature, although the studies that have been reported reflect improved methodological quality as compared to evaluations of the treatment of neurotic disorders. The pattern of results is strikingly consistent. In every instance behavioral treatment produced significantly greater weight loss at posttreatment than the alternative treatment methods irrespective of whether they were group social pressure, a form of psychotherapy, or pharmacotherapy. Moreover, in four of the five studies that reported a long-term follow-up, the short-term superiority of behavior therapy was no longer evident at follow-up. Only the Levitz and Stunkard (1974) study provides evidence of the superior long-term (nine months) efficacy of behavior therapy. These outcomes are consistent with the more general pattern of findings on the behavioral treatment of obesity (Stunkard & Mahoney, 1976).

Evaluation
Measurement Problems.   Among others, Jeffrey (1975) has pointed out that the preferred measure of treatment outcome in obesity is the weight reduction quotient defined as weight lost/overweight at pretreatment × initial weight/target weight × 100. This index controls for variations in height, weight, and percentage overweight prior to treatment. Only the Kingsley and Wilson (1977) and Öst and Götestam (1976) studies reported this measure in addition to simple weight loss. In addition to the primary objective measure of weight loss, multiple adjunctive measures of clients' physical, emotional, and social functioning are recommended on at least

Table 2-3. Obesity: Summary Tabulation of Comparative Studies

Study	Population and Problem	Treatment Methods	Measures	Results
Harmatz & Lapuc (1968)	Overweight inpatient schizophrenics	1. Behavioral (response cost) treatment 2. Group (social pressure) treatment 3. Diet control	Weight loss in lbs.	1 > 2 & 3 at four-month follow-up
Wollersheim (1970)	Overweight female students at least 10% overweight	1. Group behavioral treatment 2. Social pressure 3. Nonspecific therapy 4. Waiting-list control	Weight loss in lbs.; eating pattern questionnaire; personality & anxiety scales	1 > 2, 3, & 4 in weight loss & eating habits at post-treatment and eight-week follow-up
Penick, Filion, Fox, & Stunkard (1971); Stunkard (1972)	Obese adults at least 20% overweight	1. Behavior therapy (= modified Stuart & Davis [1972] program) 2. Psychotherapy plus dietary & nutritional instructions & infrequent use of appetite suppressants	Weight loss in lbs.	1 > 2 at post-treatment
Levitz & Stunkard (1974)	Members of TOPS (Take Off Pounds Sensibly) at least 10% overweight	1. Group behavioral treatment (modified Stuart & Davis program) conducted by professionals & TOPS chapter leaders respectively 2. Nutrition training 3. Routine TOPS program	Weight loss in lbs.	1 > 2 & 3 in weight loss & less patient attrition at post-treatment & nine-month follow-up

Table 2–3. continued

Study	Population and Problem	Treatment Methods	Measures	Results
Ost & Gotestam (1976)	Obese adults ranging from 15 to 62% overweight (mean = 35%)	1. Behavior therapy (=modified Stuart & Davis program) 2. Pharmacological treatment (fenfluramine plus advice about nutrition & exercise) 3. Waiting-list control	Weight loss in lbs.; percentage overweight, & weight reduction index	1 > 2 & 3 on weight reduction index at post-treatment; 1 = 2 at one-year follow-up
Kingsley & Wilson (1977)	Obese women at least 10% overweight	1. Individual behavior therapy 2. Group behavior therapy 3. Social pressure/motivation (adapted from TOPS)	Weight loss in lbs.; percentage overweight, & weight reduction index	1 = 2 > 3 at post-treatment; 1 < 2 = 3 at follow-up
Hall, Hall, DeBoer, & O'Kulitch (1977)	Female members of TOPS an average of about 56% overweight	1. Behavior therapy 2. Psychotherapy 3. Waiting-list control	Weight loss in lbs.	1 > 2 & 3 at post-treatment; no differences at three- & six-month follow-up

two counts. First, Stunkard (1976b) has reported the occurrence of concomitant depression with weight loss. Second, Nisbett's (1972) theory
that adults who lose weight fall below a biologically dictated "set point"
with the result that they enter a state of chronic energy deficit specifically
predicts negative side-effects of continued weight loss. Of the studies
reviewed above, only Öst and Götestam's (1976) and Wollersheim's
(1970) reports provided information relevant to these broader measurement concerns. The former found little evidence of any negative side-
effects with behavioral treatment; the latter found that weight reduction
was positively correlated with decreased anxiety ratings and generalized
positive effects. These do not support Nisbett's (1972) predictions and
Stunkard's (1976) observations.

Omnibus Treatment Packages. Omnibus treatment packages incor-
porating a broad array of different behavioral methods were used in all the
studies, making it impossible to identify the effective ingredients of
therapy. The premature standardization of an often ill-defined, multifaceted behavioral treatment program for obesity not only complicates
interpretation of comparative treatment research, but also discourages the
development of more effective treatment methods (Franks & Wilson,
1976). Several empirical findings suggest the need for greater specificity in
the assessment and treatment of obesity. One is the consistent finding of
massive interindividual variability in treatment outcome with behavioral
programs (e.g., Jeffery et al., in press; Penick, Filion, Fox, & Stunkard,
1971). Another is the finding of variability in the types of changes produced by different behavioral treatments. Kingsley and Wilson (1977), for
example, found that group behavior therapy was significantly more effective than individual behavior therapy at a twelve-month follow-up.

Comparison Treatments. Aside from Öst and Götestam's (1976) drug
treatment and Levitz and Stunkard's (1974) TOPS self-help comparison
treatments, the remaining studies employed some form of group therapy.
These alternative treatments were too diverse to permit an adequate
assessment of the efficacy of group psychotherapy, and psychotherapy
proponents are certain to question the representativeness of these treatments. However, as in the case of sexual dysfunction, there is little reason
to expect psychotherapy to be very effective even on the basis of uncontrolled case reports. Leon (1976) has pointed out that the literature
suggests that psychotherapy, consisting almost exclusively of individual
case histories in which specific statistics on weight loss are lacking, has
been successful only in "isolated cases." The comparison treatments in
the Hall, Hall, DeBoer, and O'Kulitch (1977), Kingsley and Wilson
(1977), and Wollersheim (1970) studies are most appropriately regarded as

attention-placebo control conditions than specific active forms of therapy. However, one of the methodological strengths of these comparisons is that both Hall et al. (1977) and Kingsley and Wilson (1977) established that their control treatments were as credible and as effective in eliciting expectancies of favorable outcome as their behavioral programs.

Therapist × *Treatment Confounds.*   Different therapists administered the different treatments in the Öst and Götestam (1976) and Penick et al. (1971) studies. Levitz and Stunkard's (1974) findings that professional behavior therapists were significantly more successful than nonprofessional leaders of TOPS groups in the implementation of behavioral treatment indicates that therapist factors may influence treatment outcome.

Alcoholism: Overview of the Findings.   Table 2–4 summarizes the studies reviewed in this category. Two obvious trends are evident. The first is that aversion conditioning is not more effective than the specific alternative or routine treatments. Vogler, Ferstl, Kraemer, and Brengelmann (1975) reported that their three electric shock conditions, when combined, were superior to the control group. However, the failure of the conditioning group to produce greater suppression than the random shock group indicates that any therapeutic value these treatments may have cannot be attributed to aversion conditioning. The results of several other well-controlled behavioral studies are uniformly consistent with the results of these comparative outcome studies in showing that electrical aversion conditioning is ineffective as a method of treatment for alcoholism (Hallam, Rachman, & Falkowski, 1972; Nathan & Briddell, 1977; Wilson, in press a). Wallerstein's (1957) study has been criticized by Rachman and Teasdale (1969) as an inadequate test of the efficacy of behavior therapy. For example, different diagnostic categories were confounded with the different treatments. Uncontrolled findings (Wiens, Montague, Manaugh, & English, 1976) suggest that chemical aversion conditioning may be effective with a more advantaged client population than the one studied by Wallerstein (1957).

The second trend is that multifaceted behavioral programs show evidence of significantly greater efficacy than comparison treatments. The results obtained with these broad-based behavioral approaches are especially promising in view of their apparent success even at a two-year follow-up (Azrin, 1976; Sobell & Sobell, 1976). However, the following are some methodological limitations that dictate appropriate caution in interpreting these findings.

Evaluation
Adequacy of the Comparison Treatments.   In all but the Pomerleau, Pertschuk, and Brady (1976) study, behavior therapy was compared to

routine treatment offered by a state hospital or, in the case of Miller (1975), services provided by a conventional skid row facility. Two factors suggest some reservation in interpreting the differences in favor of behavior therapy. First, it can be argued that almost any novel treatment program introduced into such conventional therapy settings would capitalize on the placebo factors of renewed interest, optimism, and enthusiasm the treatment staff might display. In other words, the two treatments might not have been valued equally highly by the therapists who administered them and/or the clients that participated in the different programs. For example, the control treatment provided clients in the Hunt and Azrin (1973) study consisted almost exclusively of didactic sessions on the negative effects of alcohol and on the workings of Alcoholics Anonymous. On face value it would be difficult to argue that such a program could have equated for the many placebo influences generated by the community-reinforcement program. Second, one reviewer has suggested an iatrogenic effect of relegating some clients to routine treatment while assigning others to a novel program (Emrick, 1974). Specifically, Emrick (1974) observes that 40 percent of the clients in Sobell and Sobell's (1976) control groups expressed resentment at having been deprived of the experimental treatment at the two-year follow-up. Another 20 percent reported that they had initially experienced feelings of resentment but then felt better. The possibility exists that the difference between the behavior therapy and control groups was in some part a function of the negative reaction of control group clients as well as the improvement shown by the behavior therapy group clients.

Measurement Issues. It is now clear that evaluation of treatment programs in terms of whether alcoholics are abstinent ("dry") or not ("drunk") (Vogler, Lunde, Johnson, & Martin, 1970; Vogler et al., 1975) is too restrictive and based on questionable assumptions of the nature of alcoholism (Baekelund, Lundwall, & Kissin, 1974; Nathan & Briddell, 1977; Pattison, 1976). Aside from abstinence, modified or controlled drinking may be a realistic alternative. Moreover, since abstinence does not ensure rehabilitation of the alcoholic (Pattison, 1976), measurement must be multidimensional. The focus should be on physical health, emotional, social, and vocational adjustment in addition to the primary data of the amount and pattern of alcohol consumption. An impressive feature of the Azrin (1976), Hunt and Azrin (1973), and Sobell and Sobell (1976) studies is the manner in which they have satisfied these measurement criteria.

Measurement of alcohol consumption has traditionally relied upon clients' self-reports, often supplemented by corroborative reports of close friends or family members (e.g., Sobell & Sobell, 1976). A more objective measure is provided by Miller's (1975) use of breath alcohol samples.

Table 2-4.   Alcoholism: Summary Tabulation of Comparative Treatment Studies

Study	Population and Problem	Treatment Methods	Measures	Results
Wallerstein (1957)	Hospitalized male alcoholics; diagnosed variously as neurotics, character disorders, & psychotic	1. Chemical aversion conditioning 2. Hypnotherapy 3. Antabuse 4. Milieu therapy (All patients also continued to receive weekly group therapy.)	Amount of alcohol consumed; social adjustment, personality measures	3 apparently more effective than 1, 2, & 4 at two-year follow-up. (No formal statistical analyses reported.)
Vogler, Lunde, Johnson, & Martin (1970); Vogler, Lunde, & Martin (1971)	Chronic, hospitalized male alcoholics	1. Electrical aversion conditioning 2. Pseudo-conditioning 3. Sham conditioning 4. Routine hospital treatment	Post-treatment abstinence; rehospitalization	1 > 2 + 3 + 4 (combined) in terms of time to relapse; no differences in number of relapses at eight-month or one-year follow-up
Hunt & Azrin (1973)	Male alcoholics who suffered withdrawal symptoms	1. Community reinforcement program, including vocational, family, & social counseling 2. Routine hospital treatment	Percent time spent drinking, working, at home, or in institutions	1 > 2 on all measures at six-month follow-up
Miller, Hersen, Eisler, & Hemphill (1973)	Hospitalized male alcoholics	1. Electrical aversion conditioning 2. Sham conditioning 3. Group therapy	Consumption of alcohol during a laboratory analogue measure of drinking	1 = 2 = 3
Miller (1975)	Chronic male alcoholics selected from jailed public drunkenness offenders	1. Contingency management program 2. Traditional services of skid row community agencies	Number of arrests, hours of employment, blood alcohol concentration (BAL)	1 > 2 on all measures; no follow-up

Study	Population	Treatment Conditions	Measures	Results
Vogler, Ferstl, Kraemer, & Brengelmann (1975)	Volunteer, chronic alcoholics	1. Electrical aversion conditioning 2. Routine hospital treatment	Abstinence rates determined by interviews with patients & collaborative source	Two of three aversion conditioning methods superior to routine treatment at one-year follow-up
Azrin (1976)	Male alcoholics with physiological withdrawal symptoms	1. Community-reinforcement program including job, family & social counseling, & an incentive program for self-administration of antabuse 2. Routine hospital treatment	Percent time spent drinking, working, at home, or in institution	1 > 2 on all measures at two-year follow-up
Pomerleau, Pertschuck, & Brady (1976)	Middle-income problem drinkers	1. Group behavior therapy 2. Individual behavior therapy 3. Traditional group psychotherapy	Ozs. alcohol consumed per week	1 & 2 > 3 in reducing drinking & less patient-attrition at six-month follow-up
Sobell & Sobell (1976)	Hospitalized male alcoholics	1. Multifaceted behavior therapy program oriented towards abstinence 2. Multifaceted behavior therapy program oriented toward controlled drinking 3. Conventional hospital treatment oriented toward abstinence 4. Conventional treatment oriented toward controlled drinking	Self-recorded drinking; general adjustment; vocational, occupational, residential, & marital status, driver's license status & use of therapeutic supports during follow-up	1 > 3, & 2 > 4 at one-year follow-up; 2 > 4 at two-year follow-up

However, while the self-reports of alcoholics about their drinking have customarily been viewed with suspicion, the data show that they are often reliable and valid (Baekelund et al., 1974; Sobell & Sobell, 1975).

Blind ratings of treatment outcome are important in eliminating rater bias. Hunt and Azrin (1973) demonstrated impressive reliability between a blind assessor and therapists' evaluations. In the Sobell and Sobell (1976) study, outcome evaluations were conducted by one of the two investigators, making it impossible to rule out unintentional distortion.

Additional Methodological Considerations.   In view of the fact that the Sobell and Sobell (1976) study is in some ways one of the most sophisticated of its kind, and because the results obtained rank among the most favorable and controversial ever reported, careful scrutiny is warranted.

Omnibus Treatment Packages.   The problems that can arise in using a very broad treatment package encompassing diverse methods is illustrated by the Sobell and Sobell (1976) study. Among others, treatment techniques comprised electrical aversion conditioning (a tested but unproven technique), various self-control procedures, direct advice, role-playing, and exposure to videotaped scenes of their drunkenness (an untested and unproven method). Yet the treatment package produced marked changes in alcohol consumption during the course of follow-up but not during treatment. Specifically, clients drank to excess during nonshock "probe" test periods but showed controlled drinking and even abstinence following the completion of the program (Nathan & Briddell, 1977). Interpretation of treatment effects is further complicated by the fact that follow-up involved a lengthy and intensive ongoing relationship between one of the investigators and the clients. It is probable that this follow-up procedure was reactive and might well have contributed in important but unspecified ways to successful outcome at follow-up. The methodological and conceptual issues involved in conducting treatment follow-ups are discussed in the following chapter.

Subject Selection and Assignment.   Clients were selectively assigned to the controlled drinking conditions in the Sobell and Sobell (1976) study because they had requested it, had significant social support in their natural environment, and/or had successfully practiced controlled drinking in the past. Comparisons between controlled drinking and abstinent conditions are thus confounded. Since behavior therapy was significantly superior to routine treatment during the second year of follow-up only within the controlled drinking condition, an interaction between subject selection factors and the long-term efficacy of behavior therapy is suggested.

Confounding Influences. A recurrent problem in comparative outcome research is equating the parameters of the alternative treatments. For example, it appears that in the Hunt and Azrin (1973) and Miller (1975) studies, the behavioral treatment groups received not just different but more therapy in the form of active contact with the therapists.

Psychotic Disorders[j]

A relatively large number of comparative studies has been completed with psychiatric patients. The studies divide into comparisons of a behavior therapy technique with general ward care or with a specific alternative treatment. Routine ward treatment consists primarily of custodial care, although several unspecified activities and small amounts of therapy of some sort may be included. Alternative treatments refer to active procedures that are more well specified than custodial ward care and are associated with an explicit rationale from which the procedures are derived.

Behavior Therapy versus Routine Ward Care: Overview of the Findings. Table 2–5 summarizes the studies reviewed in this category. Comparisons of reinforcement programs with routine ward care indicate a relatively consistent pattern. Reinforcement programs have led to improvements on measures of cognitive, affective, and social aspects of psychotic behavior, on specific behaviors in interviews and on the ward, and in global measures of adjustment or discharge from the hospital and subsequent readmission. Patient improvements in these areas are much greater for reinforcement than for routine care wards. Regrettably, comparisons of reinforcement and routine ward programs have been beset with methodological problems, including bias in subject selection and assignment, confounds of treatment with changes in the physical ward and in the hospital staff, and ancillary features of the hospital environment.

Evaluation

Subject Selection and Assignment. Ambiguities of subject selection and assignment obscure the results of studies comparing routine ward care with reinforcement. The administrative difficulties of patient assignment and care frequently militate against random assignment of patients to conditions. With few exceptions, where random assignment was used

[j] Comparative research with psychiatric disorders has focused primarily upon inpatients diagnosed as schizophrenic. Occasionally, studies include other diagnoses, multiple diagnoses, and nonpsychotic inpatients (e.g., mental retardation) because inpatients are housed on the same ward together. Research has not evaluated the relative efficacy of behavior therapy and other techniques with diverse psychotic disorders.

Table 2–5. Psychotic Disorders: Summary Tabulation of Studies Comparing Behavior Therapy with Routine Ward Care

Study	Population and Problem	Treatment Methods	Measures	Results
Schaefer & Martin (1966)	Apathy of adult schizophrenics	1. Contingent reinforcement for ward behaviors 2. Noncontingent reinforcement	Behavioral observations of apathy	1 > 2
Heap, Boblitt, Moore & Hord (1970)	Adaptive ward behaviors of chronic patients	1. Reinforcement plus self-government 2. Routine care	Number of patients performing self-care, discharge rates	1 > 2 on self-care behaviors and discharge
Birky, Chambliss & Wasden (1971)	Self-care behaviors of adult patients	1. Reinforcement for ward behaviors 2. Routine care	Discharge rates	1 = 2 on discharge; 1 > 2 with chronic patients
Gripp & Magaro (1971)	Adaptive ward behaviors of schizophrenics	1. Reinforcement for ward behaviors 2. Routine care	Rating scales and a behavior checklist	1 more gains than 2 in cognitive, affective, and social areas
Shean & Zeidberg (1971)	Self-care and social behaviors of chronic patients	1. Reinforcement for ward behaviors 2. Routine care	Ratings of adjustment; attending activities; time out of hospital; laboratory task; placement in vocational program	1 > 2 in rated cooperation on ward, communication skills, & social interaction; 1 > 2 in placement in vocational program, participation in activities, & time out of hospital

DiScipio & Trudeau (1972)	Grooming of psychotics	1. Reinforcement for personal appearance 2. Routine care	Ratings of psychotic behavior & self-esteem	1 > 2 in self-esteem & less paranoid belligerence; also, 1 slightly higher than 2 in discharge & at two-month follow-up
Maley, Feldman, & Ruskin (1973)	Self-care & social behaviors of chronic schizophrenics	1. Reinforcement for self-care & ward behaviors 2. Routine care	Standardized interview; behavioral & adjustment ratings	1 > 2 in compliance with instructions, discrimination & orientation; 1 rated as more improved & in less need of hospitalization than 2
Schwartz & Bellack (1975)	Ward behaviors of psychotics	1. Reinforcement for ward behaviors 2. Routine care	Nurses' ratings	1 > 2 in social competence & neatness & lower in manifest psychosis

(e.g., Maley, Feldman, & Ruskin, 1973; Schaefer & Martin, 1966), differences between reinforcement and routine care wards might result from pretreatment patient differences. Patients in the reinforcement and routine care wards may differ in such treatment-relevant characteristics as severity of behavior and age (Birky, Chambliss, & Wasden, 1971; Heap, Boblitt, Moore, & Hord, 1970).

To partially resolve the problem of nonequivalent groups, investigators often match patients on the reinforcement ward with those on a control ward (Schwartz & Bellack, 1975; Shean & Zeidberg, 1971). Yet, matching without subsequent random assignment of patients to treatments does not guarantee equality of groups or subsequent interpretability of group differences even when groups are equal on pretreatment matching variables (Kazdin, in press f). Matching without random assignment allows for the possibility of differential statistical regression to account for any pre-post treatment differences that might appear to result from different treatments (Campbell & Stanley, 1963).

Ward × Treatment Confounds.   In a number of programs, the physical settings of the reinforcement and routine care wards differ in significant ways. Typically, improvements are made in the ward that houses patients who receive the reinforcement condition (e.g., Gripp & Magaro, 1971; Heap et al., 1970). Aside from the physical changes in the ward, such as the addition of furniture, etc., patients in the reinforcement program often are transferred to another ward specifically designed for the program (Heap et al., 1970). The changes made in the physical characteristics of the ward and the movement of patients to a new ward have been shown to effect durable therapeutic improvements for psychotic inpatients independently of any other specific interventions (e.g., DeVries, 1968; Higgs, 1970). For example, Gripp and Magaro (1971) found that inpatients who transferred to a control ward (routine ward care) showed as many improvements as did inpatients who transferred into the ward with the reinforcement program. Thus, transferring across wards alone could account for changes in many of the programs evaluating reinforcement programs.

Staff × Treatment Confound.   Several differences in reinforcement and routine ward programs pertain to the staff, who vary across the respective wards. Different staff have been involved in reinforcement and routine ward care programs (DiScipio & Trudeau, 1972). While the association of specific staff with a given program is understandable given the constraints of institutional organization, this does not gainsay the possible interpretive problems of attributing results to the staff rather than to the programs they are conducting. The problem of the staff across reinforcement program and routine care wards is exacerbated in select studies by different staff-inpatient ratios. For example, Gripp and Magaro (1971) added staff to the reinforcement ward but did not add staff to the routine care ward. Given the possible role of staff-inpatient ratios in patient improvements (e.g., Ullmann, 1967), such confounds cannot be dismissed lightly. Added to the mere number of staff is the problem of the investigators, who may differentially attend treatment and control wards. For example, Shean and Zeidberg (1971) mentioned that they were present on the experimental (reinforcement program) ward but not on the control ward. Presumably, the presence of the investigators on the ward could have its own effects on staff and inpatient behavior independent of the specific intervention of the ward.

Other staff-related issues have obscured the comparisons of routine ward care and reinforcement programs. The behavior of staff across wards is likely to vary greatly. When staff participate in reinforcement program, many of their behaviors in relation to the inpatients are altered even though these behaviors may not be specifically programmed as part of treatment. For example, staff who implement a reinforcement program provide much more verbal and nonverbal attention to inpatients than staff on routine care wards (Trudel, Boisvert, Maruca, & Leroux, 1974). Also, staff who administer reinforcers have been shown to decrease the amount of punishment provided, increase use of approval, and in general increase overall amount of contact (Chadwick & Day, 1971; Gambrill, 1974; Mandelker, Brigham, & Bushell, 1970). Finally, staff who work on a reinforcement program become much more positive in their attitudes toward the patients than do staff who participate in a routine ward care program (McReynolds & Coleman, 1972; Milby, Pendergrass, & Clark, 1975). The differences in attitudes and behaviors of the staff on the reinforcement program ward may be a result of the program rather than a cause of inpatient behavior change. Nevertheless, the changes in staff across reinforcement and routine care wards makes unclear the precise intervention to which patient differences across wards might be attributed.

Additional Methodological Problems.   Reinforcement and routine care programs differ in ways that have no necessary bearing upon behavior modification per se. For example, in reinforcement programs, inpatients have been encouraged to engage in more activities by the staff and are informed of more opportunities to utilize resources in the hospital (e.g., DiScipio & Trudeau, 1972; Maley et al., 1973). Also, individualized treatment programs are devised for patients on a reinforcement program ward. Planning such programs with the staff or the patients may influence staff and patient behavior independently of specific contingencies that actually focus on these behaviors.

Occasionally, specific activities are clearly confounded with reinforcement and routine ward programs. For example, Heap et al. (1970) provided inpatients on the reinforcement ward with several adjunctive procedures that not only included increased activities but also group meetings and "attitude" therapy. Generally, reinforcement programs provide inpatients with extra reinforcing events that are not usually available in routine ward care programs. Thus, the effect of the reinforcement program cannot rule out the possibility that more pleasant conditions rather than operant conditioning principles partially account for the superiority of reinforcement over routine ward care. The use of noncontingent reinforcement in some studies has helped rule out the possible influences of reinforcers per se (Schaefer & Martin, 1966; Shean & Zeidberg, 1971).

Measurement of Program Effects.   While diverse types of measurement have been used, the relation of the measurement devices to the goals of treatment and the behaviors focused upon is unclear. The vast majority of reinforcement programs for psychiatric inpatients has focused upon self-care and routine ward behaviors (Kazdin, 1975d). The effects of these interventions are assessed on global ratings of psychotic behavior or overall adjustment. It is unclear how the alteration of self-care behavior affects ratings of adjustment unless possibly through stereotypic global assessments of the social desirability of patient responses. The relative severity of psychoticism, psychopathology, or maladjustment would not be expected to be as clearly related to self-care and routine ward skills as the data would suggest. This raises questions not only about the focus of treatment programs but also about the mechanisms through which their effects are achieved (Kazdin, 1977d).

The lack of specificity of treatment effects also is raised by the diversity of inpatient types who participate in a given reinforcement program. The psychiatric inpatients selected in most studies include an amalgam of diverse diagnoses. In any given study, inpatients on the ward may suffer from either chronic or acute psychosis, mental retardation, neurosis, organic brain syndrome, or other problems (Birky et al., 1971; DiScipio & Trudeau, 1972). Improvement in patients with diverse diagnoses is impressive. On the other hand, the generality of treatment effects across inpatients suggests that treatment may be effective through some change in ward atmosphere or activity rather than specific changes in the psychological status of the inpatient.

The superiority of reinforcement programs over routine ward care has been demonstrated in more favorable discharge and readmission rates, although there are exceptions (e.g., Birky et al., 1971). Discharge and readmission are important dependent measures in evaluating the success of treatment. However, they are general measures often subject to non-treatment influences (Gripp & Magaro, 1974; Kazdin & Bootzin, 1972). Indeed, discharge may not bear a direct relation to the psychological status of the inpatient but rather to social contingencies of the extratreatment environment for the inpatient or simply to a "total push" emphasis of the hospital. Favorable discharge rates for reinforcement programs have been advanced in cases where different criteria for discharge might account for the effects (e.g., Atthowe & Krasner, 1968; Heap et al., 1970).

Behavioral versus Other Specific Treatments: Overview of the Findings. Too few studies are available comparing reinforcement programs with another single technique (Table 2–6). The treatments to which reinforcement programs have been compared include role-playing, verbal-psychotherapy, play therapy, recreational therapy, and milieu therapy. The fact that three of the comparative studies have used verbal therapy should not be taken as three similar comparisons. Actually the verbal therapies have been sufficiently different to avoid classifying them as the same treatment. In almost all of the available studies, reinforcement techniques have been more effective than the comparative treatment. As in the research on routine treatments, the dependent measures have varied to include ratings of adjustment or more specific behaviors, activities, social interaction in the hospital, and behavior outside from the hospital.

From a methodological standpoint, the comparative studies have been better designed than have been the comparisons of routine ward and reinforcement programs. For example, matching followed by random inpatient assignment to treatments is commonly practiced in the comparative studies (Doty, 1975; Hartlage, 1970; Ney, Palvesky, & Markely, 1971). A few problems detract from drawing firm conclusions about the superiority of reinforcement programs.

Evaluation

Execution of Treatment.   In comparative research, an essential feature is to ensure that each treatment is administered correctly. Constraints of time, attempts to control for parameters of treatment across different techniques, predilection of the investigator for one treatment over another, and similar influences can make one of the treatments less representative of what it should be than the others. In select studies, treatments were not likely to be implemented correctly or in an optimal fashion. Hence, the study would not provide a fair comparison of treatments or easily interpretable results. For example, in the Marks, Sonoda, and Schalock (1968) study, staff delivered reinforcers to the patients at their own discretion when they recognized appropriate behavior. How-

Table 2–6. Psychotic Disorders: Summary Tabulation of Studies Comparing Behavior with Other Specific Active Treatments

Study	Population and Problem	Treatment Methods	Measures	Results
King, Armitage, & Tilton (1960)	Problem solving on a lever-pushing task with chronic schizophrenics	1. Reinforcement for problem solving 2. Verbal therapy 3. Recreational therapy 4. Routine care	Adjustment & verbalizations in interviews; ratings of ward behaviors & overall improvement	1 > 2, 3, & 4 on adjustment; 1 > 2 in ward behavior, verbalizations, & overall improvement; 1 maintained superiority at six-month follow-up
Marks, Sonoda, & Schalock (1968)	Self-care & self-awareness of chronic schizophrenics	1. Reinforcement 2. Individual psychotherapy	Ratings of adjustment; tests of mental efficiency, motor skills; association skills, self-concept	1 = 2 on most measures; inconsistent pattern on the few reliable differences
Hartlage (1970)	Adjustment of chronic schizophrenics	1. Reinforcement 2. Individual psychotherapy	Ratings of hospital adjustment & improvement	1 > 2 in improvement of adjustment & therapist ratings; 1 = 2 in self-concept
Ney, Palvesky, & Markely (1971)	Self-awareness, expression, social behaviors of childhood schizophrenics	1. Reinforcement 2. Play therapy	Developmental inventories of mental age	1 > 2 in increases in mental age

Olson & Greenberg (1972)	Social interaction, ward behaviors of psychiatric patients	1. Reinforcement for ward behaviors 2. Milieu plus group therapy 3. Milieu only	In hospital ratings of behavior, time out of hospital	1 > 2 & 3 in activities performed in the hospital & in days out of the hospital; 2 & 3 > 1 in social adjustment
Doty (1975)	Social skills of chronic patients	1. Role-playing 2. Reinforcement 3. Role-playing plus reinforcement 4. Attention-placebo 5. No treatment	Behaviors on ward & in group discussions	2 & 3 > 1, 4, & 5 in social interaction
Austin, Liberman, King, & DeRisi (1976)	Primarily psychotic or neurotic patients in day-treatment programs	1. Reinforcement program focusing on skills adaptive for community living 2. Milieu treatment including other procedures such as relaxation, music & exercise	Ratings of improvement for individual patient goals	1 = 2 at three- & six-month assessment; 1 marginally greater at two-year follow-up; in re-analysis for group 2 patients who received unscheduled behavioral treatment showed that 1 > 2 at six months

ever, staff discretion as a guideline for administering reinforcers is diametrically opposed to the basic tenets of reinforcement systems. Criteria for reinforcer delivery need to be explicit both to the staff and patient so that discretion and subjective judgment are minimized. Without clear criteria it is unclear that reinforcers were delivered for any particular behaviors or that they were delivered consistently over time. The failure of reinforcement and psychotherapy programs to produce a difference in this study would be readily dismissed by adherents of behavior modification because of the violation of basic desiderata of reinforcement programs.

Another possible clue that treatment may not be delivered properly pertains to the training of individuals who administer the different treatments. For example, in the Hartlage (1970) study, student nurses administered both psychotherapy and reinforcement conditions. Nurses received five hours of training in each technique. On the basis of so little training, adherents to either reinforcement or insight therapy techniques are not likely to endorse the adequacy in which either treatment was conducted. Even reinforcement programs, which are straightforward relative to the complexities of insight therapy, are not likely to be administered very effectively on the basis of five hours of training. Indeed, there is an extensive literature attesting to the difficulty in training staff to adequately implement reinforcement programs over protracted training periods (Hersen & Bellack, in press; Kazdin, 1976a). In any case, treatment differences in the Hartlage (1970) study might be a function of how well staff could perform the technique with brief training rather than the relative effects of different treatments per se.

A final problem unique to comparative studies is keeping the different techniques distinct. Marks et al. (1968) mentioned that to keep the reinforcement condition distinct from therapy, staff were instructed to deliver reinforcers mechanistically and impersonally. While one might argue for the advantages of keeping treatments distinct on methodological grounds, the end result may be uninterpretable. In fact, an important ingredient in reinforcement programs is the social interaction between staff and patients. The reinforcement operation is intentionally social in nature. Indeed, research was cited earlier noting how reinforcement programs may completely restructure the social behaviors of staff who administer the program (e.g., Breyer & Allen, 1975; Chadwick & Day, 1971; Trudel et al., 1974). Thus, to administer a reinforcement by minimizing interpersonal contact is an experimental test of a treatment that is not relevant to most applications of reinforcement.

On the other side of the issue, in the Marks et al. (1968) study, it would not make very much sense to delete reinforcement from therapy (e.g., Truax, 1966). To exclude contingent consequences of the therapist, whether explicitly programmed or not, may not be a test of therapy as it is normally practiced.

Measurement Problems. In general, the comparative studies have assessed behaviors focused upon directly in treatment. In a few studies, there is an unclear association with the problem focused upon in treatment and the dependent measures. For example, Ney et al. (1971) compared reinforcement for diverse behaviors (e.g., imitation, interaction, instruction following) with play therapy where children were allowed to express their conflicts and feelings symbolically with a therapist. Treatment effects were evaluated on measures of intellectual functioning. While the effects of treatment on such measures obviously are interesting, it is unclear why intellectual functioning should be the best or most appropriate measure of treatment effects. Moreover, it is unclear that intellectual functioning was the primary problem of the schizophrenic children included in the study.

A similar criticism might be leveled against the King et al. (1960) study in which patients performed on a lever-pushing task with no clear clinical relevance. However, the outcome variables included global and specific measures of adjustment and ward behavior, which presumably are important signs of treatment effects. Despite immediate appearances, the dependent measures and focus on behaviors in a laboratory task were dictated conceptually by the notion of developing problem-solving skills that would transcend the laboratory situation.

Delinquency

Overview of the Findings. Table 2–7 summarizes the studies reviewed in this category. Relatively few studies are available comparing different treatments among delinquents. Of the available studies, the differences in physical settings where the comparisons are made are great. Programs have been conducted in traditional institutional settings (Jesness, 1975), home-style family cottages (Fixsen, Phillips, Phillips, & Wolf, 1976), and the community (outpatient treatment) (Fo & O'Donnell, 1974). Also, the manner in which treatment is delivered differs markedly across studies so that some delinquents are treated on an individual basis (Fo & O'Donnell, 1974), others in a large institutional program (Jesness, 1975), and others with their families (Alexander & Parsons, 1973). Thus, the marked differences in the setting and the manner in which treatment is delivered might lead one to expect drastically different results across investigations.

A clear statement characterizing the relative effects of different treatment with delinquents would seem unwarranted for at least two reasons. First, the treatments to which reinforcement programs have been compared have varied so widely that statements about reinforcement pro-

Table 2-7. Delinquents: Summary Tabulation of Comparative Treatment Studies

Study	Population and Problem	Treatment Methods	Measures	Results
Fixsen, Phillips, Phillips & Wolf (1976)	Post-treatment adjustment of adjudicated predelinquents	1. Reinforcement for multiple behaviors (Achievement Place) 2. Reform school 3. Probation	Recidivism, grades, school attendance, school dropout, police & court contact	1 > 2 in lower recidivism, contacts with police & courts, & higher in school attendance & grades at two-year follow-up
Alexander & Parsons (1973); Klein, Alexander, & Parsons (1977)	Interaction of adjudicated delinquents & their families	1. Reinforcement for family interaction 2. Client-centered therapy 3. Psychodynamic therapy 4. No treatment	Overt behavioral measures of family interaction; recidivism Overt problem behaviors such as truancy, academic achievement	1 > 2, 3, & 4 in improving interacting and lower recidivism at six-to-eighteen-month follow-up; 1 > 2, 3, & 4 in court contacts of siblings of treated delinquent 2½ to 3½ years after treatment

Study	Focus	Treatment	Measures	Results
Fo & O'Donnell (1974)	Behavior & academic problems of adolescents	1. Social reinforcement for specific behaviors 2. Social & monetary reinforcement 3. Relationship therapy 4. No treatment		1 & 2 > 3 & 4 in reducing truancy & specific problem behaviors; no group differences in grades
Fo & O'Donnell (1975)	Follow-up of above report	1. Reinforcement program 2. No treatment	Delinquent offenses during treatment & pre-treatment years	1 > 2 in lower major offenses; youths with no major offenses increased after participating in group 1
Jesness (1975)	Routine institutional behaviors, social behaviors, academic performance & others of adjudicated delinquents	1. Reinforcement for ward, academic, & other behaviors 2. Transactional analysis	Achievement tests; multiple measures of personality; overt social behavior; parole follow-up after treatment	Great overlap across groups for multiple measures; 1 = 2 on parole violations up to two-year follow-up; 1 tend to be superior on overt behavioral measures; 2 tend to be superior on personality & self-report measures

grams and any other single treatment cannot be made. Second, the findings suggest complexities in the types of changes made with different treatments. For example, in at least one of the studies, the superiority of one treatment over another depended upon the assessment method used as the criterion (Jesness, 1975).

An impressive feature of each of the studies with delinquents is the assessment of contact with the police and courts (recidivism) after treatment. Unfortunately, the pattern of follow-up results across studies has yielded inconsistent results. Indeed, one study suggests that the follow-up results may partially depend upon the severity of delinquent behavior prior to treatment (Fo & O'Donnell, 1975), although additional demonstrations would be needed before asserting severity as a moderator variable among different treatments.

Evaluation
Design Problems.   Because of the few studies available, the specific design problems of the investigations can be treated in a single section. Initially, the lack of random assignment of subjects to conditions creates interpretive problems. The possibility exists that delinquents assigned to conditions differ initially. Initial differences do not necessarily mean that subjects differ on the measures used to evaluate treatment. Even if subjects are initially similar in their pretreatment scores, the possibility exists that the rate and magnitude of change on these measures across groups would differ even without treatment. Thus, the assignment of subjects make interpretation of the Fixen et al. (1976) study unclear.

A similar problem exists for the Jesness study (1975). Although delinquent youths were randomly assigned to conditions, the two treatment programs were conducted at different institutions. Quite possibly, differences at the institutions not relevant to treatment were responsible for the different pattern of results between groups. Essentially, randomly assigning subjects to different settings where a given treatment is conducted confounds treatment and setting.

Another instance of the treatment× setting confound is evident in the Alexander and Parsons (1973) study, where patients were assigned randomly to conditions. However, different conditions were conducted in different settings (e.g., the clinic with which the investigators were associated versus a church-affiliated treatment program). The different settings also utilized therapists with different skills, professional affiliations, and experience.

Childhood Disorders: Enuresis and Conduct Problems
Enuresis: Overview of the Findings.   The research on enuresis and conduct problems represents comparisons of different techniques and,

hence, are treated separately in terms of overall evaluation. Table 2–8 summarizes the studies comparing treatments for enuresis. A consistent pattern emerges from the literature. The bell-and-pad method appears overwhelmingly more effective than supportive and psychodynamically-oriented verbal psychotherapy and routine treatments such as increased fluid intake. The superiority of the bell-and-pad method has extended to drug treatments as well (McConaghy, 1969).

The relapse rates for the bell-and-pad method have been variable, partially as a function of treatment duration, the definition of relapse, and no doubt several other variables. For example, DeLeon and Mandell (1966) reported a relapse rate of approximately 80 percent for bell-and-pad children. However, relapse was defined as *one* enuretic episode within a follow-up period ranging from four to eighty-eight weeks. Whether a single enuretic episode over a period exceeding one and one-half years should be defined as a relapse partially depends upon the "normal" rate of enuretic episodes of individuals of the same age as the treated children who are not identified as enuretic. Even with stringent criteria, relapse is not invariably found with the bell-and-pad method (Jehu, Morgan, Turner, & Jones, 1977). However, a recent review suggests that about 41 percent of the children treated have relapsed within about six months (Doleys, 1976). The majority of these can be successfully retreated.

Overall, the effects of the bell-and-pad method both for short and long-term results do not seem to be approached by alternative treatments. Aside from the magnitude of treatment effects, the economy of the procedure has much to recommend it. Unlike alternative treatments such as psychotherapy, skilled professionals are not involved in training after the initial interview where the bell-and-pad method is explained. Indeed, professionals are not needed for this initial interview, given the nature of treatment. Parents typically conduct treatment on their own without a therapist's intervention (e.g., Werry & Cohrssen, 1965).

Conduct Problems: Overview of the Findings. For the treatment of conduct problems, comparative studies have been restricted to reinforcement versus drug treatment (Table 2–9). Because of the treatment comparisons for behavior problem children, three additional studies with mentally retarded adults are included here as well. While there is no a priori reason for including children and mentally retarded adults, comparative studies with these populations each have been concerned with behavioral management problems and have examined reinforcement and drug treatments.

The pattern of results comparing reinforcement and drug treatment with children and adults is reasonably consistent. Reinforcement of adaptive behaviors tends to be more effective in suppressing conduct problem behavior and in developing specific adaptive behaviors than alternative

Table 2–8.   Enuretic Children: Summary Tabulation of Comparative Treatment Studies

Study	Population and Problem	Treatment Methods	Measures	Results
Werry & Cohrssen (1965)	Enuretic children	1. Bell & pad method 2. Supportive-psychodynamically oriented therapy 3. No treatment	Frequency of bedwetting	1 > 2 & 3 in reducing bedwetting after 3 to 4 months of treatment
DeLeon & Mandell (1966)	Enuretic children	1. Bell & pad method 2. Individual psychotherapy separately with child & mother 3. No treatment	Frequency of bedwetting	1 > 2 & 3 in reducing wetting; approximately 80% relapse in group 1 (= one enuretic episode up to 88 weeks after treatment) but relapsed children rapidly treated
Novick (1966)	Enuretic children	1. Routine supportive therapy 2. Bell & pad method if cure not achieved (cure = 14 consecutive dry nights)	Frequency of bedwetting	2 cured 20% of children; 1 cured approximately 89% of those not affected by treatment 1; 1 > 2 with more severe cases
McConaghy (1969)	Enuretic children	1. Bell & pad method 2. Random awakening of child 3. Imipramine 4. Placebo	Frequency of bedwetting	1 = 3 > 2 & 4 after ten weeks of treatment; at one-year follow-up, 1 > 2, 3, & 4
Jehu, Morgan, Turner, & Jones (1977)	Enuretic children	1. Bell & pad method 2. Routine treatment (=such procedures as increasing fluid intake, awakening child)	Frequency of bedwetting; ratings of adjustment & parent-child relationship	1 > 2 in reducing wetting; 1 = 2 on adjustment & relationship ratings

drug treatments (using either Ritalin or Thorazine), although there are exceptions (Gittelman-Klein, Klein, Abikoff, Katz, Gloisten, & Kates, 1976). In drug research, questions always can be raised about whether dose levels were appropriate to the subjects and whether increases in dose would alter the pattern of results. In only one study were dose levels varied to address these questions (McConahey, Thompson, & Zimmerman, 1977). As noted in Table 2–9, a higher dose of Thorazine increased the efficacy of the drug in suppressing maladaptive behavior in mentally retarded adults. Even so, the results obtained with the higher dose did not approach the efficacy demonstrated with reinforcement techniques.

Increases in drug dose are not necessarily associated with increases in treatment efficacy. While drugs may suppress maladaptive behavior, they also may suppress adaptive behavior as well (Ayllon et al., 1975). Hence, increased doses would be expected to suppress adaptive behavior to an even greater extent, an effect demonstrated by McConahey et al. (1977). In general, the greater efficacy demonstrated with reinforcement techniques does not seem to be accounted for by dose levels and is not appreciably reduced by increased dosage.[k]

Evaluation.

Adequacy of Treatment.   As a general rule, comparative research both for enuresis and conduct problems has met high levels of methodological standards. However, one of the outstanding issues pertains to the adequacy of treatment. In the enuresis research, several procedures raise questions about whether the bell-and-pad procedure has been implemented properly. Although the procedure is relatively simple, it does require different steps, such as setting the apparatus each night, ensuring that the child actually is awakened by the alarm, having the child turn off the alarm, and directing the child to the bathroom to complete urination. None of the comparative studies has assessed whether parents actually implement the procedures as directed.

There are cases where the bell-and-pad procedure appears to have been conducted in a less than optimal fashion. For example, in some studies, the procedure is only implemented on some of the occasions in which it could be applied, for instance, only once a night rather than every time there is an enuretic episode or on most rather than all days during training (Jehu et al., 1977; Werry & Cohrssen, 1975). One might expect that these intermittent applications would be less effective than continu-

[k] In passing, it may be worth mentioning the combined effects of drugs and reinforcement techniques. The findings have been divided, with some studies showing that the combination of drugs and reinforcement is no better than reinforcement alone (Christensen, 1975; McConahey, 1972; McConahey et al., 1977), and other studies showing greater effects with the combination than reinforcement alone (Christensen & Sprague, 1972; Gittelman-Klein et al., 1976).

Table 2–9.   Conduct Problem and/or Retarded Children or Adults: Summary Tabulation of Comparative Treatment

Study	Population and Problem	Treatment Methods	Measures	Results
Christensen & Sprague (1973)	Hyperactive behaviors of school children	1. Reinforcement for in-seat behavior 2. Drug therapy (Ritalin) 3. Reinforcement plus drug 4. Placebo	In-seat movements	1 = 2 > 4 in reducing movements; 3 > 1
Ayllon, Layman, & Kandel (1975)	Academic behaviors & deportment of hyperactive children	1. Reinforcement for academic behavior 2. Drug therapy (Ritalin)	Overt behavior & academic performance	1 = 2 in suppressing hyperactive behaviors; 1 > 2 in improving academic performance
Christensen (1975)	Classroom behavior of institutional, hyperactive, retarded children	1. Reinforcement for working in class 2. Drug therapy (Ritalin) 3. Reinforcement plus drug	Overt behavior; teacher ratings; academic performance	1 > 2 in classroom management; 1 = 2 in academic performance; 1 = 3 in overall effectiveness
Gittelman-Klein, Klein, Abikoff, Katz, Gloisten, & Kates (1976)	Hyperactive behavior of children at home and at school	1. Reinforcement for deportment at home and at school plus drug therapy (Ritalin) 2. Reinforcement plus placebo 3. Drug alone	Teacher rating scale; overt classroom behavior; global ratings; teacher, parent, & psychiatrist ratings of overall improvement	1 = 3 > 2 on select teacher rating scales & on overt classroom behavior; 1 > 2 on global teacher & psychiatrist ratings of improvement
Shafto & Sulzbacher (1977)	Classroom behavior of a hyperactive, retarded preschool child	1. Reinforcement for play behaviors 2. Drug therapy (Ritalin) 3. Reinforcement plus drug	Overt play activity; verbal & academic behaviors; attentiveness; compliance	1 & 3 > 2 in reducing overall activity & purposeless movement; 2 > 1 in increasing inappropriate verbalizations

Study	Population	Treatments	Measures	Results
Wulbert & Dries (1977)	Clinic & home behavior of a hyperactive child	1. Reinforcement for absence of ritualistic behavior & for completion of memory, auditory, & visual tasks (clinic) or cooperation (home) 2. Drug therapy (Ritalin) 3. Placebo	Overt behaviors including task performance; rituals; distraction; eye contact with experimenter	1 > 2 & 3 in improving task performance & reducing ritualistic behaviors; 1 = 2 & 3 on distraction & eye contact which were measures of generalization
McConahey & Thompson (1971); McConahey (1972)	Adaptive (e.g., self-care, work) & maladaptive (e.g., verbal abuse) of profoundly & moderately retarded adult females	1. Reinforcement for adaptive behaviors 2. Drug therapy (Thorazine) 3. Placebo	Nurses ratings, overall improvement; multiple discrete adaptive & maladaptive behaviors	1 > 2 & 3 across multiple measures
McConahey, Thompson, & Zimmerman (1977)	Similar to above	Similar to above	Similar to above	Results similar to above; higher doses of drug slightly more effective than lower doses but 1 > 2 even at high drug doses
Rimland (1977)	Parents who rated effects of treatments their autistic children received	1. Operant conditioning 2. Psychotherapy 3. Day school 4. Residential school 5. Doman-Delacto methods 6. Diverse diet control procedures 7. Teaching machine	Global ratings of how effective treatment was	1 most effective (highest percentage of parents), 2 least effective

ous applications. Interestingly, intermittent applications are not invariably less effective and appear even more effective in alleviating high relapse rates (Doleys, 1976).

The adequacy of implementing supportive and psychodynamically-oriented therapy may be questioned as well. In general, relatively few therapy sessions have been provided in psychotherapy comparisons with the bell-and-pad method. For example, Werry and Cohrssen (1965) provided between six and eight therapy sessions; Novick (1966) provided ten sessions. The results of such comparisons, in view of the available evidence, would seem to be primarily of academic interest because the bell-and-pad method has proven to be so effective within a relatively short period of administration.

The adequacy of testing drug treatments in enuresis research also can be questioned. In the one comparative drug study, parents were instructed to administer a capsule (imipramine, amphetamine, or a placebo) thirty minutes prior to bedtime (McConaghy, 1969). Without specific checks on the frequency and timing of administration, it is quite possible that the drugs were not given as directed. Hence, the effects of treatment would be attenuated. However, the different effects across drug treatments suggests that differential adherence is not likely to explain the results.

The comparative research on conduct problems does not raise major concerns about the adequacy of treatment. In these studies, treatment is administered in institutional settings so that delivery and consumption of drugs can be monitored relatively easily. The adequacy of treatment in the drug research pertains primarily to the dose level. And, as noted earlier, the amount of the drug is not necessarily linearly related to treatment efficacy. Increased dosage level may suppress adaptive behaviors.

Select Methodological Problems.   Individual studies both in the area of enuresis and conduct problems can be criticized along particular dimensions. However, the criticisms are specific to individual studies and cannot discount the pattern of results within or across studies. For example, in the Novick (1966) study, an unambiguous comparison of supportive psychotherapy and the bell-and-pad method cannot be made because all subjects received psychotherapy. The bell-and-pad method was provided only after therapy was shown not to work. Thus, the possible influence of the sequence of treatments and the comparison of therapy alone versus therapy followed by the bell-and-pad method obscure the results. Yet, the results of this study are perfectly consistent with other comparisons of supportive therapy and the bell-and-pad method.

In cases where a consistent methodological problem might be noted, the bias would seem to operate against the bell-and-pad method. For example, the amount of contact with a professional therapist has been consistently confounded with treatment. Children and parents who receive psychotherapy consistently have more contact with a professional therapist than do children and parents in the bell-and-pad condition. The reason is that once the bell-and-pad procedure is explained, it is implemented at home by the parents. Hence, there is no need for additional professional contact other than occasional phone calls or collection of data. In contrast, psychotherapy subjects receive repeated contact with a trained therapist and frequently come to specific treatment sessions. The expectation might be that the increased contact with a therapist would enhance the nonspecific and placebo effects of supportive therapy, thereby increasing its efficacy. This might well be the case. However, bell-and-pad subjects consistently show greater treatment effects. Thus, the possible influence of the confound of therapist contact is not particularly important from a practical standpoint.

A final problem worth mentioning pertains to the assessment of behavior in the enuresis studies. The routine method of assessment is to observe the frequency of bedwetting at home. Parents monitor bedwetting and occasionally other events as well, such as the frequency of fluid intake, the time the alarm sounds, and whether medication is taken (e.g., McConaghy, 1969). Reliability (interobserver agreement) checks have not been reported in the comparative literature to assess whether parental reports are accurate. The absence of reliability is serious in light of current standards for collecting observational data (e.g., Bijou, Peterson, & Ault, 1968). Parental report of the frequency of wetting is likely to be inaccurate to some degree. The absence of interobserver agreement data makes this margin of error unknown.

While the absence of agreement data raises questions about the magnitude of treatment effects, it does not clearly explain the differential effects of treatment. Differences in parental reporting do not seem to provide a plausible explanation for the consistent treatment differences. Hence, while studies could be improved in their assessment procedures in the home, the improvements might not be expected to alter the pattern of results.

The bulk of the methodological issues raised pertained to the enuresis studies rather than to the studies on conduct problems. The reason for this is straightforward: the latter studies in general have been very well designed and carefully executed. Both within-group and between-group comparisons have been made, treatments have been carried out for protracted periods, and multiple behaviors have been carefully assessed, each with checks for interobserver agreement. High methodological standards of research have been the rule in this area rather than the exception.

One study (Rimland, 1977) included in Table 2–9 differs both in methodology and focus but is included because of its relevance to child disorders. The study is actually a survey of approximately 2500 parents of autistic children who were merely asked to rate the efficacy of the treatment their children received. As evident from Table 2–9 psychotherapy and operant conditioning treatments were rated as the least and most effective treatments, respectively. A variety of other treatments, including different diet manipulations, specific training programs, and residential care, were intermediary between the two extremes in rated efficacy. Although the survey is interesting in its own right, conclusions about the actual effects of different treatments cannot be drawn. Global ratings of treatment effects, selection factors that may have dictated which treatment was sought, and possible differences in amount of treatment or the duration of follow-up at which points parents were queried, all limit the conclusions that can be drawn.

Miscellaneous Other Problems

Overview and Evaluation.   Four studies not readily accommodated by other categories are summarized in Table 2–10. The details of these studies, all of which indicate the superiority of behavior therapy, are analyzed separately below.

Rush et al. (1977) found that what might be called cognitive behavior therapy resulted in significantly greater reduction in depression and client attrition rate during therapy.[1] These findings are impressive on several counts. The comparison treatment provided a stringent control. Tricyclic pharmacotherapy has been shown to be more effective than other treatments, including psychotherapy, and is widely viewed as the recommended therapy for depression. Moreover, the results produced by pharmacotherapy in this study were comparable to previous findings with antidepressant drugs, suggesting that it was adequately tested as an alternative form of therapy. Treatment-produced improvement was clinically as well as statistically significant, over 70 percent of clients who received cognitive behavior therapy showing marked improvement or total remission of what Rush et al. (1977) term "depressive symptomatology" as compared to less than 30 percent of clients treated with pharmacotherapy. These results were maintained at a six-month follow-up. Any therapist×treatment confound can be dismissed, since eighteen different therapists administered the treatments. The majority of these therapists were committed to a psychoanalytic approach, had no minor expertise in behavior therapy, and participated in the study solely for didactic and training reasons.

---

[1] Rush et al. (1977) describe their treatment method as "cognitive therapy." However, as Beck (1976) makes clear, *behavioral* procedures are used to facilitate the goal of cognitive change. In this sense, Rush et al.'s (1977) methods clearly fit contemporary conceptualizations of behavior therapy (Mahoney et al., 1974; Wilson, 1977b).

Table 2-10. Miscellaneous Adult Disorders: Summary Tabulation of Comparative Treatment Studies

Study	Population and Problem	Treatment Methods	Measures	Results
Liberman, Levine, Wheeler, Sanders, & Wallace (1976)	Distressed married couples	1. Behavioral marital group therapy 2. Interactional therapy	Behavioral observation of in-session interaction; self-report of marital satisfaction	1 > 2 on behavioral observations
Ritchie (1976)	Medical patients with chronic pain	1. Reinforcement for participating in diverse activities (e.g., swimming, learning a skill) 2. Routine hospital care	Time spent in activities, self-report & objective tasks estimating pain	1 > 2 in time in activities; 1 = 2 in measures estimating pain
Rush, Beck, Kovacs, & Hollon (1977)	Moderately to severely depressed outpatients with neurotic depression	1. Cognitive behavior therapy 2. Tricyclic pharmacotherapy	Self-ratings & clinical ratings by clinical assessors who were aware of the treatment patients received	1 > 2 across all measures of depression; results maintained at six-month follow-up
Taylor, Farquhar, Nelson, & Agras (1977)	Adult outpatients suffering from hypertension	1. Relaxation treatment 2. Nonspecific therapy 3. Medical treatment	Blood pressure	1 > 2 & 3 in reducing blood pressure at posttreatment; 1 = 2 = 3 at six-month follow-up

Two criticisms can be made of this study. First, measurement consisted of standardized client and clinical ratings. The assessors who completed these ratings were not blind to the treatment clients had received. Rush et al. (1977) suggest that the high consistency between client self-ratings and the clinical ratings argue against the notion of bias on the part of the assessor, but the problem remains. Second, the cognitive behavior therapy group had more contact with the therapist than did the pharmacotherapy group. Technically, this constitutes an experimental confound, although Rush et al. (1977) point out that in another study comparing pharmacotherapy with psychotherapy (Covi, Lipman, Derogatis, Smith & Pattison, 1974), the former was more effective despite the fact that the latter received more therapist contact.

Taylor, Farquhar, Nelson, and Agras's (1977) study provides a well-controlled demonstration of the efficacy of relaxation treatment as an adjunct to medical treatment in the management of hypertension. Several commendable methodological features distinguish this study. The availability of an objective measure (blood pressure) and the use of blind assessors provided a more convincing evaluation of outcome than the majority of studies reviewed in this paper. Similarly, Taylor et al. (1977) provided evidence that their nonspecific treatment condition was perceived by the patients as highly credible and effective, the defining criteria of an adequate placebo control condition. As with much of the research covered here, however, the superiority of the relaxation treatment was no longer statistically significant at six-month follow-up.

Liberman, Levine, Wheeler, Sanders, and Wallace's (1976) study is distinguished by the use of multiple objective and subjective outcome measures. Instead of relying upon an independent assessor's clinical ratings obtained during a conventional interview (e.g., Sloane et al., 1975), Liberman et al. (1976) obtained reliable behavioral observations by blind raters of actual samples of marital interaction. In our analysis of the studies on neurotic reactions we argued that specific, objective measures of behavior are more likely to reveal differential treatment effects than more global clinical ratings. Thus, it is significant to note that whereas Liberman et al. (1976) found few differences on client ratings, direct behavioral observations provided significant between-treatment differences.

Finally, Ritchie (1976) found that a token reinforcement program produced a marginal increase in activity levels in chronic pain clients in comparison to a control group on a routine hospital activity management schedule. There were no differences on measures of pain. Inadequate specification of the nature of the control group and the absence of any follow-up data undermine the value of this study.

CONCLUSIONS AND IMPLICATIONS

The clinical treatment outcome studies reviewed in Tables 2–1 through 2–10 vary enormously in methodological adequacy. A relatively small number of studies were sufficiently well designed and executed so as to permit unequivocal conclusions. For the majority of studies, however, fundamental conceptual difficulties and design deficiencies greatly complicate meaningful interpretation. Several studies contain little useful information. Many of these methodological flaws have been discussed in our analyses of the different categories of studies; a more extended appraisal of the limitations of the sort of traditional comparative outcome studies reviewed above is presented in the following chapter.

Although many interpretive problems in evaluating the comparative treatment outcome literature exist, conclusions of far-reaching significance are likely to be drawn anyway. These conclusions about the relative efficacy of different treatment approaches have major consequences for the funding of future research and clinical training programs in this country. These exigencies compel us to pay serious attention to the existing comparative outcome studies, despite our considered opinion that the inadequacies of the data base are for the most part so pronounced, and the conceptual model that guided these comparisons sufficiently misguided, that meaningful interpretation is often impossible. The present discussion attempts to distill some overall findings from the heterogeneous mass of different data summarized above and to compare these findings with the conclusions reached by previous reviews of essentially the same outcome literature.

Unlike Luborsky et al. (1975), grades were not assigned to the studies reviewed here according to some selected methodological criteria. The first objection to such an undertaking is that it is arbitrary. For example, the two studies that Luborsky et al. (1975) graded the highest (B +) were Gelder et al. (1967) and Sloane et al. (1975). Yet both studies are characterized by major methodological problems, as discussed previously in the section on neurotic disorders. At the lower end of the scale, Luborsky et al. (1975) assigned a "C" grade to studies by Cooper et al. (1963, 1965) and Marks and Gelder (1965) that were excluded from the present review because of fundamental design deficiencies. All were retrospective designs.

The second objection to arbitrary methodological grading of this sort is that even if grades were assigned reliably, their utility is doubtful. Presumably the rationale behind such a grading system was to see whether different grades were related systematically to specific outcome results. Thus, in discounting the potential criticism that inadequate outcome measures explain the failure to find differences among different therapeutic approaches, Luborsky et al. (1975) appeal to their grading system. They assert that *"the best designed studies do not show a very different trend from those that are less well designed"* (p. 1004), suggesting that this argues against accounting for their results on the basis of considerations of experimental control. Unfortunately, the value of this comparison is vitiated by the restricted range of methodological quality in the studies they reviewed. All the studies contained methodological flaws and fall far short of the optional design criteria for outcome research. To use an analogy, Luborsky et al. (1975) graded on a "curve." An absolute standard of comparison results in a heavily positively skewed distribution in which there are few well-controlled studies.

Despite the methodological limitations of the research reviewed in this chapter, certain observations can be made that could materially influence the acceptance of behavior therapy by public, professional, and political agencies. First, in not a single comparison among the studies reviewed was behavior therapy found to be significantly inferior to the alternative treatment, which in most instances was some form of verbal psychotherapy. On the contrary, in the majority of studies behavior therapy was either marginally or significantly more effective than the alternative treatment. This superiority is clear cut in the treatment of childhood disorders such as enuresis and hyperactivity; it is also apparent in the modification of neurotic depression, addictive behaviors (at least in the short-term), and the institutional management of psychotic disorders. To repeat, the evidence that forms the basis of these observations is often sparse and the data such that the greater efficacy of behavior therapy is not always compelling, yet these findings command attention.

The statement that behavior therapy at the very least is not less effective than alternative treatments against which it has been compared is significant. In its early stages during the late 1950s and early 1960s, behavior therapy was widely rejected as ineffective at best, dangerous at worst. A comprehensive survey of the comparative outcome studies on therapy outcome that provided no evidence for the de facto truth that psychotherapy was superior to behavior therapy would have come as a major surprise to the therapeutic establishment. Although some extremists still persist in making sweeping denunciations of behavioral methods as harmful to patients (e.g., Bruch, 1974), they are few and far between. The prevailing consensus, even among critics of behavior therapy such as Strupp (1976), is that behavior therapy is of definite value to the informed practitioner (American Psychiatric Association, 1973). The debate has shifted to *how* effective behavior therapy is and *when* it should be applied, rather than *whether* it should ever be employed.

Behavior therapy was originally alleged to be dangerous to patients largely because of fears that it was a superficial treatment that would result in symptom substitution. Contrary to earlier conceptual confusion, more recent theoretical analyses have shown that behavior therapy is not a symptomatic form of treatment that ignores the causes of behavior (Bandura, 1969). Both behavioral and psychodynamic treatments attempt to modify the "underlying causes" of behavior; the difference is what the respective approaches regard these "causes" to be. Psychodynamic formulations favor hypothetical unconscious determinants of behavior; behavior modification, in contrast, considers the causes to be antecedent, mediational, and consequent variables which are controlling or maintaining the inappropriate response patterns.

The discussion of symptom substitution has been clouded by the conceptual ambiguity of the notion itself and implicit assumptions about the causes of behavior (Cahoon, 1968; Ullmann & Krasner, 1965). In fact, whatever substitute symptoms are, there is some agreement that they are not likely to occur. Several studies explicitly designed to uncover negative side effects of treatment have not reported evidence for symptom substitution (see Leitenberg, 1976b; Mahoney et al., 1974; O'Leary & Wilson, 1975). Typical of the findings in this regard is Sloane et al.'s (1975) comment: "Not a single patient whose original problems had substantially improved reported new symptoms cropping up. On the contrary, assessors had the informal impression that when a patient's primary symptoms improved, he often spontaneously reported improvement of other minor difficulties" (p. 100).

The notion of symptom substitution has been a conceptual red herring devoid of clear empirical meaning and corresponding evidence. Of course, the conceptual problems of symptom substitution do not extend to the more empirically based notion that changes in the treated behavior may be associated with concomitant behavior changes. In fact, behavior therapy studies have shown that when one behavior changes, others may change as well (e.g., Nordquist, 1971; Sajwaj, Twardosz, & Burke, 1972; Wahler, Sperling, Thomas, Teeter, & Luper, 1970). Some of these changes may be judged desirable; others may not. More often than not, the correlated changes in behavior are positive (e.g., Gripp & Magaro, 1971; Maley et al., 1973; Paul, 1967). In rare instances, maladaptive responses have been reported after behavior therapy (Balson, 1973; Meyer & Crisp, 1966). Rather than substitute symptoms, these emergent responses can be explained more parsimoniously.

Behaviors are not necessarily discrete and independent units of an individual's response repertoire. Evidence suggests that behaviors may cluster or covary in larger units than single responses (Wahler, 1975). Changes in one behavior may be expected to result in changes in other behaviors. Also, behavior change does not occur in a social vacuum.

Given the reciprocal interaction of behavior and the environment, one would expect that behavior changes will influence the social environment in which the individual functions (Bandura, 1977c; Goldiamond & Dyrud, 1968). Changes in the social environment in turn are likely to alter further responses of the individual outside those focused upon in treatment.

The initial criticism of behavior therapy as hazardous to one's health was soon modified in the direction of a grudging acceptance. It was said to be effective in a few limited situations such as the treatment of monosymptomatic fears and simple habits. The treatment of more complex problems of adjustment was still reserved for psychotherapy. The third conclusion from this review is that there is no evidence that behavior therapy is any less broadly applicable to complex disorders than psychotherapy. Luborsky et al.'s (1975) conclusion that behavior therapy (in effect, imaginal systematic desensitization) is especially suited for circumscribed phobias cannot be sustained given the available evidence. On the contrary, the available evidence is that behavior therapy is more suitable for a broader range of clients even within the relatively narrow category of adult neurotic problems considered by Luborsky et al. (1975) in their review (e.g., DiLoreto, 1971; Sloane et al., 1975).

Luborsky et al. (1975) claimed to have reviewed those studies consisting of "the general run of patient samples who seek psychotherapy" (p. 1006). In fact, their analysis is restricted almost exclusively to neurotic clients of the YAVIS type and thus is thoroughly unrepresentative of the different individuals with diverse problems whom community clinics, mental health centers, and other psychiatric services are supposed to help. Deliberately excluded were all childhood disorders and a wide range of common adult problems including addictive behaviors, different sexual problems, and psychotic disturbances. These massive omissions are particularly puzzling coming from those who dismiss the relevance of so-called analogue research on grounds that it is not generalizable to the general client population. The consideration of the utility of any treatment approach based upon psychological principles must include the numerically and clinically significant non-YAVIS population and those clients with disorders other than neurotic reactions. One of the advantages of behavior therapy is that it has been applied to diverse types of problems. Aside from the conventional psychiatric disorders (e.g., Craighead, Kazdin, & Mahoney, 1976; O'Leary & Wilson, 1975), important applications have been made in education (e.g., Drabman, 1976), medical care (e.g., Katz & Zlutnick, 1974; Knapp & Peterson, 1976), and environmental and social problems (e.g., Kazdin, 1977b). The point can be made that whereas behavior therapy has been applied to an unusually wide range of problems, appropriate comparative studies with alternative treatments such as psychotherapy have not been conducted. This is so. Many of the problems tackled by behavior therapists—described in the previous chapter—have long been shunned by psychotherapists, and little if any systematic outcome data exist. This paucity of outcome data is the telling point (Azrin, 1977).

A frequent assumption in the comparative psychotherapy literature has been that behavior therapy might have greater influence on "symptom-outcome measures" (e.g., Luborsky et al., 1975). The fourth conclusion drawn from this review is that there is no satisfactory evidence that behavior therapy produced fewer changes in either specific target behaviors or more general measures of adjustment than psychotherapy. The overall trend of the data contradicts this assumption, which implies the stereotyped view of behavior therapy as a limited and relatively superficial form of treatment that can on occasion be used as an adjunct to traditional psychotherapy. Behavior therapy affected changes not only in target behaviors but also in measures of more general psychological functioning in many of the categories of disorders.

In sum, it can be concluded that the available comparative outcome studies provide no evidence that behavior therapy is less effective, more dangerous, less broadly applicable, or produces less extensive change in psychological functioning than alternative treatments such as psychotherapy. On the contrary, with at least some types of problems behavioral treatment methods appear to be more effective than other treatments to which they have been compared. Behavioral methods are demonstrably more applicable to a much broader range of human problems than verbal psychotherapy, and there is clear evidence of broad-gauged treatment effects across specific target behaviors as well as more general measures of personal, social, and vocational adjustment.

The consistent conclusion of recent reviews of the treatment outcome literature has been that "everybody has won and all must have prizes" (Luborsky et al., 1975), that "all roads lead to Rome" (Garfield, 1976), that "the temple of truth may be approached by different pathways" (Marmor, 1975), and that the alleged superiority of behavior therapy over alternative therapies is "negligible" (Smith & Glass, 1977). The evaluative strategies which produced this conclusion must be emphasized. Smith and Glass (1977) invented what they term "meta-analysis" to conduct a sweeping review of a large number of unspecified studies, cavalierly disregarding the methodological quality of individual studies. Luborsky et al.'s (1975) "box score" strategy lead them to categorize an arbitrarily selected, methodologically flawed, and very limited group of studies as "for" or "against" behavior therapy. In a competition between behavior therapy and psychotherapy, the tally of thirteen "tie scores" and six in favor of behavior therapy was interpreted as demonstrating the equivalence of behavior therapy and psychotherapy.

Both Smith and Glass's (1977) and Luborsky et al.'s (1975) evaluative strategies are criticized in the following chapter. Suffice it to note here that although some studies indicate the greater efficacy of behavioral methods with some behavior disorders, the conceptual and methodological limitations of many of studies reviewed in the present chapter do not permit an adequate evaluation of whether behavior therapy or psychotherapy has been convincingly demonstrated to be superior to appropriate control treatments. Nor do the data allow the eclectically pleasing but potentially stultifying conclusion that there are no differences among equally effective therapies. As noted in Chapter 1, there are well-documented differences among specific behavioral methods, contrary to Luborsky et al.'s (1975) presumption of no such differences and Smith and Glass's (1977) unclear assessment of relative efficacy of individual behavioral techniques. Moreover, differences that clearly favor behavioral methods are evident in the treatment of some types of disorders. With respect to adult neurotic reactions, that class of limited studies that has traditionally been the overworked focus of comparative outcome research, potential differences have been obscured or blunted by the use of inappropriate methodologies. More discriminating methods and measures are required to provide answers to the question of therapy outcome. Alternative strategies that derive from a conceptual model of behavior change different from that which has guided traditional comparative outcome research are discussed in Chapter 4.

Chapter 3

Conceptual and Assessment Issues

Virtually all the comparative treatment outcome studies reviewed in the last chapter were conceived and conducted within the conventional model of outcome research. This research has been directed toward answering the basic underlying question, "Is one form of therapy (e.g., 'behavior therapy') more effective than another (e.g., 'psychotherapy')?" A number of uncritically accepted assumptions are implicit in such an approach:

1. The terms "behavior therapy" and "psychotherapy" refer to well-defined, internally consistent sets of concepts and readily reproducible operations that can be usefully compared to each other or to something labeled "routine treatment."
2. Generally applicable and standardized measures exist (e.g., clinical ratings) that can be used to evaluate the relative efficacy of these alternative forms of therapy.
3. Treatment outcome can be evaluated in terms of qualitative concepts such as "cure," "relapse," and "remission."
4. Outcome studies can be evaluated in a summary, qualitative fashion as showing that a particular therapy is significantly superior to, inferior to, or no different from an alternative therapy, and
5. A balance sheet or box score can be derived in which diverse studies are assigned to one of these discrete categories and the resultant cumulative totals meaningfully compared.

The assumptions have impeded rather than illuminated the nature of therapy outcome. The fundamental question about the relative effectiveness of different approaches need not be discarded. However, it is clear that thinking about treatment outcome evaluation is in need of major revision. The critical question must be rephrased. It is not a matter of whether "behavior therapy" is superior to "psychotherapy," but what treatment administered by which therapist is most effective for what problem in which patient? *Specificity* and *operational precision* are the hallmarks of this more relevant reformulation of treatment outcome research. In this chapter, the conceptual and methodological inadequacies of the conventional model of outcome research are identified and their implications for therapy evaluation are discussed. In the next chapter, alternative evaluation strategies for treatment outcome are described.

INADEQUACIES OF THE CONVENTIONAL OUTCOME RESEARCH MODEL

The Therapy Uniformity Assumption

In addressing himself to the problems inherent in research on the outcome of psychotherapy, Kiesler (1966) identified several "uniformity assumption myths." One of these myths was the assumption that "psychotherapy" refers to a uniform, homogeneous treatment. Comparative research has taken special interest in contrasting techniques representative of different therapeutic schools. Thus, "psychotherapy" is contrasted against "behavior therapy" given that the traditions from which these derive most clearly conflict. However, there is no "psychotherapy" to which other approaches can be compared in any general sense. There are only different methods of psychotherapy. The same point applies to behavior therapy. There is no "behavior therapy" in the sense of a specific technique that could be compared to another technique. There are several different techniques subsumed under the rubric of behavior therapy (Bandura, 1969). Many of these techniques within behavior therapy are based upon different assumptions and therapeutic procedures (Wilson, in press c). A characterization of some of these techniques inevitably will misrepresent others, despite the fact that they are jointly referred to as "behavior therapy."

In the abstract, the point that general categories such as "behavior therapy" or "psychotherapy" include different techniques seems sufficiently obvious not to warrant mention. Yet, despite Kiesler's (1966) warning about the problematic consequences of the therapy uniformity assumption, global entities labeled "psychotherapy" and "behavior therapy" are still compared in specific empirical investigations (e.g., Sloane et al., 1975) and in reviews of psychotherapy outcome research (e.g., Luborsky et al., 1975). In their analysis, for example, Luborsky et al. (1975) attempt to justify their comparative evaluation of "behavior therapy'' by asserting that different behavioral treatment techniques do not differ from each other in terms of relative efficacy. However, there is overwhelming evidence that some behavioral treatment methods are significantly more effective than others. To take but one example, performance-based methods such as participant modeling are superior to techniques that rely upon imaginal (e.g., systematic desensitization) or vicarious (e.g., symbolic modeling) sources of behavior change (Bandura, 1977b; Kazdin, 1977c; Marks, 1975; Wilson. in press b).

Another facet of the therapy uniformity myth is that there is no uniform ''routine treatment.'' Comparison treatments labeled as ''routine'' vary enormously in composition, ranging from those that include several active treatment components to those that are minimal control conditions. More often than not, only cursory information is provided about ''routine treatment,'' such as summary statements that refer to ''group psychotherapy'' of ''milieu therapy.'' Proper evaluation of comparative outcome research necessitates detailed information on the specific methods used, their credibility for the subjects, and the time and treatment personnel involved in therapy.

Implications for Therapy Evaluation.   Typical of the comparative outcome research, Sloane et al. (1975), contrasted psychotherapy to behavior therapy that embraced a wide range of procedures, including relaxation training, systematic desensitization, specific advice and direct intervention in problems assertion training, role-playing, and aversion conditioning. Several reasons argue against the use of such omnibus treatment packages in outcome research. First, evaluations of ''behavior therapy'' are especially vulnerable to distortion if therapy uniformity is assumed. Behavior therapy encompasses numerous techniques that are constantly being developed, tested, modified, and refined. For example, two of the techniques used in the Sloane et al. (1975) study—systematic desensitization and electrical aversion conditioning—were among the most important methods of behavior therapy in its earlier stages. However, as noted above, it is now clear that there are more effective alternatives to systematic desensitization in the treatment of anxiety-related disorders. Electrical aversion conditioning, once the preferred method of treatment for problems such as alcoholism and sexual deviance, has been shown to be ineffective for the most part and replaced by more effective methods in treating these and other problems (Bancroft, 1974; Wilson, in press a).

Second, omnibus treatments obscure identification of the critical behavior change variables (Franks & Wilson, 1976). Once therapeutic change is produced there is no means of isolating the specific feature of the omnibus package that accounted for change. As discussed in the next chapter, there is a point in the evaluation of a given therapy technique at which an omnibus treatment is appropriate. This is when a technique is initially developed and the effective components and appropriate areas of application remain to be determined. By the time comparative research is conducted, sufficient information about the technique should be known to apply the technique specifically to a given therapeutic problem (Kazdin, in press f).

Third, and more complex from a methodological standpoint, multifaceted treatments may include components that have competing effects on outcome. It is one matter to assess the effects of desensitization but quite another to include it in a package with several other treatments. The effects of desensitization are well established, but little is known about its use as part of a package with other techniques. The other techniques in which it is embedded themselves may influence the efficacy of desensitization or any other behavioral technique.

Consider the following examples. Meichenbaum, Gilmore, and Fedoravicius (1971) found that both systematic desensitization and self-instructional training were significantly more effective than a no-treatment control group in the treatment of speech anxiety. The combination of systematic desensitization and self-instructional training was consistently less successful than either technique applied singly across all measures. On some outcome measures the combined group was not significantly superior to the control group. Similarly, McReynolds and Paulsen (1976) reported that a treatment for obesity that focused specifically on stimulus control procedures produced greater weight loss than the typical omnibus behavioral self-control program in which stimulus control is but one of many different procedures. Sherman, Mulac, and McCann (1974) compared four different groups in the treatment of speech anxiety: rehearsal feedback, self-relaxation, a combination of relaxation/rehearsal, and no treatment. In marked contrast to the results of Meichenbaum et al. (1971) and McReynolds and Paulsen (1976), only the combined group showed significantly reduced speech anxiety. Neither rehearsal nor relaxation alone resulted in significant improvement as compared to the control group. Sherman et al. (1974) suggest that the combination of the two treatment methods produced a synergistic effect that neither alone could duplicate.

The considerations involved in the use of multifaceted treatment programs are complex and beyond the scope of the present chapter (Franks & Wilson, 1977). Suffice it to say here that broad-spectrum treatment approaches are not always more effective than more circumscribed interventions. The reasons for the tendency towards lesser efficacy of combined treatments are not clear. One possibility is a simple operational limitation: if a combination of two techniques is compared to the administration of a single method then less time is spent on each of the combined methods than on each method applied singly (e.g., Meichenbaum et al., 1971). Another possibility is that as the number of treatment methods increases, the client's adherence to therapeutic prescriptions with respect to specific methods declines (e.g., Blackwell, 1976; Franks & Wilson, 1976). Nor is it currently possible to rule out some more fundamental conflict among competing therapeutic mechanisms. A final issue is that of temporal parameters. The timing of *when* a technique is introduced in an overall therapeutic program can be more important than *how* many techniques are employed. For example, Barlow et al. (1973) showed that in the initial stages of their uniquely successful treatment of a male transsexual, aversion conditioning was ineffective in decreasing inappropriate sexual attraction. However, in the later stages of the program, after the client had acquired some basic heterosexual skills, the same aversion conditioning was effective.

Recommendations. Comparative research requires contrasting well-specified treatments. Those techniques with discrete components are more easily investigated than those that depend upon more global processes and nebulous factors. The degree of specificity of the technique determines in part the extent to which a meaningful comparative study can be conducted. It makes little sense to contrast techniques with ill-defined components. The specification is essential so that one can experimentally evaluate whether the technique was conducted properly. Replication also depends upon having well spelled-out components that can be restated and implemented by investigators unfamiliar with the original research.

Once treatments are specified, data need to be collected to determine whether the specifications in fact were met. A comparative study is meaningful only insofar as there are assurances that the treatments were conducted properly, i.e., consistent with their original specifications. Data can be collected either through video or audio tapes, transcripts, direct observations, and so on to ensure that the original specifications were followed (Kazdin, in press f). A good illustration of this check upon the success with which different treatment methods are actually administered is provided by Sloane et al. (1975). Analyses of tape recordings of the fifth session indicated several differences between the therapeutic behavior of the psychotherapists and behavior therapists. It is important to distinguish between determining whether the treatments are distinct (i.e., can be separated by blind judges) from whether the specifications of treatment have been met. Treatments can be distinct from each other on process measures. However, this does not necessarily argue for an adequate test of either of the techniques. Comparative research requires empirical verification of whether the different techniques have been adequately tested. The adequacy of a test is not dependent upon the data reflected in outcome but upon whether the treatment ingredients have been conducted in the manner specified in advance of the investigation.

A central issue for comparative research is ensuring that the test of a given treatment will fairly represent that treatment. As alluded to above, without precise specification of treatment components, this criterion cannot be met. Assume for a moment that the techniques to be compared are well specified. Other problems arise in ensuring that the techniques are adequately tested. Initially, experimentation holds dimensions of treatment constant so that they will not be confounded with treatment. For example, the number of therapy sessions across different treatments may be held constant. The rationale for this, of course, is to hold the amount of treatment constant so that it is the type, rather than the amount, of treatment that might explain any group differences. Gelder et al.'s (1967) study is an example where violation of this methodological stricture made the results largely uninterpretable. Even if the group that receives more treatment shows *fewer* changes at outcome relative to another treatment, the interpretation of the findings is ambiguous. Having more treatment cannot be assumed to provide a more or less conservative test of treatment.

In the laudable attempt to control parameters of treatment, the specific techniques may be distorted or misrepresented. Holding the number of sessions constant presupposes that therapeutic change for each technique operates in the same time course. Conceivably, different treatments could reach a similar outcome but require different durations. Comparative research that holds the duration of treatment constant may not be a test of differential efficacy of treatment. Rather, the comparison addresses the differential efficiency of treatment or the relative effects of different techniques under particular time constraints. Presumably, for some therapy techniques the amount of treatment given is not an incidental component but one of the initial treatment specifications.

It is important to specify the criterion to be used for terminating therapy. For some techniques, duration of treatment may not be relevant as long as the specific tasks have been completed. In systematic desensitization, for example, the goal of treatment is for the client to complete a hierarchy of previously anxiety-eliciting stimulus situations without experiencing distress. For other techniques, presumably, processes assumed to take extended periods will need to unfold if treatment is to be adequately tested. As a general rule, whether parameters such as the number of sessions, duration of individual sessions, spacing of sessions, and similar factors are held constant depend upon the techniques to be compared and the centrality of these parameters to the technique.

Another concern in comparative research is keeping treatment techniques distinct. This concern is based upon the notion that any test of different treatments probably should minimize their overlapping components to provide the best possible experimental test. The concern is based upon sound methodology. Presumably, if the techniques either on an a priori basis or in actual practice are too similar there is no purpose in conducting a comparative study. Also, the more similar the techniques in practice, the more likely that there will be no differences across groups at outcome. Finally, if there are no group differences at outcome it will be unclear whether the unique components of the respective treatments are equally effective or whether the commonalities of the treatments account for change. For example, Zitrin et al. (1976) noted that "many of the patients in supportive psychotherapy, on their own initiative, proceeded with in vivo desensitization," and that "the differences between the two therapeutic modalities may become blurred . . ." (p. 15). Independently of the outcome of the different treatments, it would be difficult to interpret results where treatments become blurred.

In light of the commonalities among treatments, comparative studies occasionally have taken special care of keeping treatments distinct. In the process, however, treatments are evaluated that have no counterpart in clinical practice. The techniques tested, even if under the most relevant clinical conditions, may only be distant analogues of therapeutic practice. For example, in their comparison of psychotherapy and reinforcement techniques with psychiatric patients, Marks et al. (1968) mentioned that they attempted to keep treatments distinct. As noted earlier, to keep the reinforcement condition distinct from therapy, staff were instructed to deliver tokens mechanistically and impersonally. Thus, relationship factors, assumed to be central to the therapy to which reinforcement was compared, would not intrude into the reinforcement. However, a reinforcement program administered mechanistically and impersonally has no real bearing upon reinforcement practices. An impressive body of research has established that social interaction changes considerably in reinforcement programs (see Kazdin, 1977d). Thus, to administer a reinforcement program that minimizes interpersonal contact and social interaction is a test of a treatment not relevant to clinical applications of reinforcement. Moreover, it would make little sense in the Marks et al. study to delete reinforcement in the psychotherapy condition. Evidence already has suggested that therapy may include strong, although implicit, reinforcement (e.g., Truax, 1966). To exclude contingent interpersonal consequences on the part of a therapist might keep psychotherapy and reinforcement distinct, but this is not a test of either procedure as it is normally applied. As a general point, the attempt to keep treatments distinct may provide tests of treatments that have no counterpart in actual practice. Hence, the results of such comparative research might have little bearing or generality to treatment techniques used in practice.

The Measurement of Therapeutic Outcome

The lack of adequate measures of treatment outcome has possibly been the most serious deficiency of the treatment literature to date. Conceptually, the problem has been that the measurement strategies employed have derived from the conventional outcome research model in which abnormal behavior is regarded as a quasi-illness. Viewing abnormal behavior in this way lends itself to qualitative rather than quantitative measures. Thus, judgments are made whether the client is cured, markedly or partially improved, or shows no effect of treatment. Although these states are on a continuum of improvement, they are discussed as qualitatively different, something akin to illness. Directly related to this conception of abnormal behavior is the prediction of outcome measures upon traditional assumptions about the nature of personality. Briefly, these assumptions reflect the belief that personality consists of a number of broad underlying dispositions that pervasively influence the client's behavior across different situations and over time. These personality characteristics are not measured by direct observation of actual samples of relevant behavior, but inferred either directly or indirectly from behavioral signs (see Mischel, 1968, 1977).

Guided by these assumptions about the nature of abnormal behavior and personality, outcome measures have traditionally been restricted to various personality tests (e.g., the Rorschach or MMPI) or global clinical ratings of the client's overall psychological functioning (Meltzoff & Kornreich, 1970). Inferring underlying personality dispositions from indirect signs based on psychological tests or the clinical interview has been the standard psychodynamic measure of therapy outcome. However, the evidence seems quite clear that these clinical judgments of personality structures are not very useful (e.g., Mischel, 1968; Peterson, 1968). Mischel (1973) has summarized the evidence:

> The accumulated findings give little support for the utility of clinical judgments even when the judges are expert psychodynamicists, working in clinical contexts and using their favorite techniques. . . . clinicians guided by concepts about underlying genotypic dispositions have not been able to predict behavior better than have the person's own direct self-report, simple indices of directly relevant past behavior, or demographic variables (p. 254).

Clinical ratings are usually made by the therapist and an independent psychiatric assessor who may or may not be blind to the type of treatment the client has received. On rare occasions an attempt is made to obtain comparable ratings of the client's psychological status by interviewing a close friend or relative. Although most behavioral researchers have abandoned the use of traditional personality tests, clinical ratings continue to be widely employed as the major measures of treatment outcome. The serious limitations of clinical ratings are discussed in the analysis of the Sloane et al. (1975) study in the last chapter. Since this investigation represents the best attempt of its kind yet to conduct adequate measurement of therapeutic outcome using clinical ratings, its failings are all the more revealing. In that study, ratings of different aspects of the client's functioning were made by the therapist, client, independent assessor, and an informant. Therapists' and patients' ratings are subject to obvious bias, and there are basic problems with assessors' and informants' ratings as well. The former were based, as is typical, on a single clinical interview. As such, it is consistent with personality trait theory and the assumptions of psychodynamic therapy that the clinical interview is the primary vehicle through which change takes place and is to be evaluated. The behavioral model, however, emphasizing situation-specific effects on behavior, dictates that a client's behavior during the clinical interview—an artificial setting replete with numerous demand characteristics for what is deemed to be appropriate verbal behavior—does not necessarily allow one to generalize to actual behavior in the natural environment (Wilson & Evans, 1977). Informants' ratings are vulnerable to distortions introduced by the fact that the informant might be directly affected by the client's problem and thus it is not free from bias, has limited access to direct observation of the problem, or is in collusion with the patient. In this instance the correlations among these different measures were so low that Sloane et al. (1975) concluded that different raters used different goals and/or different criteria.

A clear example of the pitfalls involved in relying on clinical rating scales to evaluate outcome is reported by Teasdale et al. (1977). They found a marked discrepancy in the rating scales developed by Gelder and Marks (1966) and used by at least one group of investigators at Oxford, and a modification of these scales by Watson and Marks (1971) used by other groups of investigators at the Maudsley Hospital in London and elsewhere. The discrepancies were in terms of pre-treatment assessments and in mean changes as a result of treatment, the Watson and Marks (1971) scales yielding improvement almost twice as great as that of the Gelder and Marks (1966) scale. Understating the problem, Teasdale et al. (1977) drily remark: "There is a need for workers in this field to agree on methods of measurement."

Recommendations.   Specific behavioral measures of therapy outcome should be obtained wherever possible, for several reasons. First, it is dictated by the recent reconceptualization of personality and behavioral assessment (Mischel, 1968; Peterson, 1968). The evidence indicates that a person is best described and understood by determining what he or she thinks, feels, and does in particular life situations. Mischel (1973) has summarized this view of personality assessment:

> The focus shifts from attempting to compare and generalize about what different individuals are like to an assessment of what they *do*—behaviorally and cognitively—in relationship to the psychological conditions in which they do it. The focus shifts from describing situation-free people with broad adjectives to analyzing the specific interactions between conditions and the cognitions and behaviors of interest (p. 265).

Accordingly, direct assessment of actual samples of behavior in the natural situation provides the most relevant information about therapeutic improvement.

Second, specific behavioral measures usually provide the most discriminating means of demonstrating differential efficacy among techniques. Global clinical ratings all too often obscure actual treatment outcome differences and reflect differences among assessors' subjective views rather than changes in actual functioning. For example, Crowe et al. (1972) compared three different methods of behavior therapy—systematic desensitization in imagination, flooding in imagination, and reinforced practice in vivo—in the treatment of phobic clients. Behavioral avoidance measures showed significant differences among these techniques, whereas the Gelder and Marks (1966) clinical rating scales failed to reflect any differential treatment effect. Moreover, the objective behavioral avoidance measure revealed a significant difference in specificity of effect on treated and untreated phobias among the three forms of treatment. The clinical rating scales once again indicated no differences. The importance of these findings on the measurement of treatment effects can be readily appreciated when it is remembered that the same clinical rating scales were the major dependent measures used in the studies by Gelder and Marks (1966) and Gelder et al. (1967). Behavioral measures were omitted. Crowe et al.'s (1972) results document the conclusion reached in the previous chapter that the methodological limitations of these latter studies—frequently cited in traditional analyses of the comparative outcome literature—are such that they simply blunt and obscure significant differences among opposing methods. Numerous other studies have demonstrated important differences in behavioral measures where clients' self-reports have shown no significant evidence of differential treatment effects, particularly in the fear reduction literature (e.g., Franks & Wilson, 1976; Lick & Bootzin, 1975) but also in the treatment of other problems with different behavioral methods (e.g., Kazdin, 1975b; Liberman et al., 1976).

Third, objective behavioral measures are less subject to distortion and bias than are less direct measures that rely upon clinical judgment, verbal self-report, or questionnaire responses. For example, judgments of others as to the improvement of a client may bear little or absolutely no relation to overt behavioral measures of the rated behavior (e.g., Kazdin, 1973b; Schnelle, 1974). In addition, the biases of those individuals completing the assessment devices are more likely to enter into global ratings than into specific measures of overt behavior (see Kazdin, 1977a; Kent & Foster, 1977).

Fourth, behavioral measures facilitate replication of findings across studies. Because the measures refer to overt behavior, they are less dependent upon inferences on the part of raters or judges than are more global ratings. Thus, variability in the observations due to the *assessor* rather than the *assessee* can be minimized.

Of course, it is easier to obtain meaningful measures of behavior in the treatment of a homogeneous sample of snake-phobic clients than with a heterogeneous selection of different phobias. Gillan and Rachman (1974), for example, reported considerable difficulty in obtaining reliable behavioral-avoidance measures in their investigation of mixed phobic disorders in an outpatient population. Indeed, this is one of the most powerful reasons for conducting well-controlled studies of homogeneous problems in what has been called "analogue research," a point developed in the next chapter. In certain cases, direct behavioral observation is not very feasible, e.g., the treatment of sexual dysfunction (Lazarus, 1961). However, in instances such as this, behavior therapists have extended the breadth of their outcome measures while enhancing the objectivity by including psychophysiological indices of treatment effects. The use of the penile plethysmograph and the vaginal photoplethysmograph has resulted in important advances in the measurement and modification of sexual behavior (e.g., Abel & Blanchard, 1976; Barlow, 1977).

One of the most impressive features of behavior therapy has been the development of a wide range of different measurement methods for the assessment and modification of various disorders (see Ciminero, Calhoun, & Adams, 1977; Hersen & Bellack, 1976a). A full description of these advances in measurement is beyond the scope of the present paper. Suffice it to note the following: reliable and valid coding systems for direct behavioral observation of diverse behaviors across different situations (e.g., Kazdin, 1975a); blood alcohol measures and free operant drinking rates in seminaturalistic settings with alcoholics (e.g., Miller, 1975; Nathan & Briddell, 1977); audio and video taping to secure samples of behavior as it occurs in the problem situation (e.g., Kazdin, 1975b; McFall & Twentyman, 1973; Saudargas, 1972); psychophysiological monitoring systems for problems ranging from asthma through depression (Shapiro & Schwartz, 1972); stabilometer chairs to measure hyperactivity

(Christensen & Sprague, 1973); urine alarm systems and electric potty chairs (e.g., Schwitzgebel & Schwitzgebel, 1973); and other instruments to assess an extremely wide range of responses (Rugh & Schwitzgebel, 1977).

Adequate assessment of outcome must entail *multiple measures* of both objective and subjective measures. Specifically in the treatment of anxiety-related disorders, for example, explicit measures of three response systems—overt behavior, physiological reactions, and self-report—seem necessary. The rationale for a multiple measurement strategy in psychological research in general has been elaborated by Campbell and Fiske (1959), who clarified the need to provide convergent validation among several independent means of assessing given construct. For treatment evaluation in particular, the need for broad yet specific multiple measures has been addressed in the last chapter and by several other authors (e.g., Lang, 1969; Rachman & Hodgson, 1974). Aside from methodological reasons for using multiple measures, the possibility exists that different modalities of assessment may be differentially affected by, or relevant for, particular treatment methods or therapeutic problems. For example, certain therapeutic techniques are concerned explicitly with some modalities (e.g., self-report of feelings) rather than others (e.g., overt performances in everyday life). Similarly, select problems may vary in the modality of primary relevance. Measures of overt behavior may be particularly relevant for some problems (e.g., conduct disorder) but somewhat less relevant for other problems (e.g., affect disorders). The issue is not merely one of relevance but rather one of priority. Presumably, different problems seen in therapy can be measured across different modalities. However, these modalities may differ in the priority with which they are viewed depending upon the problem. For example, in the treatment of depression, self-report and overt behavioral measures might reflect changes in mood. However, self-report may more clearly discriminate depressed individuals and the efficacy of treatment than overt performance in a given clinical case.

The emphasis on multiple objective and subjective outcome measures does more than reflect the complexity yet specificity of therapeutic change along different dimensions of functioning. It also indicates that a broader approach to outcome evaluation is taken than the stereotype of the extreme behavioristic position that concerns itself solely with overt behavior, downgrading subjective experience as irrelevant, nonscientific, or epiphenomenal (Skinner, 1971). For example, a common clinical phenomenon is the depressed client who constantly "puts himself down" and who considers himself worthless and incompetent even though it is clear to the objective onlooker that he is competent and that he is distorting reality. In cases like these, behavior is mainly under the control of internal, self-generated stimuli rather than environmental events. Different people might respond differently to the same objective stimulus situation depending on how they subjectively perceive or interpret what is happening to them. In these instances behavior therapy attempts to correct the faulty cognitions that produce depression and emphasizes explicit measurement of relevant subjective experience (e.g., Beck, 1976).

Therapy outcome investigators mired in the conventional research model have consistently proposed that "quality" of improvement be considered in addition to the "amount" or "quantity" of therapeutic change. Thus, confronted with the apparent phenomenon that different treatment approaches do not differ from each other on conventional statistical analyses of outcome, Luborsky et al. (1975) suggested that some therapies might still produce differences in quality as opposed to amount of improvement. Detailed measures of multiple-response systems, objective as well as subjective, would decide the fate of tours de force of this nature. Yet this assumes that therapeutic goals are measurable according to established scientific criteria, an assumption not always well founded. Strupp and Hadley (1977), for example, have proposed that in addition to the client's self-report and society's judgment of therapeutic improvement, the "quality" of the client's functioning should be the third major criterion of therapy outcome. This estimate of quality of life experience is to be derived not from the multiple measures proposed above, but from the subjective clinical judgment of the client's character structure. This is a reaffirmation of psychodynamic theory that assumes that behavioral adjustment and improved subjectively experienced improvement are not treatment goals per se, but merely reflections of the underlying personality structure that is the object of therapeutic reorganization. As noted above, this belief fares poorly in the light of available experimental evidence and has done much to retard significant progress in the field (Bandura, 1969; Mischel, 1968; Peterson, 1968).

CRITERIA FOR EVALUATING PSYCHOTHERAPY

Traditionally, controversies over outcome criteria have included such issues as the manner in which therapeutic change is assessed (e.g., subjective ratings, projective tests, overt behavior), the source of evaluation (e.g., patient versus therapist), and the generality or specificity of assessment (e.g., global personality measures versus circumscribed overt behaviors) (Bergin & Strupp, 1972; Mischel, 1971; Strupp & Hadley, 1977). Although the specific measurement issues raised in discussions of outcome are vitally important, broader issues pertaining to the criteria for evaluating therapy have yet to be addressed adequately either conceptually or empirically. These issues embrace the manner in which patient change is evaluated, and the efficiency, cost, and consumer evaluation of treatment.

Client-Related Criteria

In therapy research, conclusions about treatment or the relative effects of different treatments are drawn on the basis of comparing mean sources of patients receiving various treatment or control conditions on a particular dependent measure (e.g., therapist ratings). Statistical analyses serve as the basis for concluding that groups differ. From group differences, conclusions are reached about the one therapy being more or less effective than another or, in the case of no difference, equally effective. Indeed, on the basis of comparisons of groups receiving different treatments, major conclusions have been drawn about the relative merit of different techniques (Luborsky et al., 1975; Sloane et al., 1975).

Yet, group differences in mean performance provide an extremely limited criterion for comparing treatments or for evaluating a given treatment. Several other related criteria need to be considered, including the importance of change, the proportion of treated individuals who change, the breadth of the changes, the durability of the change, the efficiency and cost of treatments, and consumer evaluation of treatment. These criteria, highlighted below, are not necessarily subordinate to the commonly used criterion of group differences, particularly when making recommendations for individual treatment or policy decisions about health care in general.

Importance of the Change. For clinical research, a major, if not *the* major, criterion for evaluating treatment is the clinical significance or overall importance of the improvement effected in the client. Clinical significance of change refers to whether improvement enhances the client's everyday functioning. The question is simply: "Did therapy ameliorate the problem for which the client sought treatment?"

Recent research has begun to examine the overt performance of individuals after treatment to determine whether a major change has been made in their everyday functioning. A criterion for determining whether the change made in treatment is clinically important is whether the clients engage in normative levels of the behavior after treatment. Using normative data as criterion, diverse applications have found clinically significant changes in such areas as treatment of social withdrawal (e.g., O'Connor, 1972; Walker & Hops, 1973) and conduct problems of children (e.g., Kent & O'Leary, 1976; Patterson, 1974), self-care skills of the mentally retarded (e.g., Azrin & Armstrong, 1973), social skills of adults (e.g.,

McFall & Twentyman, 1973), communication skills, achievement orientation, and self-concept of delinquents (e.g., Eitzen, 1975; Minkin, Braukmann, Minkin, Timbers, Timbers, Fixsen, Phillips, & Wolf, 1976) and others (see Kazdin, in press b, for a review).

Assessment of normative data is not without problems, including defining the normative group, determining the subject and demographic variables that determine the normative level, and so on (Kazdin, in press b). For many populations (e.g., the mentally retarded), normative standards may not be an appropriate criterion. Yet, the limitations of normative data as a universal criterion need not detract from the problem areas where individuals can be returned to normative levels of functioning.

In general, the magnitude of therapeutic change needs to be given much more attention in the treatment literature. The magnitude of change does not merely refer to categorizing patients as "much improved," "very much improved," and so on, which has been commonly done in the therapy literature (Goldstein & Dean, 1966; Meltzoff & Kornreich, 1970). Rather, the extent to which treatment restores adequate or acceptable levels of functioning needs to be assessed directly. In many ways, evaluating treatment in light of the *importance* of the therapeutic changes seems to be a more appropriate criterion than is the statistical comparison of group differences.

Proportion of Patients Who Improve. The problem with a statistical comparison of group differences is that it averages the amount of change across all clients within each treatment group. Obviously, the average (mean) change of patients may have no counterpart in reality. No patient in a given treatment group may have changed in an amount equal to this average. Indeed, the average does not necessarily represent the extent of improvement of most individuals. The very nature of an average is to distort individual performances to achieve an overall summary of treatment effects (Chassan, 1967).

It is important to look beyond the average to the effects of treatment on individuals. For example, Gelder et al. (1967) found no significant differences among systematic desensitization, individual psychotherapy and group psychotherapy at their post-treatment evaluation. However, they also reported that the number of clients whose phobias were rated as much improved by two or three raters at the final evaluation were: systematic desensitization, nine of sixteen (fifty-six percent); individual psychotherapy, three of ten (thirty-three percent); and group psychotherapy, two of sixteen (12.5 percent). In terms of this criterion, systematic desensitization was clearly more effective.

Conceivably, one treatment may make more clients worse on a given dependent measure than another treatment, but still produce a better overall average effect than the other treatment. One might wish to recommend treatment on the basis of the proportion of treated clients who are likely to improve rather than on the basis of a group average. Selecting a treatment that produces improvements in the largest number of clients maximizes the probability that a given client will be favorably affected by treatment. In contrast, selecting a treatment that produces the greatest average change may not improve the highest proportion of clients. Directly related to the proportion of change is the issue of the importance or magnitude of change, addressed earlier. One technique may, on the average, be inferior to another. Yet, techniques might be evaluated on the number of individuals in a treatment group who achieve a clinically important change.

Breadth of Changes.   The efficacy of treatment is most appropriately judged on the basis of how well it alters the original problem for which the patient sought treatment. Yet, another criterion that might be invoked to differentiate treatments is the breadth of the changes produced. Both in clinical cases and research, investigators have discussed the breadth of changes produced by treatment, which suggests that treatment effects commonly extend beyond the areas for which the client sought therapy (e.g., Maley et al., 1973; Paul, 1967a; Sloane et al., 1975).

Related to the breadth of therapeutic change are the side effects of treatment. Conceivably, two treatment techniques might be equally effective in altering the problem for which the client sought treatment. However, the side effects might differ in such a way as to recommend one treatment over the other. For example, Ayllon et al. (1975) found that reinforcement techniques and methylphenidate (Ritalin) equally suppressed hyperactive behavior of children in a classroom situation. However, the drug suppressed, whereas the reinforcement contingency accelerated, academic performance. Thus, the treatments differed in side effects. A comparison of treatments based only upon the direct focus yielded no differences and lead to the unfortunately misleading conclusion that the treatments were equally beneficial.

To take another example, Rush et al. (1977) showed that the cognitive-behavior therapy was more effective than tricyclic antidepressant drugs in the treatment of depression. Perhaps as important as the statistically significant difference in favor of cognitive-behavior therapy, however, was the fact that it also resulted in significantly less attrition than the pharmacotherapy. One reason for patients dropping out of the latter treatment was the occurrence of unpleasant drug-associated side effects.

Generally, the breadth and nature of changes are important criteria for evaluating a given treatment or for comparing the relative utility of different treatments. Presumably, different treatments develop different skills in clients and are likely to vary in the generality of effects produced. While the primary criterion for change necessarily is improvement in the problem for which treatment is sought, the nature and extent of changes beyond this focus also are important.

Durability of the Improvements.   An important, and widely recognized criterion for evaluating treatment is the durability of therapeutic change. The relative paucity of follow-up data in clinical research makes the long-term effects of many techniques a matter of speculation. However, durability of therapeutic change remains a major criterion for evaluating therapy and for comparing different therapies. Treatments that are equally effective at the end of treatment may differ considerably in the course of change during follow-up. It is quite possible that one treatment evinces greater improvement at post-treatment assessment but shows a more rapid decline of therapeutic change during follow-up than a less effective treatment at post-treatment. For example, Kingsley and Wilson (1977) showed that individual behavior therapy for obesity produced significantly greater weight loss at post-treatment than a group social-pressure treatment. However, at a one-year follow-up the social pressure treatment was superior.

To take another case, tranquilizers might be more effective than psychotherapy in alleviating anxiety while both treatments are in effect. However, at follow-up, when both treatments have been terminated, psychotherapy should have the edge. Tranquilizers are not likely to develop in the client an ability to handle stress in the drug-free state. Therapy is more likely to achieve this end.

Even if the two techniques are equally effective at post-treatment assessment, it is quite possible that the course of behavior change during follow-up would be quite different. For example, some techniques attempt to develop coping and problem-solving skills that transcend the specific problem for which clients sought treatment (Goldfried & Goldfried, 1975). If these techniques accomplish their goal, improvement might be maintained during a follow-up period as clients continue to apply the skills in the face of problematic or aggravating circumstances. In contrast, a more narrowly focused therapy technique may address only the specific problem for which the client sought treatment and not develop a means of handling new problems as they arise.

Debates over the relative effects of different treatments are usually based upon immediate therapy treatment effects. It is likely that debates, insofar as they are profitable at all, will increasingly look to long-term effects. In light of contemporary literature, durability rather than short-term outcome appears to be the great equalizer of treatments.

Efficiency and Cost-Related Criteria

The above criteria refer to the effects of treatment on patients and the diverse ways in which these effects can be examined. Each of the criteria is important for evaluating a given therapy technique as well as comparing different techniques. However, patient change is not the only criterion upon which therapy evaluation can be based. There are other criteria related to the efficiency and cost of treatment.

Efficiency in Duration of Therapy. Assuming that different techniques are equally effective on a particular outcome measure, the rapidity with which these results are achieved is a very important consideration. Obviously, a technique that reaches a specified level of improvement in a shorter period of time is to be preferred. For example, psychodynamic treatment traditionally has fostered the notion that treatment needs to be intense and protracted. An alternative treatment need not be more effective than psychodynamic therapy but only show that the same magnitude of change can be achieved in a shorter period of time. For example, Bancroft (1974) has estimated that the combined success rate of several behavior therapy programs for the treatment of homosexuality of approximately 40 percent is not dissimilar to the results achieved with psychoanalytic treatment (Bieber, Dain, Dince, Drellich, Grand, Gundlach, Kremer, Rifkin, Wilbur, & Bieber, 1962). However, the average duration of treatment for the most effective behavioral treatment program was only six to seven hours (Feldman & MacCulloch, 1971), whereas 75 percent of the clients in the Bieber et al. (1962) study received more than 150 hours or more of treatment, with more than a third of the sample receiving 350 hours or more. With only two exceptions, improvement was limited to those clients who received 150 or more hours of psychoanalysis.

It is often argued that comparisons of behavioral methods with psychodynamically-oriented treatment methods place the latter at a disadvantage since these empirical investigations are brief. Psychotherapy is said to require more time than behavior therapy, the implication often being that this is because more fundamental changes in personality structure are effected as opposed to the more symptomatic relief afforded by behavior therapy. In the Paul (1966) study, for example, the apparent inferiority of the psychotherapy condition in relation to systematic desensitization has been attributed to the brevity of therapy—five hours over a six-week period. What form of psychotherapy, it has been asked, can be expected to be effective after so short a trial? This objection notwithstanding, the point is that while a longer duration of psychotherapy treatment might have produced results equal to those of systematic desensitization—an open empirical question—the treatment of choice under these circumstances is systematic desensitization if for no other reason than its greater efficiency.

Efficiency in the Manner of Administering Treatment.   Aside from the amount of time required to administer treatment, efficiency can be measured by the manner in which treatment is administered. Traditionally, administration of outpatient treatment has been conceived of primarily as an individual enterprise where one client is seen by a professional who is responsible for treatment. An obvious question that comes to mind is whether the treatment can be administered in groups rather than on an individual basis. Group treatment, of course, allows professionals to treat more clients within a given time period and in this sense is more efficient.

A distinction can be made between therapy *in* groups versus therapy *through* groups (Franks & Wilson, 1973). In the former the use of a group setting is more in the interests of economy of time and effort on the part of the therapist than a deliberate attempt to capitalize on the group process itself. The group application of systematic desensitization is a good example of this efficiency-oriented purpose (Lazarus, 1961; Meichenbaum et al., 1971; Paul & Shannon, 1966). Interestingly, there is no evidence that this economical application of systematic desensitization is any less effective than time-consuming individual administration. Research and clinical reports with other techniques have suggested that group treatment is at least as effective as individual treatment and hence more efficient in terms of therapist time and effort (e.g., Hand, Lamontagne, & Marks, 1974; Kingsley & Wilson, 1977; Lazarus, 1971; Teasdale et al., 1977). These findings encourage the expanded use of what are economic and efficient applications of behavioral methods in groups.

The extent to which a technique can be widely disseminated also is a measure of efficiency. A technique that can be widely disseminated, but is only moderately effective, may have greater impact on client care than a technique that is more effective but less easily disseminated. For example, behavior therapy research has revealed that modeling is effective in reducing avoidance behaviors (e.g., Bandura, 1971; Rachman, 1976b). Modeling can be accomplished by providing patients with a live demonstration or films of individuals performing the desired behavior. Such modeling demonstrations effectively reduce avoidance but work less well than does a modeling demonstration in which patient is subsequently guided through each of the behaviors in the actual situation (Bandura et al., 1969; Röper et al., 1975). On the other hand, film modeling as a therapeutic technique can be easily disseminated by showing films to large groups of individuals en masse who share similar phobias. The reduction in efficacy of film modeling over modeling with guided participation is compensated for in part by the ease with which film modeling is extended on a large scale.

By invoking a criterion related to the ease of dissemination, traditional psychoanalytically-oriented psychotherapy, or worse, psychoanalysis proper, would not fare particularly well. Even if psychoanalytic therapy were unquestionably effective in overcoming client disorders, the difficulty of disseminating this technique widely means that mental-health professionals need to look elsewhere for effective treatment. Recent techniques are characterized by their ease of dissemination.

One of the most effective ways in which treatment can be widely disseminated is through bibliotherapy. Self-help manuals may also reduce costly professional interventions. Although self-help books based on several different therapeutic approaches are currently available, by way of example, this discussion focuses on behavioral bibliotherapy. Behavior therapy self-help manuals have been used with varying degrees of therapist contact. Glasgow and Rosen (1977) have distinguished among self-administered programs in which the written manual constitutes the sole basis for treatment; minimal contact in which there is some contact with the therapist such as phone calls or even periodic meetings; and therapist-administered programs in which there is regular contact with the therapist, who guides the client in the use of the manual. Which of these different degrees of therapist involvement is appropriate for a particular client will depend on a number of factors, including the nature and severity of the problem and the type of self-help program or manual.

Numerous behavioral self-help programs exist, including manuals for the treatment of anxieties, lack of personal assertion, sexual dysfunction, obesity, cigarette smoking, excessive alcohol consumption, child behavior problems, toilet training, and study skills (Glasgow & Rosen, 1977). Of course, the extent to which these sorts of self-help programs are useful will depend on how effective they are demonstrated to be. At present few have the benefit of empirical support, and some can be criticized for prescribing clinically unsound procedures (Rosen, 1976). On the brighter side, Hagen (1974) found no difference between a minimal contact and therapist-directed program in the treatment of obesity. Moreover, Rosen, Glasgow, and Barrera (1976), for example, have reported a well-controlled clinical investigation demonstrating that totally self-administered systematic desensitization was as effective as its therapist-directed counterpart in the treatment of phobias. However, even if a self-administered program is less effective than a therapist-administered procedure, its use may still be indicated on the grounds of cost-effectiveness and greater disseminability.

Costs of Professional Expertise. Several different costs are important in evaluating therapy techniques. One infrequently discussed in evaluating therapy is the cost of professional training required of individuals who conduct treatment. Traditionally, becoming a therapist, either through psychiatry or psychology, entails lengthy and expensive training. However, there is a sufficient therapy literature both for outpatient and inpatient treatment that shows that untrained or moderately trained individuals may do just as well as professionals in effecting client change (e.g., Poser, 1966; Rioch, Elkes, Flint, Usdansky, Newman, & Silber, 1963).

Training nonprofessionals to apply treatment in real world settings beyond the therapist's office and the laboratory has become an integral feature of behavior therapy. The use of nonprofessionals is best understood in terms of Tharp and Wetzel's (1969) triadic model—the professional consultant acting through a natural mediator to produce changes in the behavior of a third person. Mediators are important because they have the most contact with the individual, for whom they also control powerful natural reinforcers. Parents have been widely used as mediators of change in behavioral intervention programs (e.g., Berkowitz & Graziano, 1972). Other demonstrably successful uses of behavioral mediators have included psychiatric nurses and hospital attendants (e.g., Kazdin, 1976a); classroom teachers (e.g., O'Leary & Drabman, 1971); siblings (e.g., Lavigueur, 1976); elementary school children (e.g., Solomon & Wahler, 1973); preschool children (e.g., Cash & Evans, 1975); mentally retarded children (e.g., Drabman & Spitalnik, 1973); and even neurologically impaired children (e.g., Nelson, Worell, & Polsgrove, 1973).

A related issue is the frequent use of nonprofessional therapists who are similar in some obvious sense to the client. The self-help groups like Alcoholics Anonymous (AA) and Take Off Pounds Sensibly (TOPS) fall into this category. Although often accepted as fact, the real value of relying upon these nonprofessional sources of therapy has never been systematically determined. Yet, other evidence suggests that nonprofessionals in general can achieve therapeutic changes and with some training are just as effective as professionals (e.g., Jordan & Levitz, 1973; Kent & O'Leary, 1977). Presumably, treatments may differ according to whether professionals or nonprofessionals are required for their administration. Treatment that requires less professional training to implement would be highly preferred.

Client Costs. Many costs to the clients can be used to distinguish treatments. The most obvious is the actual monetary expenditure clients provide for their treatment. Actually, client costs are influenced by other factors, such as the cost of professional training and the disseminability of treatment. Esoteric techniques that require professional training to administer and are restricted to professional settings necessarily are more expensive for the client than more widely available techniques.

In addition to time and monetary considerations, the treatment experience can be weighed in terms of its emotional cost to the client. For example, a particular technique might be discounted in favor of an alternative technique that is less taxing on the client. If the temporary emotional distress evoked by therapy itself is sufficiently intense, an alternative treatment might be preferred even if relatively less effective. This analysis has been made of systematic desensitization versus flooding in the treatment of anxiety-related disorders. In contrast to the gradual, sugar-coated "seduction" quality of desensitization, flooding involves protracted exposure to high-intensity aversive stimulation. Often the immediate effect of that exposure is greatly to increase anxiety levels to frightening proportions. Investigators have reported adverse effects of flooding during and between treatment sessions (Barrett, 1969; Emmelkamp & Wessels, 1975).

Aside from the emotional cost, a particular therapeutic method might pose a threat to the client's physical well-being. In these instances, as is almost routine in medical science, the potential risk of the treatment must be weighed against its potential benefits in the context of what other methods are available. In general, more benign and less intrusive procedures are tried first with potentially more dangerous methods reserved for the last resort. For example, unlike alternative treatment methods for the modification of cigarette smoking, rapid smoking has shown considerable promise (Lichtenstein, Harris, Birchler, Wahl, & Schmahl, 1973). Yet there is also evidence that it might have adverse physical effects, including an elevated risk of cardiac abnormalities (Horan, Hackett, Nicholas, Linberg, Stone, & Lukaski, 1977; Horan, Linberg, & Hackett, 1977). Given the well-known health risks of smoking, including cancer and cardiovascular disorders, the risks of treatment might be considered well worth taking.

The emotional costs or stress-inducing characteristics of treatment are extremely important considerations in evaluating treatment. The significance of these characteristics can be seen in the context of aversion therapy (Rachman & Teasdale, 1969), which is not as widely used as it once was in behavior therapy. There are many aversion therapy techniques, some of which employ aversive stimuli directly (e.g., electric shock, nausea-inducing drugs) or in symbolic form (e.g., imagined aversive events). A number of reports have indicated that clients refuse treatment either upon hearing the prospect of aversion techniques or after being exposed to treatment itself (Azrin & Powell, 1968; Hedberg & Campbell, 1974; Wilson & Tracey, 1976). Thus, for many patients the emotional or stress-inducing costs of some treatments override concerns about amelioration of the therapeutic problem.

Of course it is not easy to arrive at a priori decisions about the emotional cost of the treatment experience for the client. Consider the use of chemical aversion conditioning in the treatment in alcoholics (Wiens et al., 1976). Undergoing this therapy is a taxing experience, including extreme nausea, repeated vomiting, and the associated physical malaise. Yet, many clients actively seek such a treatment program when afflicted with the problems of excessive alcohol consumption. The reason is that the entire inpatient therapy program takes no more than two weeks. Regular follow-up and maintenance services are offered and often made use of by clients, but by this time their lives are in greater order and they can concentrate on maintenance of sobriety without undue disruption. The brevity of the program, the sense of predictability about a structured, specifically time-limited program, the attitude of "let's get it over and done with," all appeal to these clients. The analogy is to something they know and understand, namely, medical treatment where a physical disorder may require brief hospitalization. Compared to the prospect of continuing a protracted therapy regimen that might involve repeated questioning and disclosure of intimate personal experiences that the problem drinker or alcoholic may not consider relevant to his or her immediate purpose of gaining control over the urge to drink, the perceived aversiveness of the aversion therapy might be subjectively far less.

Cost-Effectiveness. Increasingly, questions are likely to be raised about whether the returns from psychological treatment are worth the costs and whether treatments differ in terms of a cost-effectiveness analysis. Various criteria already mentioned will be relevant to such considerations in terms of costs of professional training, disseminability, client costs, and so on. The effectiveness of treatment in light of these costs is likely to be scrutinized more closely in the future. Contemporary treatment applications certainly raise questions about whether the effectiveness of treatment is warranted by the cost of many client concerns.

For example, consider the Sloane et al. (1975) study which compared behavior therapy, psychotherapy, and a waiting-list control group. The administration of different therapists required considerable resources of investigators, therapists, and clients alike over a protracted period. Certainly, a question can be raised about whether treatment was worth the cost. The ratings of target symptoms, the dependent measure that most favorably reflected the outcome of the two therapy groups, are not cause for enthusiasm. At the end of a year after treatment, *all* groups were in the "trivial to mild range" in terms of severity of target symptoms.

Given the results, it might be difficult to justify the time, effort, and money involved in the conduct of either formal behavior therapy or psychotherapy by acknowledged experts in the two fields. A treatment conducted by less expert, less expensive therapists in a less time-consuming manner might have reduced still further the less than massive differences obtained between formal therapy and the most minimal of therapist contact.

Consumer Evaluation of Treatment

A neglected area in therapy research is consumer evaluation of treatment. Alternative treatments for a given problem may not be equally acceptable to prospective clients. Presumably, acceptability of treatment would be influenced by efficiency and cost considerations, but there are in addition considerations about the inherent procedures used to effect change and their appeal to the client.

Effective treatments may not be acceptable to clients if specific aspects of the procedures are objectionable in their own right (e.g., McConaghy, 1969). As noted earlier, clients may avoid treatment initially or withdraw if aversive treatment methods are used. The acceptability of the treatment procedures per se is very important and may override treatment efficacy in dictating preferences. For example, clients in the study by Crowe et al. (1972) preferred desensitization over flooding, even though the latter was more effective on objective outcome measures.

Many people may be reluctant to attend treatment in general. For example, Bernstein and McAlister (1976) note that a recent Gallup poll showed that only 34 percent of people who wish to stop smoking are interested in attending a smoking clinic. The majority seem to favor a self-help program (Schwartz & Dubitzky, 1968). Although self-administered programs may prove to be less effective than therapist-directed programs, there might still be a place for the former on the grounds of greater acceptability among certain segments of the population.

Different therapy methods may have different treatment objectives that are more or less acceptable to certain individuals. A case in point concerns alcoholism. In contrast to the traditional insistence on abstinence as the only possible therapeutic goal, the possibility and even desirability of controlled drinking as a goal of therapy, at least in some cases, has been seriously proposed (Pattison, 1976).

Many individuals who begin to experience drinking problems refuse to seek professional help. One is that they are unwilling to consider a lifetime of imposed abstinence. Controlled drinking provides these individuals with a specific alternative to excessive alcohol consumption which, unlike abstinence, does not preclude the numerous sources of social reinforcement that are bound up with drinking in our society. In a related point, the greater acceptability of a controlled drinking treatment program might encourage clients to enter therapy who refuse to identify themselves as alcoholics (Miller & Caddy, in press).

Implications for Evaluating Therapy. Evaluation of therapy techniques either on their own or in relation to each other has been based upon narrowly defined outcome criteria. Yet, treatment evaluation always is in relation to a particular criterion or subset of criteria of those available. There can be no definitive answer to the question of whether one treatment is better than another unless the criterion in any given comparison is specified. Techniques are likely to be differentially valuable across the available criteria. This statement is *not* a typical compromise proposing that all techniques are worthwhile on at least some criterion. It is likely that some techniques are not very useful or are readily surpassed by a viable alternative on a number of criteria.

In general, the criteria used to evaluate treatment need to be greatly expanded. The value of treatment includes diverse measures of change for the individual client. However, beyond that, considerations about efficiency, cost, disseminability, acceptability, and several other criteria mentioned above often outweigh simple calculations of change on a narrowly defined outcome measure. Whether a given technique should be used at all or in relation to alternative techniques depends upon multiple criteria that have been neglected almost entirely in therapy evaluation.

In advance of a broad evaluation of therapy outcome, definitive claims made about the relative efficacy or utility of different treatments would seem premature. It is quite possible that treatments will fare differently across the diverse outcome criteria so that the superiority of one technique may be limited to one or a few criteria. Claims made about treatment efficacy will need to be much more analytic in the future in order to specify precisely the outcome dimension that is addressed and how relevant it is for the problem or patients studied. The treatment of choice for a given patient may vary depending upon the particular outcome criterion relevant to the individual patient's problem.

FOLLOW-UP EVALUATION AND THE MAINTENANCE OF THERAPEUTIC IMPROVEMENT

The Nature of the Problem
The Quasi-Disease Model. Conventional approaches to outcome evaluation have been rooted in the quasi-disease model of abnormal behavior with its emphasis on such qualitative concepts as cure, spontaneous remission, and relapse (Bandura, 1969; Ullmann & Krasner,

1975). Although these concepts appropriately describe the treatment of many physical diseases, they are less useful in conceptualizing changes in behavior that are the product of social-psychological variables. Much of psychologically-based treatment has been heavily influenced by the view that abnormal behavior is a function of some intrapsychic personality conflict that is relatively unaffected by environmental events. To the extent that intrapsychic conflict of this sort is resolved, abnormal behavior is altered independent of environmental changes. The recurrence of previous problems is viewed as a relapse. Relapse, as Marlatt (1977) notes, "implies that one has 'lapsed' back into the disease." The original treatment is regarded as incomplete or insufficient and additional therapy focuses on the same intrapsychic conditions initially assumed to underlie the presenting problem.

The Social-Learning Model. Within the social-learning framework, most abnormal behavior is seen as a function of antecedent and consequent environmental events and cognitive mediating processes that may vary in different situations, in different people, and often, at different times in the same person. Behavior is neither a product of largely autonomous internal forces nor a simple function of external environmental contingencies. Psychological functioning involves a reciprocal interaction between a person's behavior and the environment; the person is both the agent and the object of environmental influence. Given this perspective, when one asks if a treatment effect lasts, one has to consider a number of factors, including the problem being treated and the circumstances under which it occurs.

Different behaviors will vary in the degree to which they are likely to generalize to new situations and to be maintained over time (cf. Eysenck, 1963). To the extent that a newly acquired behavior has immediate and powerful reinforcement value (e.g., orgasmic responsiveness), the probability of its generalization and maintenance would appear to be especially high. Other newly acquired behaviors such as eating less or ceasing to drink have few, if any, immediately strong positive consequences, in contrast to the instant gratification afforded by eating and alcohol consumption. These newly acquired behaviors appear to be highly vulnerable to disruption, at least in their initial stages, a theoretical prediction that is amply borne out by the clinical evidence (e.g., Hunt, Barnett, & Branch, 1971).

The settings in which behavior occurs may be the decisive factor in determining generalization and maintenance of therapeutic improvement (Atthowe, 1973; Kazdin, 1977d; Stokes & Baer, 1977). For example, Fairweather (1964) compared two intervention programs in the treatment of institutionalized psychotic inpatients. One was a conventional hospital program in which the hospital staff was responsible for making decisions for inpatients and supervising their daily activities. In this condition, inpatients occupied the usual passive and subordinate role they normally play in treatment programs. The other program was based on an intensive small-group training in problem-solving and decision-making skills in which inpatients themselves were trained to make decisions, regulate their own activities, and evaluate their own progress. Incentives such as money and pass privileges which were made contingent upon the achievement of progressively more complex levels of social and self-directive behavior were distributed according to the inpatients' decisions. The hospital staff acted as consultants rather than as direct overseers of activities.

The results of Fairweather's study during the twenty-seven weeks it was in progress revealed the consistent superiority of the self-managed program over the control procedure across a variety of different outcome measures. Inpatients in the self-management group demonstrated significantly greater improvement in interpersonal responsiveness, verbal communication, mutual concern and awareness, and reduction in bizarre behavior. Moreover, inpatients in the group-administered incentive condition were discharged sooner than inpatients in the conventional hospital program.

Despite these impressive group differences in outcome within the hospital setting, the recidivism rates for inpatients who received the different forms of therapy were basically similar. In a manner consistent with most previous findings, 80 percent of those persons who had been hospitalized for brief periods adjusted successfully to community life, whereas 45 percent of persons who had been institutionalized for more than two years avoided rehospitalization at the six-month follow-up. Results such as these indicate that the natural environment to which inpatients return upon discharge is a decisive factor in determining whether they readjust to society or end up being readmitted to a mental hospital (Anthony, Buell, Sharatt, & Althoff, 1972).

In addition to the nature of the target behavior and the natural environment in which it occurs, variables such as self-control skills and expectations of self-efficacy may influence the generalization and maintenance of behavior change (Bandura, 1977b; Mischel, 1973). With respect to generalization, for example, Bandura, Adams, and Beyer (1977) analyzed the performance of snake-phobic subjects treated with participant modeling in both similar and dissimilar threat situations (interactions with snakes of similar and markedly different physical characteristics). All subjects had completed in treatment all of the behavioral tasks that were subsequently assessed in the post-test of approach behavior toward the different snakes. However, subjects differed in terms of independently assessed expectations of efficacy regarding their fear of snakes. Efficacy expectations proved to be a significantly superior predictor of performance in the dissimilar threat situation than past behavior with the snake in the treatment situation. These findings suggest that not past behavior, but the effect of past behavior on specific expectations of individuals is the better predictor of generalized behavior change. In terms of social-learning theory, these efficacy expectations also may determine how long and with what effort and persistence clients will engage in coping behavior following therapy (Bandura, 1977b). Accordingly, it is probable that maintenance of treatment-produced behavior change is influenced by specific outcome and efficacy expectations (Marlatt, 1977; Wilson, 1977).

One of the major weaknesses of the literature on treatment methods based upon psychological principles is the relative lack of long-term follow-up studies. Behavior therapy is no exception. In their analysis of the contents of the four major behavior therapy journals[a] for the year 1973, Cochrane and Sobol (1976) found that only 35 percent of studies where follow-up was appropriate actually included follow-ups. Less than a third of these follow-up investigations (only ten out of 113 studies reviewed) took place more than six months after the end of therapy. In a similar analysis of three behavioral journals[b] for the years 1972–1973, Keeley et al. (1976) estimated that about 12 percent of studies reported follow-up data of more than six months duration.

Recommendations. From a social learning perspective, outcome evaluation must distinguish among the initial induction of therapeutic change, its transfer to the natural environment, and its maintenance over time. It is important to distinguish among these different phases of treatment since they appear to be governed by different variables and require different intervention strategies at different times. Generalized behavior change, for example, should not be expected unless specific steps are taken to produce generalization. Several different strategies have been demonstrated to facilitate generalization of treatment-produced improvement (e.g., Bandura et al., 1975; Kazdin, 1977d; Marholin, Siegel & Phillips, 1976; Stokes & Baer, 1977).

In a similar fashion, a given treatment might produce highly significant improvement at post-treatment compared to appropriate comparative control groups, but show no superiority at a subsequent follow-up owing to the dissipation of the initial therapeutic effect over time. It would be premature to conclude that such a treatment method is ineffective; a more

[a] *Journal of Applied Behavior Analysis, Journal of Behavior Therapy and Experimental Psychiatry, Behavior Therapy,* and *Behaviour Research and Therapy.*
[b] *Journal of Applied Behavior Analysis, Behavior Therapy,* and *Behaviour Research and Therapy.*

specific analysis may indicate that it is effective in inducing change, but fails to maintain change. It may be that by complementing the treatment method with different strategies designed to facilitate maintenance of change, long-term improvement may be effected. Within this expanded framework it may be that a specific treatment technique and a specific maintenance method are both necessary, although neither may be sufficient for durable therapeutic change.

The point is that it is inappropriate to use follow-up information as the sole criterion for a dichotomous all-or-nothing judgment about the success or failure of treatment. Even without long-term follow-up data of treatment efficacy, a method that produced an initial effect may represent a useful starting point for the design of a more enduring treatment. As Azrin (1977) argues, this would seem particularly true in the case where no other treatment has been effective.

There is a need for greater specificity of analysis in differentiating among initial treatment-produced change and its generalization and maintenance. For example, the relationship among these different phases of treatment will vary according to the specific behavior that is the target of change. In the treatment of obesity, weight at post-treatment has been shown to bear no relation to weight at one-year follow-up (Jeffery et al., in press). However, the initial treatment response of obsessive-compulsive patients appears to be an accurate predictor of long-term success (Marks et al., 1975).

BETWEEN-STUDY COMPARISONS: THE BOX-SCORE STRATEGY AND META-ANALYSIS

The preceeding analyses have indicated that the conceptual and methodological problems inherent in the majority of studies reviewed in the second chapter make it difficult if not impossible to draw firm conclusions from between-treatment comparisons within the same study. These interpretive problems are compounded in an attempt to compare different studies using the box-score approach (e.g., Beutler, 1977; Luborsky et al., 1975). Using a dichotomous measurement criterion—statistically significant versus nonsignificant—the results of various treatment outcomes are indiscriminately summed across the different studies and represented as three distinct categories: "better than," "worse than," or "no different from" an alternative therapeutic approach. This qualitative, global evaluative strategy is an effort to provide overall answers to the questions (e.g., "Is behavior therapy more effective than psychotherapy?") that we have maintained are unanswerable in any meaningful sense.

Glass (1976) has criticized the box-score methodology as biased in favor of studies with large *n*s that are statistically significant but may show only weak results. Gardner (1966) has similarly criticized the box-score methodology in literature reviews. As an alternative to box-score methodology, Smith and Glass (1977) have proposed an approach they call meta-analysis. The basic unit of meta-analysis is an "effect size," defined as the mean difference between the treated and control subjects divided by the standard deviation of the control group. In their analysis of therapy outcome studies, Smith and Glass (1977) calculated effect sizes for any type of outcome measure reported in the literature. Thus, they mixed together more than 830 effect sizes from 375 studies. Anticipating criticism for treating different outcome measures as equivalent, Smith & Glass (1977) countered that "all outcome measures are more or less related to 'well-being' and so at a general level are comparable." But an appeal to the notion of generality of outcome is not good enough. Research on personality assessment has shown that what is needed are *specific* measures of particular behaviors (Mischel, 1977).

Several compelling reasons discourage both the box-score and meta-analysis strategies of outcome evaluation.

1. A series of methodologically inadequate studies that to one degree or another repeat basic errors in design and/or implementation is no better than a single inadequate study. If within-study comparisons between alternative treatments obscure potential differences, collapsing numerous studies into a box score simply exacerbates the confusion. Meta-analysis provides a more discriminating means of quantifying how different features of studies relate to their measured effects. However, no matter how sophisticated the statistical meta-analysis of outcome results is, the findings are only as good as the quality of the original data. Smith and Glass (1977) disregard the methodological quality of individual studies and criticize attempts to restrict evaluation to better controlled studies, as in the previous chapter.

2. The foregoing sections have emphasized the importance of specificity of assessment, measurement, and treatment in therapy outcome research. Both the box-score strategy and meta-analysis derive sweeping conclusions from inchoate and inadequate studies comparing often ill-defined treatment methods, different therapists, heterogeneous patients and problems on the basis of nonuniform measures. Statistical adjustments by regression analysis do not necessarily correct for specific differences in design and execution among studies. Moreover, Gardner's (1966) point about the pitfall in box-score methodology of capitalizing on chance applies equally well to meta-analysis. Both are ex post facto methods, and since there is no obvious limit on the procedural variations among studies that can be submitted to a regression analysis, patterns may be demonstrated that have little value.

3. The box-score methodology treats different treatment techniques

within a therapeutic approach such as behavior therapy as equally effective, a fallacy exposed earlier. In Smith and Glass's (1977) meta-analysis different behavioral techniques are said to differ in efficacy, but the validity of the claims made is dubious. For example, they conclude that systematic desensitization is markedly superior to implosive therapy. However, the evidence is quite clear that flooding—a variant of implosion therapy—is at least as effective, if not more so, than systematic desensitization (e.g., Crowe et al., 1972; Gelder et al., 1973; Leitenberg, 1976a; Marks et al., 1971; Rachman & Hodgson, in press). The only studies in which implosion has been shown to be inferior to systematic desensitization (Morganstern, 1972) tended to use less fearful subjects in ways that failed to test adequately the technique of flooding. Subsequent studies that were better controlled and more relevant to the clinical situation failed to support the superiority of systematic desensitization. This underscores the hazards of disregarding the quality of individual studies. Poor data are not always better than nonexistent data. Ignorance can be bliss where weak results from faulty studies can seriously confuse and mislead.

4. In the box-score strategy, equal weight is ascribed to different studies despite the heterogeneity of treatment variables and the lack of standardized evaluation criteria. As Gardner (1966) observed, this results "in a kind of majority rule whereby two poor experiments are given twice as much weight as a single sound one" (p. 416). As an example, in the Luborsky et al. (1975) review, the ambitious and in some ways impressive Sloane et al. (1975) study of ninety-four patients with neurotic and personality disorders is regarded as roughly equivalent to Crighton and Jehu's (1969) brief report of twenty-three students treated for test anxiety. Or consider the hypothetical case in which one study (involving a particularly effective method) resulted in a massive, clinically significant treatment effect for therapy X as compared to therapy Y. Yet three other studies (involving somewhat different methods than those employed in the first study) found therapy Y marginally but statistically superior to therapy X. Does the numerical score of 3:1 reflect a substantive difference in clinical reality?

5. The box-score strategy contributes further to the reification of the concepts of "behavior therapy" and "psychotherapy." Different labels can be applied to slice up selected studies in arbitrary ways. Beutler (1977), for example, chose a different categorization of therapeutic approaches from Luborsky et al. (1975). The five categorizations used by Beutler (1977) for cross-comparisons were "cognitive modification," "cognitive insight," "behavior therapy," "behavior modification," and "affective insight." The first category, cognitive modification, is exemplified by the methods described by Mahoney (1974a). These methods are more usually identified as part of behavior therapy or modification, and there seems little good reason for distinguishing between them in this

manner. Beutler (1977) makes the distinction on the grounds that "cognitive modification" methods are verbally mediated, whereas "behavior therapy" techniques involve imagery. There is no compelling experimental or clinical evidence to justify such a separation between what, after all, are *both* symbolic processes (cf. Bandura, 1977c; Wilson, in press b).

6. A logical error is committed. In the Luborsky et al. (1975) analysis, for example, "tie scores" were implicitly regarded as equal in evidential value to comparisons in which one therapy was said to be superior to another. However, the null hypothesis cannot be proved, and the demonstration of a statistically significant difference must still carry more weight than the failure to show a difference. There is undoubtedly a place for the careful reporting of negative results (Kazdin, in press f). However, the possibility that an outcome indicating no difference between treatment variables is more a function of inappropriate design or poorly executed procedures provides an alternative interpretation to the assumption that no differences actually exist. These considerations are particularly relevant given the inadequate methodologies of comparative treatment studies that inexorably tend to obscure potential differential treatment effects.

7. Box-score categories and Smith and Glass's (1977) meta-analysis suggest a substantial empirical backing—simply in terms of number of studies and quantity of data—that upon critical scrutiny is shown to be largely illusory.

8. Finally, given the box-score tabulation of studies, what conclusion is to be drawn from distribution of scores? Luborsky et al.'s (1975) tabulation of studies comparing behavior therapy and psychotherapy showed thirteen tied scores and six scores in favor of behavior therapy. In no instance was psychotherapy superior to behavior therapy. They concluded that there is no difference between behavior therapy and psychotherapy. The arbitrary nature of such a judgment requires no emphasis. One wonders if the figures were eleven versus eight, for example, whether the verdict of "not different" would still have been registered? Logically one might expect a statistical analysis of these numbers to establish whether the distribution is attributable to chance or not. The prospect of juggling these numbers in a statistical analysis serves to emphasize the assumptions of homogeneity that were violated in compiling the basic score.

Chapter 4

Research Strategies for Therapy Evaluation

Research in psychotherapy and behavior therapy has given special emphasis to two major questions: Does psychotherapy work? Does one therapy work better than another? Of course, the specific outcome issues that can be addressed in research extend well beyond these questions. The overall goal of clinical research is to develop effective therapy techniques. Developing effective treatments may begin with the basic question of whether treatment works and finally end with a comparison among techniques demonstrated to work. There are, however, many intervening stages.

Traditionally, outcome research is highly praised when conducted in clinical settings because such research is touted as the final testing ground for therapeutic efficacy. While the clinical situation *is* the final testing ground, it may be highly overrated as the place to develop and experimentally establish the basis for effective treatment. The sacrifice of experimental control often associated with treatment in clinical situations may obscure important mechanisms and processes that account for change. As a result it can be argued that well-controlled research that evaluates treatment methods in laboratory-like conditions is likely to provide the greatest empirical yield. Moreover, large-scale group research is only one alternative for clinical research. Single-case experimentation represents an alternative methodological approach that has contributed greatly to treatment evaluation.

In the present chapter, different treatment evaluation strategies designed to develop effective therapies are discussed. Different strategies, the questions they address, and control conditions essential for evaluating outcome are presented. In addition, the notion of so-called analogue research, the generality of findings from laboratory and other clinical research, and the conditions under which therapy techniques appear to be most appropriately investigated are evaluated. Finally, single-case experimental methodology is highlighted as a tool for a treatment evaluation with individual clients.

TREATMENT EVALUATION STRATEGIES

There are several ways to evaluate psychotherapy techniques depending upon the specific question asked and the corresponding research strategy employed. The comparison of different therapy techniques in applied clinical settings (reviewed in Chapter 2) represents only one research strategy, one that has received more emphasis in the literature than is warranted. Fundamental questions about a given treatment need to be adequately addressed prior to raising comparative questions. Indeed, comparing different treatments without adequately addressing other research questions can just as easily impede as promote progress in the development of effective therapy techniques.

It is important to consider the diverse research strategies for evaluating therapy and the specific questions that each strategy addresses. The different evaluation strategies include the treatment package, constructive, dismantling, parametric, comparative, client-therapist variation, and internal structure or process strategies (Kazdin, in press f).

Treatment Package Strategy

The treatment package strategy refers to evaluating the effects of a given treatment as that treatment is normally conducted or advocated by proponents of the technique. The notion of the treatment as a "package" denotes that several components of the treatment may be distinguishable both on conceptual and operational grounds. For example, participant modeling includes treatment components such as specific therapeutic instructions, symbolic modeling, guided practice, self-observation, and positive reinforcement (Bandura, 1971; Leitenberg, 1976a). Yet in this strategy the technique is evaluated in toto without concern about the contribution of component parts to the effects of overall treatment.

A treatment package approach often is the first approach used to evaluate a therapy technique. Through clinical practice, extrapolation from experimental research, or theoretical derivation, an individual may advocate a particular therapy technique. The initial question is whether the technique alters the problem for which it was designed. To answer this question, the minimal comparison conditions are treatment and no-treatment control conditions. Ideally, an additional procedure may be included which provides subjects with the opportunity to attend treatment sessions but receive a placebo control treatment. In the case of systematic desensitization, for instance, the initial evaluation of this nature was conducted by Lang, Lazovik, and Reynolds (1965). Comparing the treatment technique to a placebo control treatment, technically, goes beyond addressing the question of whether treatment works and raises questions about the reasons for the change.

Evaluation of the efficacy of a single therapeutic technique (e.g., systematic desensitization) in the treatment of a particular problem is an example of *technique-oriented* outcome research. The relatively restricted conditions of highly controlled research of this nature demand that all clients be treated in the same way with the same single technique. In other words, different clients are treated as if they are a homogeneous group. However, clinical experience and experimental evidence show that the assumption of homogeneity among a large group of clients is questionable. Even in the limited classification of phobias the variables that maintain phobic behavior may vary from one individual to another, especially in frequently complex anxiety cases. To the extent that multiple maintaining variables determine a clinical problem, a multifaceted treatment program is required to modify them. Clinical practice requires a *problem-oriented* approach; multiple treatment techniques are tailored to an individual client's particular problem (Goldfried & Davison, 1976).

In technique-oriented outcome research this flexibility is sacrificed, and as homogeneous a sample of clients as possible is selected to fit the method, rather than the methods being moulded to fit the client. A large sample of clients, however, will be heterogenous almost by definition. If the single method results in improvement despite this heterogeneity among patients, it is an impressive demonstration of effectiveness (O'Leary & Wilson, 1975). If the outcome is mixed or negative, the researcher is in a dilemma. It might be that the method simply is ineffective. Or it might be that as a result of differences among the clients the method was inappropriately applied to some instances. A more complete behavioral assessment might require a multifaceted therapy program that may or may not include the specific technique under consideration. However, in these cases where mixed results are obtained without an adequate behavioral assessment, the results need not be nugatory (Wolpe, 1977). It may be fruitful, for example, to conduct post hoc internal analyses of the data to discover whether any specific client characteristics were related to treatment outcome. These client variables can then be included as independent variables in subsequent research of this nature (Paul, 1969a).

In the problem-oriented approach, a complex multifaceted approach may be necessary to effect clinical change. With the emphasis on helping the clients, treatment may comprise all sorts of ingredients, including some that are unnecessary and perhaps even ineffective. Yet, at this point the extra ingredients are not too important. Only after the main question is resolved (Does this treatment package alter the problem?) is a finer analysis warranted. In any case, the development of a treatment package often derives from concern with treating and ameliorating a specific problem.

The priority of the treatment package approach also stems from a concern for experimental efficiency. If the entire treatment package with all of its distinguishable components changes behavior, then the researcher can scrutinize particular components more analytically. Presumably, the package is likely to be the most effective variation of treatment. If it does not change behavior, it probably makes little sense to delve further into the technique. Essentially, exploring the effect of the treatment package serves as a screening device to assess whether further analytic research on the technique is warranted.

The importance of the package approach to clinical research cannot be overestimated. In clinical work, the highest priority is given to effecting maximal behavior change. To this end Azrin (1977) has advocated the use of package programs that "include as many component procedures as seem necessary to obtain, ideally, a total treatment success" (p. 144). The applied commitment of clinical research makes effecting change of greater immediate import than analyzing the reasons (package components) for the change. A treatment package approach emphasizes the importance of outcome or changing behavior, whereas the analysis of the components of treatment emphasizes understanding the reasons for the change.

While the priority of producing clinical change often dictates the use of treatment packages consisting of multiple methods, this strategy is not without problems. From the standpoint of treatment evaluations and analysis it is important to ensure that the program is not so complex and wide-ranging that it is difficult to identify the specific techniques in such interactive programs. Similarly, it should not be so diverse that there is difficulty in keeping the program distinct from other methods both in concept and practice.

The use of a limited multifaceted treatment package that is still problem-oriented is illustrated in a study by Kent and O'Leary (1976). Children with conduct problems and academic difficulties were randomly assigned to a no-contact control group or a behavioral intervention program. The latter comprised a structured but flexible twenty-hour individualized program that specified several intervention methods and provided clear guidelines for when they were to be implemented. Attesting to the replicability of this carefully specified treatment program, a therapy team of professional psychologists and B.A. level psychological assistants achieved results comparable to those produced by the professionals alone in a subsequent study (Kent & O'Leary, 1977).

Constructive Treatment Strategy

The constructive treatment strategy refers to developing a treatment package by adding components to enhance therapy-effects technique (McFall & Marston, 1970). With the constructive approach, the investigator usually begins with a basic treatment component that is relatively narrowly circumscribed in focus. Research that adds various ingredients to the basic treatment is conducted to determine what enhances treatment effects. As research continues, effective components are retained and a large treatment package is constructed. The addition of techniques to the package may not necessarily be the result of theoretical considerations. Indeed, the characteristic of this approach is empirically establishing components that when added to treatment enhance the therapeutic effects. Essentially, the constructive treatment approach addresses the following question: What can be added to this treatment to make it more effective? Phrased in this way, the question is never really answered. However, research can continue to develop a given technique by adding components.

Research in the area of modeling has illustrated the constructive treatment approach. Modeling usually consists of a client observing someone else perform a particular behavior (Bandura, 1971). Characteristically the observer merely views someone else engaging in those behaviors the observer wishes to develop. Modeling conducted in this general fashion has been effective in altering a variety of behaviors (e.g., Rachman, 1976b; Rosenthal & Bandura, in press). Interestingly, research has demonstrated that modeling effects are enhanced when the client not only observes the model but also practices engaging in the modeled behavior during treatment (Bandura et al., 1969). Thus, adding participation of the client during treatment, developed out of a constructive treatment approach, surpasses the effects of modeling without this procedure. Further research has shown that adding supplementary performance aids to the modeling and guided participation components produces still greater therapeutic change (Bandura, Jeffery, & Wright, 1974).

The constructive approach need not merely make procedural additions to treatment, as in the case of participant modeling. Sometimes entirely different and conceptually unrelated treatments might be combined. The question is still whether adding new components to an existing intervention makes a difference. However, comparisons across different treatments also may enter in the research. For example, Greenberg et al. (1975) compared the effects of a reinforcement program alone versus a reinforcement program combined with milieu therapy on the behavior of institutionalized psychiatric patients. Both groups received a reinforcement program designed to improve adaptive behaviors in the hospital. One of the groups also received small group discussions and decision-making tasks related to the patients' own treatment. The results suggested that the combined reinforcement-milieu program was superior on out-of-the-hospital measures (i.e., days spent working in the community, days spent on home visits, and days in the community after discharge) but not on inpatient measures (i.e., self-care skills, attending activities, in-hospital work). The superiority of the combined procedures on measures of extrahospital adjustment is important for programs that might rely upon a behavior modification approach alone.

The advantage of the constructive treatment approach is that it empirically establishes a treatment package. Components that are shown to enhance treatment outcome are added to the basic procedure. As this process continues, the efficacy of the package increases. The empirical development of a treatment package is especially refreshing in clinical psychology and psychiatry, where treatment methods seemingly proliferate to no end. Most therapies that emerge have no established body of empirically-validated information. Rather, proponents of most therapeutic approaches advance particular techniques based largely upon clinical practice, uncontrolled observations, anecdotal material, and a theory of human woes and their amelioration based upon personal experience. This contrasts sharply with relying on empirical verification of the utility of particular treatment components.

As a scientific and applied endeavor, clinical psychology has the dual goals of developing treatment and understanding of the reasons for the effects of treatment. Yet, a constructive approach may not necessarily shed light on the mechanisms of behavior change. Research along these lines can proceed atheoretically so that components are added to treatment without understanding how they operate or interact with other components (McFall & Marston, 1970). Ideally, however, the components added to treatment in a constructive approach would derive from some theoretical context, so the investigator has guidelines of the components to add to treatment. The development of participant modeling within the social learning theory framework is a case in point. Also, theoretical guides of this nature allow not only for constructing effective treatments but also for testing theoretical propositions (see Bandura, 1977a, 1977b).

Dismantling Treatment Strategy

Once a treatment package has been shown to work, research may begin to analyze the precise influence of specific components. The purpose of dismantling treatment research is to understand the basis for behavior change effected by the overall package. To dismantle a given technique, individual treatment components are eliminated from treatment. Comparisons usually are made across groups that receive the treatment package or the package minus the specific components. Essentially, different components of treatment can be viewed as separate independent variables. Each component may be withheld from some clients and presented to others or presented in varying degrees across clients. Also, the separate and combined effects of different components can be evaluated. Differences across groups, depending upon the specific design, can suggest whether certain components are necessary and sufficient to effect behavior change and whether specific components produce additive or interactive effects.

The results of a dismantling strategy usually go beyond the implications of conducting treatment and bear upon theoretical notions that served as a basis for the derivation or explanation of the technique. By dismantling the treatment package, the investigator can comment upon whether the ingredients thought to be crucial for behavior change in fact are. Thus, dismantling research often has important theoretical implications and may produce results that call for revision of the theory.

The dismantling strategy has been used extensively in the evaluation of systematic desensitization (Lang, 1969). Part of the reason for this is that when desensitization was formally proposed as a therapy technique, specific ingredients were carefully described as essential for behavior change (Wolpe, 1958). The clarity with which specific ingredients were spelled out immediately led to research examining whether the ingredients contributed to behavior change. Desensitization, as originally proposed, included three essential ingredients for the treatment of anxiety-based disorders. First, the client needed to learn a response, usually relaxation, that was incompatible with anxiety. Second a hierarchy of anxiety-provoking situations needed to be constructed. Finally, the response incompatible with anxiety needed to be paired with the hierarchy items in order of progressively increasing anxiety. Pairing of the hierarchy items usually is accomplished by having clients imagine anxiety-provoking scenes while relaxed. Extensive desensitization research using the dismantling strategy has addressed the role of these components in changing behavior. Dismantling studies have compared systematic desensitization (all three components) with diverse variations that exclude or alter the supposedly crucial components. For example, desensitization without relaxation or with tension instead of relaxation, and desensitization without a graded hierarchy or with only intensely fearful items, have been contrasted with desensitization proper. The findings across several studies, with few exceptions, have suggested that original assumptions about the ingredients thought to be crucial to the success of the technique are in error (Kazdin & Wilcoxon, 1976; Wilkins, 1971; Wilson & Davison, 1971). Specific components of desensitization can be omitted without loss of efficacy. The only component that appears to be important is imagined or overt rehearsal of the response that is to be developed. These findings have had important implications for the theory about the mechanism of behavior change by ruling out interpretations that depend upon the ingredients originally thought essential.

The dismantling strategy requires that the treatment package consist of well-specified ingredients and that these ingredients be limited to some reasonable number. For example, Vogler, Compton, and Weissbach (1975) used a dismantling strategy in evaluating the efficacy of a broad-spectrum behavioral approach with chronic hospitalized alcoholics. One group received the following combination of treatment techniques: video-taped self-confrontation of drunken behavior, blood-alcohol discrimination training, electrical aversion conditioning for excessive consumption within the laboratory, alcohol education, behavioral counseling, and "alternative training." Another group received only the latter three techniques. "Behavioral counseling" consisted of a remarkably diverse range of procedures, including the identification and reinforcement of behavior incompatible with drinking, contingency contracting, instruction in problem-solving techniques, role-playing and assertion training often coupled with the use of video-taped feedback, relaxation training, communication skills development, and role modeling. All subjects also received elements of the standard hospital treatment program that included large group therapy meetings, art therapy, and Alcoholics Anonymous (AA) meetings. In addition, booster sessions were administered to both groups on a weekly basis during the first month after treatment and then monthly for the next eleven months.

The results of this study were ambiguous (Franks & Wilson, 1976). However, the important point is that given the multitude of treatment influences that subjects in both groups received, it would be extremely difficult to interpret meaningfully even more convincing intergroup differences than those obtained by Vogler et al. (1975). Data derived from such an evaluation strategy do little to establish the utility of behavioral techniques either singly or in combination in the treatment of alcoholism.

In addition, a theoretical notion as to the nature of the ingredients and their relative importance also is very helpful. Without a theoretical framework in which to view treatment, it is easy to trivialize the components. Actually, there are an indefinite number of components within any given therapy technique, some of which might be theoretically important (e.g., content discussed in therapy, therapist behavior) and others which are not (e.g., ratio of client to therapist verbalizations, distance between client and therapist). The priority of components for research is determined by the technique's theoretical basis, which specifies the mechanism of therapeutic change and, hence, the necessary conditions for behavioral change.

The notion of components of a given treatment technique varies as the theoretical basis for treatment changes. Dismantling research may show that a particular theory can not plausibly account for the results of a given technique. In this case, the components of the technique might be reanalyzed along different dimensions to assess the plausibility of another theory. Thus, no specific components of treatment are the basic elements. Rather, these are defined by the theoretical interpretation of the technique. As the theoretical basis changes, so may the components studied.

Parametric Treatment Strategy

The parametric treatment strategy refers to varying specific aspects of treatment to determine how to maximize therapeutic change. This strategy resembles the constructive treatment strategy insofar as the purpose is to examine dimensions that can be used to enhance treatment effects. However, in the constructive strategy, components of treatment usually are added to an existing treatment. The constructive approach usually evaluates the effects of adding or combining *qualitatively* distinct interventions to an existing treatment. Indeed, different treatment packages might be combined in a constructive evaluation approach. In contrast, the parametric strategy usually varies one or more dimensions within the existing treatment package. New treatments are not added. Rather, variations of dimensions within the existing treatment are studied. In parametric research, the variation often is made along *quantitative* dimensions by providing more or less of a given portion of treatment. For example, parametric investigations have focused upon such variables as the amount of treatment, and the number, spacing, and duration of individual sessions. With such parametric variations, each of the groups studied might receive the same general treatment and differ only in quantitative dimensions of variables associated with that treatment.

Parametric research also can vary qualitative aspects of a given treatment. Most therapy techniques leave unspecified many dimensions of treatment. Working within the technique, many aspects can be altered to determine their effect on outcome. For example, in a therapeutic procedure such as modeling, the basic ingredient is observing or imagining someone perform a particular behavior. Yet, the treatment leaves unspecified *who* the model should be (e.g., whether someone similar or dissimilar to the client) or *how* the model behaves while performing the behavior. Yet, each of these factors contributes to treatment effects (Kazdin, 1973a, 1974a). Thus, aspects of the treatment may be varied and reveal parameters of that treatment that can enhance therapeutic change.

An example of this parametric treatment approach is provided in an investigation that evaluated flooding as a technique to treat agoraphobic clients (Stern & Marks, 1973). Flooding consists of confronting the individual with the stimuli that cause distress until the adverse reaction habituates. Stern and Marks (1973) evaluated two parameters, namely the duration of continuous exposure to the feared stimuli (one long period of exposure versus several short exposures) and the mode of flooding (in imagery or in actual situations). Neither long nor short exposure periods in imagery produced much reduction in anxiety as rated by the patient and a blind rater. However, the longer period of exposure in vivo produced much more reduction in anxiety than did the shorter periods of exposure. These results suggest that in vivo is superior to imagery-based flooding and that longer continuous exposure periods are more effective than shorter periods for a given amount of total exposure. The results of this parametric study show specific variations of dimensions within flooding that can be altered to enhance treatment.

The parametric evaluation strategy is useful in many of the same ways as the constructive evaluation strategy is. The evaluation of specific treatment parameters can help build an effective treatment strategy. In addition to maximizing treatment outcome, the parametric approach can reveal important information about the theoretical basis of the technique and the mechanisms responsible for change. The process of varying the specific dimensions of treatment might yield information that supports or is incompatible with the mechanism assumed to account for change.

Comparative Treatment Strategy

The question of comparative research usually holds wide interest because theoretical battles over the basis of different therapies and vested interests in particular techniques all reduce to "whose is better?" Indeed, as discussed in the previous two chapters, the enthusiasm that inappropriate comparative questions have raised may well have impeded the development of more sophisticated evaluation strategies.

Despite the apparent simplicity of comparing different treatments, comparative research is beset by numerous methodological and conceptual difficulties. The nature of these difficulties was detailed in the previous chapter. In brief, objection was made to the comparison of ill-defined omnibus treatment programs with heterogeneous behavior disorders using unsatisfactory and global outcome measures. Yet the fact that traditional comparative outcome research has been methodologically marred in this manner does not mean that well-controlled comparative studies are not feasible under certain well-defined circumstances. For example, Bandura et al. (1969) demonstrated that a performance-based method participant modeling is significantly superior to techniques that rely upon symbolic representation of events (e.g., imaginal systematic desensitization and symbolic modeling). Not only has this laboratory-based research program shown the relative efficacy of different behavioral methods, it has also provided a theoretical testing ground in which the mechanisms of behavior change have been analyzed (Bandura, 1977b).

In another successful application of the comparative evaluation strategy, Gelder et al. (1973) compared specific treatment methods (systematic desensitization and flooding) to an attention-placebo control condition in the treatment of phobic disorders. Treatments were carried out by experienced therapists explicitly trained in the administration of the different methods. An attempt was made to induce a high expectancy of success in half of the subjects by describing the treatment and therapist chosen in very favorable terms and showing them a video tape of a client who had benefited from the treatment they were to receive. Treatment effects were evaluated in terms of measures of behavioral avoidance, blind psychiatric ratings, client self-ratings, physiological responsiveness, and standardized psychological tests. The adequacy of the control group in eliciting expectancies of treatment success comparable to those evoked by the two behavioral methods was assessed directly.

Half of the clients were agoraphobics, the other half a mixed group of specific phobias. Agoraphobics are regarded as more difficult to treat than simple phobias. They represent the typical sort of client Sloane et al. (1975) regarded as the appropriate focus of treatment outcome studies, and show the more generalized kind of anxiety disorder for which behavior therapy is often alleged to be unsuited. Clients were assigned to treatments and therapists in a factorial design that permitted an analysis of the possible interactions among treatment effects, therapist differences, type of phobia, and levels of expectancy. Treatment duration was fifteen weekly sessions, similar to the Sloane et al. study, with three-month and six-month follow-ups.

In sum, the Gelder et al. (1973) study was sufficiently well designed and well executed to answer the question of what treatment method has what specific effect on what problem in whom. It provides one methodological model according to which specific treatment methods can be compared with each other and with an interpretable placebo control condition.

Client and Therapist Variation Strategy
The discussion of evaluation strategies to this point implies that specific techniques have certain effects in a relatively straightforward fashion. Little mention has been made of the clients and therapists who are involved in treatment and the influence their attributes and behavior may have on therapeutic outcome. The client and therapist variation strategy examines these influences in two different ways. Initially, clients and therapists can be selected for specific attributes. Alternatively, behavior of the clients or, more likely, of the therapists can be experimentally manipulated.

Clients might be selected because of their differences in age, sex, socioeconomic standing, marital status, education, or in personality measures such as introversion-extraversion, suggestibility, and so on (Garfield, 1971; Meltzoff & Kornreich, 1970). Therapist variables have been studied in a similar fashion by looking at such characteristics as therapist training, years of experience, age, interests, various personality traits, empathy and warmth during the sessions, and so on (Meltzoff & Kornreich, 1970; Truax & Mitchell, 1971). Finally, client and therapist variables can be combined to look at particular combinations of subject variables or variables derived from a particular client-therapist dyad (e.g., Parloff, 1961).

When clients and therapists are classified along some dimension according to particular subject variables, the main question asked is whether treatment is more or less effective with certain kinds of participants. Essentially, the question is one of external validity. An interaction of treatment with the characteristics of the client or therapist suggests that treatment is more or less effective depending upon the variable used to classify either the therapist or client. Such findings are potentially useful in making decisions about the type of treatment appropriate for clients with certain types of characteristics.

The client and therapist evaluation strategy also embraces direct manipulation of independent variables rather than merely subject selection. Rather than selecting therapists' attributes (e.g., empathy or warmth) and correlating them with outcome (e.g., Sloane et al., 1975), these characteristics can be manipulated experimentally. Therapists can behave differently across clients according to the dimension that is to be varied. For example, Morris and Suckerman (1974a, 1975b) have evaluated the effect of therapist warmth in changing behavior of college students afraid of harmless snakes. Treatment, systematic desensitization, was presented via tape recorder, where a therapist verbalized the hierarchy items to be imagined. The tapes for some subjects included the therapist speaking in a "warm" fashion by making his voice soft, melodic, and pleasant. In contrast, other subjects received the identical tapes with the therapist speaking in a "cold" fashion by making his voice harsh, businesss-like, and impersonal. Both treatments reduced anxiety to a greater extent than did no treatment. Also, subjects who received the warm voice condition showed greater improvement.

The selection of clients and therapists according to specific dimensions increases the precision of the evaluation of treatment outcome. It is unlikely that a simple question such as which treatment produces greater change or which components enhance treatment will be the most productive approach. To these questions need to be added stipulations about characteristics of the clients as well as of the individuals who deliver treatment. The study of variables with which treatment effects are associated begins to define the boundary conditions associated with a given technique and the areas where different techniques produce different advantages. Essentially, the client and therapist variation strategy allows more refined questions to be asked about a given technique and its merits relative to other techniques. Hence, this strategy adds to other strategies already mentioned.

Internal Structure or Process Strategy

The above research strategies refer to what traditionally has been known as outcome research. Outcome research addresses the general question of what happens to the client at the end of therapy; in other words, did therapy work? Each of the strategies discussed to this point addresses this question in the sense that performance after treatment serves as the criterion for evaluating treatment, variations of treatment, or different treatments. Traditionally, process research has been distinguished from outcome research. Process research addresses questions that pertain to the transactions between the therapist and client and the type of interactions and their interim effects on client and therapist behavior (see Shlien, 1968; Strupp & Luborsky, 1968).

As usually discussed, process and outcome research are dichotomized. Process research is viewed as the study of activity within the therapy session and while treatment is still in process. In contrast, outcome evaluates the final effect of treatment when treatment has been terminated. While the distinction holds in certain types of research, for much of research it is profitable to reject the dichotomy (Kiesler, 1971). Much of process research examines the effects of different variables on client behavior within the treatment session. Insofar as the client changes in behaviors during treatment sessions are desirable, in-session behavior actually is an interim measure of outcome. The effects of specific variables on client behavior during treatment is one measure of the beneficial effects of treatment and, hence, is an appropriate outcome measure.

A well-known example from the therapy literature illustrates the focus on the process of change and its relevance for outcome. A frequently cited study by Truax (1966) examined excerpts from tape recordings of one successful therapy case conducted in the tradition of client-centered (nondirective) psychotherapy by Carl Rogers. As is well known, in nondirective therapy certain therapeutic conditions (e.g., empathy and acceptance or positive regard) supposedly are provided to the client unconditionally. Truax found empathy and acceptance were likely to be verbalized by the therapist when the client made insightful statements, focused upon the problem, or expressed herself in a way that was similar to the therapist. The significance of the study was that it demonstrated that "nondirective" therapy, contrary to its theoretical rationale, is very directive in reinforcing certain kinds of behavior. This study examined the process of therapy rather than improvement of the client. Yet the nature of the investigation makes it more than an examination of the internal structure of treatment. Presumably, according to the theoretical basis of client-centered therapy, how clients speak about themselves and perceive the world is the important outcome of successful treatment. Changing relevant verbalizations during the sessions thus is very much an outcome measure in the sense that it reflects whether therapy is achieving its intended objective.

Not all research on the processes of therapy can be reinterpreted as an interim measure of outcome. For example, research on the internal structure of therapy may examine aspects of the therapist's behavior over time, which is purely a study of internal changes in treatment that says nothing directly about how or what the client is doing. In addition, the responses evaluated in the client may not bear directly on the problem for which the client sought treatment. For example, process research may focus upon the perception of the client and therapist of the therapy session itself and the correlates of different impressions of treatment (e.g., Orlinsky & Howard, 1975). In this kind of research, the characteristics of events in treatment are the focus and may or may not bear on therapeutic behaviors related to improvement of the client. Rather, the goal is to understand the mechanisms of change and the course of events in therapy.

Research on the internal structure of treatment presumably is most appropriate after the treatment package itself has demonstrated therapeutic effects. While the interaction between a therapist and client might be of interest in its own right, the value of selecting a particular therapy for process evaluation would be unclear if treatment was not shown to effect change. As a general rule, internal structure or process research raises questions about techniques rather than treatment problems. However, by isolating particular processes associated with successful outcome, hypotheses can be generated and tested about the essential components of a given treatment. Hence, "process" and "outcome" research, even as traditionally conceived, are quite related.

Treatment Evaluation Strategies: General Comments

The foregoing treatment evaluation strategies address different but complementary questions. The strategy that is relied upon most heavily for a given technique may depend upon the extent to which the technique has been well investigated. Preliminary research of a therapeutic technique is likely to adopt the package, constructive, or parametric evaluation strategies. After the technique is demonstrated to be effective in altering a particular problem, it is likely to be evaluated more analytically in dismantling, client-therapist variation, or internal structure strategies. Along with this, investigators increasingly will compare the newly established package with techniques that claim effectiveness for a particular problem. In any case, there tends to be an evolution of the type of research strategy adopted that is suited to the development of the technique. However, this evolution is not fixed. Indeed, a dramatic way to develop visibility of a given technique, long before it has been carefully established in package evaluation research, is to conduct a comparative study. If the technique can be shown to be superior to an existing technique, this is likely to generate a flurry of enthusiasm in the field more quickly than the treatment package evaluation strategy would. Thus, comparative research may be the first strategy adopted. However, comparative research usually requires greater effort than treatment package research in terms of the number of subjects, therapists, and groups needed. Thus, unless there is some preliminary assurance that the new treatment will be fruitful, the extra effort of comparative research might be profitably deferred for later studies.

Another reason for holding comparative questions in abeyance pertains to development of the individual treatments that are to be compared. Early in the development of a given therapy technique, the parameters that maximize treatment efficacy are not well known. Research that examines parametric variations that maximize treatment effects needs to precede comparative work. Once the variation of treatment that will be maximally effective has been shown, it makes sense to compare it to another treatment that has achieved similar status.

Aside from the status of research for a given technique, the priority of the investigator in terms of applied or basic research aims determines the treatment evaluation strategy adopted. As mentioned earlier, if the primary commitment is to discover a treatment that ameliorates a clinical problem, then treatment package, constructive, and comparative approaches are likely to be adopted. In the applied clinical context, effecting the greatest amount of change as efficiently as possible, is more important than is understanding the theoretical basis for the technique or the mechanisms of change. In contrast, in laboratory-based research, where there is less urgency to affect client change, greater priority can be given to dissecting treatment to isolate its effective components. The goals of effecting change and understanding the basis for the change are not incompatible, but, they usually do vary in priority across investigations and treatment evaluation strategies (see Kazdin, in press f).

Control Groups for Treatment Evaluation

Evaluation of the efficacy of therapy depends upon careful experimental control over rival hypotheses that might account for therapeutic change. Several different control conditions can be used depending upon the research evaluation strategy and the purpose of the investigation. The range of available control procedures cannot be reviewed here (cf. Kazdin, in press f). However, it is useful to discuss briefly two major control conditions that address basic questions in evaluating the efficacy of treatment.

No-Treatment and Waiting-List Control Groups.   An obvious issue in treatment research is demonstrating whether therapy induces greater changes than would be obtained without treatment. Research designed to assess the efficacy of a given treatment usually needs to include in the design a group that does not receive treatment. The purpose of a no-treatment control group is to assess whether treatment effects greater change than that which would occur over the same time period without formal treatment. Methodologically, a no-treatment group controls for several threats to internal validity, such as history, maturation, the effects of repeated assessment, instrument decay, statistical regression, and similar factors that could contribute to or account for change (Campbell & Stanley, 1963; see Kazdin, in press f).

In the psychotherapy literature, changes that occur independently of formal treatment are referred to as *spontaneous remission* (e.g., Bergin, 1971; Meltzoff & Kornreich, 1970; Rachman, 1971). Although a detailed discussion of spontaneous remission is beyond the scope of the present chapter, a few points are worth noting in passing. Spontaneous remisssion refers to changes made without receiving formal treatment in a given investigation. Yet, individuals who do not receive treatment in the investigation may seek alternative treatments. This is difficult to trace directly because the sources of treatment most often sought are outside of the mental health professions (physicians, clergymen) (Frank, 1961; Gurin, Veroff, & Feld, 1960). Aside from receiving help outside of the investigation in which clients serve as no-treatment controls, improvement may result from a host of other factors (e.g., change in situations that may have precipitated the problem) (see Subotnik, 1972). Whatever the reasons for these changes, they need to be controlled for in the evaluation of a particular treatment package.

For control purposes, it would be desirable to know the level of improvement to be expected for a particular population of clients with a given disorder so that treatment could be evaluated using a no-treatment control group. At present, there is debate about the proportion of clients who improve without formal treatment (Bergin, 1971; Kiesler, 1971; Subotnik, 1972). The rate of improvement appears to be a complex function of several variables, including severity of the problem, patient diagnosis, age, the criteria used to evaluate change, and other factors. Hence, a no-treatment control group is essential because the level of improvement for a given set of clients cannot be precisely identified in advance of an investigation.

There are obvious practical and ethical obstacles in using a no-treatment control group. Initially, assigning patients to a no-treatment group is likely to result in high levels of attrition. Clients in need of treatment invariably will need to seek alternative treatments if treatment is not provided in the investigation in which they agree to participate. Attrition can limit the conclusions that can be drawn because the clients remaining in the group are likely to be highly select. The amount of attrition is likely to be a function of the duration that clients are required to serve as no-treatment controls in the investigation. To maintain clients in a no-treatment group, they are often promised that treatment will eventually be provided after a waiting period. This waiting period corresponds to the duration required to provide other clients in the study with treatment. When clients serve in a group that eventually receives treatment, this is referred to as a waiting-list control group. A waiting-list control group allows comparison of treatment with no treatment only for the period in which treatment is provided (Sloane et al., 1975). This does not allow long-term comparison of treatment and no-treatment groups, because the no-treatment group is eventually given treatment. Hence, the waiting-list control group is only a partial solution. It is quite possible that in the long run, treatment and no-treatment groups would prove to be no different. That is, the effects of treatment may be attenuated over time and/or the no-treatment group may improve over time.

For example, Kent and O'Leary (1976) found that a behavioral program for conduct problem children greatly improved behavior both in the home and at school relative to a no-treatment control group. Interestingly, the highly favorable effects of treatment were no longer significant on a number of dependent variables at a nine-month follow-up. The no-treatment group improved over the follow-up interval across diverse measures, with some exceptions. In this study, the conclusions drawn would have differed if a waiting-list rather than a no-treatment control group had been used. The central findings at follow-up would have been unavailable because subjects in the no-treatment condition eventually would have received treatment.

Aside from the practical problems of using a no-treatment group, there are obvious ethical constraints (e.g., Stuart, 1973). When clients seek treatment, it is difficult to justify withholding all attempts at intervention. Even an unlikely treatment that may exert little influence can be better defended than providing no treatment at all, in part because of the placebo treatment effects that are likely to accrue to any treatment. Overall, in clinical situations, no-treatment and waiting-list control groups often are difficult to implement, which presents problems for conducting basic research on evaluating the efficacy of a given treatment package. Alternative strategies for evaluating treatment outcome often can avoid using a no-treatment group because the questions asked pertain to different treatments or to variations of treatment rather than to treatment versus no treatment.

Nonspecific Treatment Control Groups.   A frequently discussed issue in psychotherapy research is the influence of such factors as the therapist-client relationship, suggestion, client belief in the curative effects of treatment, attending therapy, and similar influences that may contribute to client improvement. Virtually all therapies share such general characteristics as providing a client with a rationale that places his or her problem into a coherent theoretical framework, engaging in specific procedures designed to ameliorate the problem, an attentive and interested therapist who is committed to the treatment process, and similar factors (Frank, 1961). The components of treatment, such as therapist support, that are not specific to any particular form of therapy may well contribute to client change. The components associated with attending treatment per se have been referred to as "nonspecific treatment factors." The therapeutic changes resulting from these factors have been referred to as "nonspecific treatment effects."[a]

Nonspecific treatment factors present an obstacle for therapy evaluation whenever investigators wish to attribute the effects of a given treatment or the relative effects of different treatments to specific active ingredients peculiar to a specific therapy. Yet, to draw conclusions about active ingredients requires controlling for the effects of treatment per se. In treatment research, the nonspecific effects of treatment have been controlled in one of two ways. First, an investigation can include at least two treatment groups in the study, as would be done in such research strategies as the dismantling, constructive, comparative, and parametric strategies. Each treatment would include many of the nonspecific treatment factors such as a rationale about therapy, establishing a therapeutic relationship, providing several treatment sessions, and so on. Hence, any differences between groups would be attributed to specific ingredients of treatment rather than nonspecific treatment effects.

A second and more recent approach toward controlling nonspecific treatment effects is to include in the investigation a pseudotherapy, or

---

[a] The term "nonspecific" is unfortunate. The many therapeutic factors lumped together under this rubric are quite specific. It is more realistic to propose that, although many "nonspecific" influences still remain to be specified, they are neither intrinsically unspecifiable nor qualitatively very different from other independent variables involved in planned behavior change (e.g., Kazdin, in press f; Wilson, in press d; Wilson & Evans, 1976).

attention-placebo group (e.g., Lang et al., 1965; Paul, 1966). The purpose of this group is to provide all of the nonspecific factors of treatment without presenting a veridical therapy procedure. Clients might meet with a therapist and engage in tasks considered by the therapist to be therapeutically inert. In general, a nonspecific treatment control group is modeled after the placebo in drug research, where clients receive a treatment, albeit one that should not effect change. If a treatment group can be shown to effect greater change than the group that receives the inert control condition, specific active ingredients of treatment can be inferred as responsible for change.

At first glance, the practical problems of using a nonspecific treatment control group appear less formidable than those in using a no-treatment control group. In a nonspecific treatment control group, clients can engage in a plausible task that is not designed to offer specific therapeutic ingredients. The difficulty stems from determining those agents that are nontherapeutic. Depending upon the conceptualization of the investigator, merely discussing the therapeutic problem and historical factors may be interpreted as either an active treatment or as a control condition (Kazdin, in press f). Despite the debates that might be entertained about active therapy ingredients, there are several examples from the literature with nonspecific control procedures based upon having clients imagine material not related to their problem, engage in discrimination and motor tasks, discussing issues only tangentially related to their problems, or even engaging in recreation (Kazdin, in press f). The practical problem is compounded by the ethics of providing treatment that is specifically employed because it is thought to be inert. Essentially, using a nonspecific control procedure instead of a presumably more effective treatment, based upon theoretical if not empirical grounds, may be a questionable practice. Of course, the ethical problem may lead to practical obstacles as well. A nonspecific treatment control group that in fact is not achieving improvement is likely to show attrition as well. A group receiving a treatment that actually is inert may suffer from attrition as clients seek more effective alternatives.

Recently, research suggests that nonspecific treatment effects may not be as easily controlled as originally thought. Treatment and frequently used nonspecific treatment control conditions have been found to differ in the extent to which they are credible to the clients and generate in clients expectancies for improvement (Borkovec & Nau, 1972; McReynolds & Tori, 1972; McGlynn & Walls, 1976; Nau, Caputo, & Borkovec, 1974). Credibility of treatment or expectancies for improvement refer to the faith generated in clients on the basis of the specific treatment to which they are assigned and may be measured in different diverse ways, including ratings of the believability of treatment, simulated performance after exposure to treatment or control condition rationales, or performance on bogus measures of therapeutic change (Kazdin & Wilcoxon, 1976).

The problem of controlling for differential credibility and expectancies for therapeutic improvement across treatment and control conditions has emerged from research in behavior therapy, particularly work on systematic desensitization. Investigations have shown that nonspecific control groups to which desensitization has been compared frequently are less believable to the subjects and lead subjects to expect less improvement. Comparisons of desensitization with control treatments that generate lower levels of expectancies for success invariably show superior effects of desensitization on outcome measures (Kazdin & Wilcoxon, 1976). Yet, when desensitization is compared to control conditions that are as credible and generate as much expectancy for success as does desensitization, desensitization tends not to differ from the control condition. The purpose of the discussion is not to impugn the effects of desensitization. Rather, the problem revealed in the desensitization literature is likely to have broad methodological implications for therapy research in general.

Whether the differential credibility of treatments is a problem in a given study is a matter of the conclusion the investigator wishes to draw. If the investigator is interested only in showing that a treatment technique is more effective than no treatment or than an alternative treatment, there is no need to be concerned with, or to control for, the possible influence of the credibility of the expentancies for success generated by treatment. However, if the investigator wishes to make claims as to *why* change has occurred or the reason that one treatment works better than another, then differential credibility across alternative treatments must be ruled out as a rival hypothesis (Kazdin & Wilcoxon, 1976). The need to control for differential credibility across conditions appears to be essential for dismantling, constructive, comparative, and parametric therapy evaluation strategies, at least if the investigator wishes to make claims about the reasons for differences across groups.

The importance of controlling for differential credibility and expectancies generated by treatment and control conditions has been recognized repeatedly in the literature (e.g., Frank, 1961; Kazdin & Wilcoxon, 1976; Jacobson & Baucom, 1977; Rosenthal & Frank, 1956; Thorne, 1952; Paul, 1966). Only recently has research begun to utilize groups to control for nonspecific treatment effects on a systematic basis. However, distinctions can be made among the different factors that are controlled by simply including a nonspecific treatment control group in the investigation. Even when select factors are controlled, such as providing some form of treatment for the client, the possibility exists that the control group may differ simply in believability and for that reason differ from treatment in the effects produced at outcome. Additional research needs to focus upon developing control groups that adequately control for expectancies for success that may serve as a plausible rival interpretation of differences across treatments (Kazdin, in press f; Kazdin & Wilcoxon, 1976).

Control Groups in Relation to Treatment Strategies. The function of the control groups mentioned above is primarily to rule out such specific threats to internal validity as the effects of client changes over time independently of treatment and the nonspecific effects of treatment. Aside from ruling out specific artifacts, control conditions help reveal the mechanisms of change. A nonspecific treatment control group may do this, at least by negation, by showing that contact with treatment and the expectancies generated by the treatment cannot plausibly account for the results. Yet, more specific types of control conditions can isolate the components of a veridical treatment that account for change. The above discussion only examines a few of the commonly used control groups. Additional groups that are used to isolate mechanisms of treatment cannot be discussed in a general sense because they depend upon the specific treatment that is evaluated and hypotheses about the nature of treatment.

The research strategy and the control conditions used to evaluate treatment evolve together as the nature of the questions change. In an early stage of research, major attention is likely to be given to treatment package or constructive strategies. Control conditions consist of no-treatment or waiting-list control groups. As the package is shown to be effective more analytic work is likely to begin. Dismantling and parametric strategies may receive a greater attention. The control conditions then include treatment groups that differ in select and often subtle dimensions that help isolate factors that contribute to or enhance change. Research on the mechanisms of change is a highly important stage, because it helps develop the basis for an effective treatment. The principle, theory, or mechanisms through which treatment attains its effects can be revealed through such analytic work.

After treatment is well developed, it is especially meaningful to raise questions about its efficacy relative to a viable alternative, i.e., comparative research. The comparative question is most appropriately asked only after there are assurances that each of the treatments effects change and the appropriate application of each of the treatments is known. For example, dismantling, parametric, and client-therapist variation research strategies should warrant priority over direct comparative research. The dismantling and parametric research is likely to reveal dimensions that can be varied within a treatment to enhance its effects. The client-therapist variation research is likely to reveal the applicability of treatment across client variables (e.g., diagnosis, age) and therapist character-istics (e.g., degree of training). Comparative research presupposes that considerable information is known about each of the treatments so that the test is meaningful to begin with. It would be a mistake to compare different treatments when the appropriate application of each treatment—to what sorts of clients and therapeutic problems—is un-known. The comparison is only important when each technique is known to be effective in some specific area and presents an alternative to an existing treatment with similar evidence.

Occasionally, comparative research contrasts global treatment pack-ages applied to a wide range of clients. The Sloane et al. (1975) study comparing behavior therapy and psychotherapy constitutes such an example. While such a comparison eventually may provide meaningful results, it presupposes that each technique is specifically defined and applied to a specific set of problems. Prior evidence is needed to suggest that each separate, well-defined technique has in fact carefully demon-strated change with the particular problem to be treated and that the parameters that contribute to each technique are at least partially known. Hence, a comparative study ideally is preceded by background evidence that suggests the efficacy of treatment (treatment package research) and reveals variables contributing to its efficacy (parametric, client-therapist, variation, dismantling research). Otherwise, the comparison is neither a fair test of the individual treatments nor a meaningful application.

By way of analogy, it would not be very meaningful to compare two different "drugs" to treat all or most patients who came for treatment at a clinic. Initial research would be useful to establish that each of the drugs worked on its own, and to establish the ideal dose and the specific client conditions for which the drug was suited. Drugs are not applied to patients in general but depend upon a precise condition usually narrowly defined. The medical approach toward specification of treatment *and* the disorder to which treatment is applied has not been fully exploited in evaluating psychological treatment. The utility of the medical approach is quite evident in comparing different treatments, each of which may be known to alter a particular problem. Once such information is known, it is particularly meaningful to compare the two different drug treatments.

"Analogue" Therapy Studies

The different treatment evaluation strategies discussed earlier raise several questions about therapy. Aside from the specific evaluation strategy, the most direct means of addressing questions about the efficacy of treatment might seem to be studying therapy techniques as they are practiced in the clinical situation with "real" clients and therapists. To conduct such research, clients who come for treatment can be assigned to appropriate treatment and control groups, and assessment devices can be administered to evaluate treatment. Although the basic requirements can be highlighted in a straightforward fashion, meeting these requires a Herculean effort in the face of nearly insurmountable obstacles. A host of practical problems—recruiting experienced therapists for the project, keeping clients in the project—and ethical obstacles—withholding treatment, assigning patients to control groups (O'Leary & Borkovec, 1977)—can make clinical research difficult if not impossible (e.g., Candy et al., 1972) and often, if completed, uninterpretable (Chapter 2).

One solution to the problem is evaluating treatment under conditions analogous to those available in the clinic. Research that evaluates treatment under conditions that only resemble or approximate the clinical situation has been referred to as "analogue" research. An "analogue" study usually focuses upon a carefully defined research question under well-controlled conditions. The purpose of the investigation is to illuminate a particular process or to study an intervention that may be of importance in actual treatment. The ultimate goal of "analogue" research is to reveal empirical relationships that can be generalized to actual treatment settings.

An important issue in the therapy literature is the extent to which "analogue" studies contribute to understanding therapeutic processes and outcome in clinical settings. It is generally acknowledged that "analogue" studies provide an important link in extrapolating from basic laboratory research to therapy (Bernstein & Paul, 1971; Heller, 1971). "Analogue" studies allow careful experimental control by studying circumscribed and well-defined behaviors. Also, careful control can be achieved by minimizing sources of variances that might otherwise obscure the effects of treatment. Thus, subjects can be selected because of their similarities on the target problem and subject and demographic variables. Similarly, therapists can be selected for homogeneity of training interests and experience. In addition, control groups not easily used in clinical situations can be readily employed in laboratory conditions where client treatment is not the highest priority. Thus, clients can be assigned to a nonspecific treatment control condition which is not expected to effect change, or indeed not be assigned to treatment at all. In "analogue" studies, treatment-specific ingredients of treatment as well as treatment itself can be more readily withheld than in the clinical situation. Freedom in providing or withholding specific ingredients of treatment greatly expands the range of questions that can be asked about therapy. This, perhaps, is the greatest advantage of laboratory "analogue" research.

There are different paradigms of "analogue" therapy research, including interviewing (Heller, 1971) verbal conditioning (Kanfer, 1968; Heller & Marlatt, 1969), and mild fears that may resemble clinical phobias

(Bernstein, 1973; Bernstein & Paul, 1971). Research in each of these areas has permitted extremely well controlled investigation of specific hypotheses. Yet the advantages of methodological rigor afforded by research in these areas notwithstanding, there is the lingering concern about external validity. In other words, can the results be generalized to clinical situations?

The problem of generalizing results can be illustrated by the "analogue" research on relatively mild fears that has been exploited in behavior modification. Various behavioral treatments such as desensitization and flooding have been explored with college students who have mild fears of small animals such as harmless snakes. Often these college students have been recruited for an experiment with the external incentive of course credit. These subjects were not motivated to obtain treatment for a personal problem of pressing concern. Major concerns have been voiced about the generality of research in these studies to clinical situations (e.g., Cooper, Furst & Bridger, 1969). The issue is whether results from these "treatment" studies can be extended to clients with more generalized problems of greater severity. There is reason for this concern. Recent research has shown that fear of small animals in college students typically habituate more quickly in response to the presence of the anxiety-provoking stimulus and are more influenced by suggestion than are fears in social situations (Borkovec, Stone, O'Brien, & Kaloupek, 1974; Borkovec, Wall, & Stone, 1974; Singerman, Borkovec, & Baron, 1976). It is very likely that research on behaviors that habituate less rapidly than fears of small animals and are less amenable to suggestion will be more generalizable to clinical problems that presumably share these characteristics.

The issue of generalizing from well-controlled laboratory studies of behavior change methods to therapy as practiced in the clinical situation transcends the target problem under investigation. There are several dimensions along which "analogue" studies depart from the clinical situation, including the type of therapists used and the extent of therapist training, the setting in which treatment is conducted, motivation of clients for treatment, and others (Kazdin, 1977 f). The crucial issue is whether or not, or to what extent, departures from the clinical situation on each of these dimensions limit the generality of results to therapeutic practice.

Implications for Therapy Evaluation.   Therapy investigations are usually discussed in the clinical literature as either "analogue" or "nonanalogue" research. Dichotomizing clinical research in this fashion may obscure interpretations of research findings in different ways. First, the distinction tends to overlook the inherent limitations and analogue nature of *all* clinical research, including those studies conducted in clinical situations with patient populations. Second, and more important, the categorization does not provide clear guidelines to distinguish among analogue studies.

All psychotherapy and behavior therapy research is analogue research insofar as it constructs a situation in which the phenomenon of interest can be studied (Kazdin, 1977e). The experimental version of the phenomenon may resemble the naturally occurring phenomenon in varying degrees, but in an important sense is only an analogue. Even when therapy research is conducted in a clinical situation, it is only an analogue of treatment as usually conducted. There are several reasons for the analogue nature of clinical research.

Initially, the ethics of clinical research require that all subjects be fully informed that they are participating in a research project and are exposed to the contrived arrangements that entails. Such potential artifacts as demand characteristics (Orne, 1969), pretest sensitization (Lana, 1969), and subject roles (Weber & Cook, 1972) are sources of bias that may influence the results by virtue of the experimental arrangement. The use of special pretreatment assessment devices, screening procedures, and careful arrangements that keep intake workers, therapists, and assessors "blind" all contribute to the experimental nature of the investigation and move it away from the conditions of clinical practice.

The assessment of behavior on psychological measures make an investigation an "analogue" in an important sense. It is not the responses on psychological measures or therapist ratings per se that are of interest but rather the construct assumed to be represented by these measures. The measures used in research are of interest because they may reflect or relate to changes occurring in the natural environment in the client's ordinary circumstances. Yet, the measured responses are only an analogue of the responses and situations of direct interest.

In this sense, many of the "analogue" studies that have been dismissed as clinically irrelevant are, in fact, more relevant tests of behavior change methods, since they more directly measure changes in the subjects' natural environment. In contrast to interview-based ratings of outcome in comparative clinical studies (e.g., Gelder et al., 1967; Sloane et al., 1975), so-called "analogue" investigations such as DiLoreto's (1971) and Paul's (1966) that have assessed behavioral change in the criterion situation are closer to the reality of the client's problem. On the dimension of relevance of measurement the typical "clinical" outcome study is thus more of an analogue than the much criticized "analogue" research study.

Viewing all therapy research as an analogue to clinical practice—presumably the situation to which one would like to generalize—has important implications for conceptualizing and evaluating treatment research. Initially, it is essential to keep in mind that investigators are interested in extrapolating research findings to some area, problem, setting, or subject population that itself is not studied directly. There is always the possibility that that extrapolation is not justified. The difference between the clinical situation and an experiment might be precisely along dimensions that restrict generalizing from one area to the other. *A major implication of this view is that it is not only fruitless but also counterproductive to speak of "analogue" versus "nonanalogue" or "clinical" research.* Rather, research can be viewed on the basis of the extent to which it resembles the situation to which one wishes to generalize (see Kazdin, 1977e).

There are several dimensions along which therapy research may vary from the clinical situation. This itself does not necessarily limit the extent to which the results can be generalized. The results often can be generalized across dimensions that seem very discrepant. For example, many findings in the psychology of learning have been established with infrahuman species. Specific learning paradigms and principles have had generality to human behavior despite differences between humans and infrahumans and the importance of considering uniquely human characteristics (see Weimer & Palermo, 1975). The fact that research does not focus upon a problem or population of direct interest is not always critical.

In evaluating therapy research, there are two important questions. First, to what extent do the conditions resemble the situation to which the investigator wishes to generalize? Second, to what extent are the departures from the clinical situation relevant for generalizing the results? There are several dimensions along which studies may depart from the clinical situation. These dimensions include the target problem, the population studied, the manner in which subjects or clients are recruited or the motivation of the subjects for treatment, characteristics of the therapists, the "set" and expectancies of the client, instructions about the nature of treatment and its effects, the variation of treatment and its departure from clinical practice, the assessment measures, the context in which the measures are administered, and so on (see Kazdin, in press f).

The generality of an investigation depends upon where the investigation lies with respect to these and similar dimensions vis-à-vis the clinical situation. Each dimension can be viewed as a separate continuum along which studies can vary. The continuum reflects the degree of resemblance of the study to the clinical treatment situations to which the results are to be generalized. The task for evaluating *any* therapy outcome study— whether arbitrarily designated as "analogue" or not—depends upon where it falls on the continuum with respect to each dimension. More important, generalizability of the results depends upon how the dimension relates to treatment efficacy. An explicit assumption is that resemblance of a study along a particular dimension necessarily increases generality of the results of the study to the clinical situation. The negative side of this assumption is more important to focus upon: the greater the dissimilarity of the study along a particular dimension, the less likely that the results can be generalized to the clinical situation.

With many dimensions, it is possible, indeed likely, that the assumed relationship is accurate. Thus, studies that only faintly resemble the clinical situation might produce changes that are not likely to occur in the clinical situation. However, with other dimensions it is reasonable to expect that the results might be quite generalizable from the laboratory to clinical setting. Possibly the *less* resemblance of a study to the clinical situation for a given dimension, the *more* difficult it would be to change behavior (Kazdin, 1977e). That is, departure from the clinical situation may make behavior changes more difficult to achieve. In these cases demonstration of behavior change in the nonclinical situation might even be a more convincing demonstration of an effect of treatment than would application in the clinical situation. For example, consider the therapist dimension. If therapists who bear very little resemblance to those who normally practice therapy (i.e., less experience, education, and training) effect marked behavior change in their clients, the generality of this finding to highly trained therapists is quite plausible. Similarly, consider the treatment dimension. If behavior change is shown with a variation of treatment that deviates from the clinical version, the results might be even greater for the technique as normally practiced. With respect to client commitment and motivation it might be that the client who seeks therapy in distress is more likely to continue in therapy and to adhere diligently to therapeutic prescriptions than the less severely disabled subject who is recruited for a research study (Franks & Wilson, 1973). In many cases, the laboratory-based version of treatment is an important test because it minimizes the parameters of treatment that are likely to enhance change (e.g., individualization of therapy content and duration) (O'Leary & Wilson, 1975).

A problem in therapy research is that "analogue" studies have been rejected on the grounds that, by their very nature, they provide a weak test of the relationship between a treatment variable and client change in the clinical situation (Luborsky et al., 1975; Marks, 1976a). Yet this is not necessarily the case. The relation between a laboratory-based study and generality to clinical situations for a given dimension itself is an area of research. The importance of a given dimension to the generality of the results needs to be evaluated directly. Research is needed that investigates the influence of departures from the clinical situation along various dimensions and the implications of such departures for generalizing results to clinical situations. Comparisons of varying degrees of resemblance of research to the clinical situation for a given dimension can reveal whether departure from the clinical situation attenuates, enhances, or has no effect on treatment.

An uncritical bias against alleged "analogue studies" has obscured some important distinctions among studies. Thus, any study using subjects other than clients who have sought treatment through conventional channels is labeled "analogue"; its findings are then queried on account of "volunteer" (usually "student") subjects (e.g., Marks, in press). Ethical imperatives require that all subjects in this research be "volunteers," so the specific nature of the subject-selection process is the issue at hand. For example, the subjects in Bandura's treatment outcome research program were recruited through advertisements placed in community newspapers (Bandura et al., 1975). These subjects were described as highly phobic, afflicted with various debilitating problems as a consequence of their years. The assertion that these subjects are qualitatively different from "real clients" who have sought psychiatric assistance is weak.

The generality of findings based on "real" clients seen in clinical settings is not intrinsically greater than data derived from laboratory investigations. It is often the case that subject selection processes in these clinical outcome studies admit only highly select clients with particularly favorable chances of improvement (Candy et al., 1972; Sloane et al., 1975). Moreover, the treatment motivation of "real" clients seen in clinical practice and the severity of their behavior disorders may vary as widely as they do in laboratory-based studies. Arbitrarily categorizing research investigations as "analogue" versus "clinical," designed to study qualitatively different "nonclinical subjects" versus "real clinical clients," represents what Bandura (1977a) has described as a recycling of mental disease ideology under clinical euphemisms.

The representativeness of subjects that participate in laboratory-based research is frequently questioned; however, the question is seldom if ever asked about clients treated in clinical settings. The representativeness of these clients of the nature and extent of behavior disorders in the wider community is open to question. It appears that the phobic individuals that are clinic clientele may not be a representative sample of the fears and phobias in the broader population from which they are drawn (Agras, Chapin, & Oliveau, 1972). In a related fashion, Cameron and Spence (1976) have indicated that factors that cause hospitalization and result in the diagnosis of alcoholism are not necessarily directly linked to alcohol consumption. Rather, they seem to be a function of disintegration of the individual's social support.

Recommendations. The general model of laboratory-based "analogue" research is to be strongly encouraged in the literature. There are different types of "analogue" studies, so called, depending upon how minutely dissected treatment might be, whether processes assumed to operate in treatment are isolated from other components, and whether traditional questions of process or outcome are raised. The approach afforded by "analogue" research is unique and provides a model for scientific evaluation in general. Laboratory-based "analogue" research allows for careful specification of treatment. The specification of treatment is essential to ensure that the causal agent can be identified once experimentation is completed. And, of course, specification of treatment permits replication of research and treatment by others. Related to this is the precise assessment and evaluation of behavior change. Also, homogeneity of client selection allows for precise evaluation of the problems and behaviors for which treatment is suited.

Laboratory research permits careful control over treatment. Dimensions that would normally be allowed to vary can be standardized or controlled in such a way as to avoid confoundings that would ordinarily occur in the clinical situation. The careful control of laboratory-based research is evident in the types of questions that can be asked. The basis questions about a given treatment and parameters that contribute to its efficacy are difficult if not impossible to answer adequately in a clinical situation. Adequate control strategies to vary subtleties or even to provide major ablations of treatment rarely are available in clinical situations, where research questions are necessarily subordinate to analysis of the procedures.

Of course, advocating use of laboratory research does not ignore the extension of findings to clinical situations. The importance of testing the generality of findings in the clinical situation need not be reiterated. However, many studies simultaneously attempt to establish the internal validity and external validity of treatment in a single project. In psychotherapy research, this has often been disastrous. The recent study by Sloane et al. (1975) illustrates this problem well, because it represents an excellent example of studies strongly committed to questions of internal and external validity. The study sought to evaluate treatment with "real" clients, experienced therapists, and under ordinary clinical circumstances. This led to necessary sacrifices which, from the standpoint of internal validity, were quite serious. The effects of treatment could not be evaluated unambiguously because of confounds of treatment with therapists, amount of treatment during the follow-up period, and other factors. While the research is commendable in its attempt to evaluate treatment in a clinical situation, the predictable methodological sacrifices had their eventual toll.

Rarely can comparative psychotherapy research rigorously evaluate the internal validity of a variable without sacrificing external validity, and vice-versa (cf. Kazdin, in press f). This suggests that clear findings need to be established under controlled conditions, replicated, and then evaluated under conditions where less control is possible. *The empirical foundations for behavior therapy and psychotherapy may not derive from the situation in which the techniques are normally used.* Once techniques are evaluated in controlled situations and parameters that contribute to change are assessed, they can be extended and evaluated in less well controlled situations.

In addition to direct tests of treatment in the clinical situation, additional bridging work is needed to assess the effect of departures from the clinical situation. As noted earlier, it is *not* necessarily the case that analogue evaluation of treatment in a situation that departs from the clinic limits generality of the results. The dimensions that contribute to generality of laboratory-based findings need to be evaluated. Such research will help establish the relevance and limitations of controlled studies that depart from clinical practice.

Single-Case Experimental Methodology

Evaluation of therapy has been based almost exclusively upon group research and the examination of the average amount of changes among a large number of clients. However, given that treatment of the individual is the hallmark of clinical practice, the reliance upon group experiments and average client performance has been called into question. An alternative approach to developing and evaluating effective treatments is to investigate the individual case directly. Developing and evaluating treatments at the case level is not an endorsement of the case study as traditionally conceived. While the case study may provide insights and hypotheses about treatment, it characteristically has relied upon anecdotal information and impressionistic accounts of treatment. Indeed, the limitations of the case study in demonstrating a causal relationship between treatment and behavior change are widely known and discussed (Hersen & Barlow, 1976; Kazdin, in press f; Lazarus & Davison, 1971; Paul, 1969a). Yet studying the individual case does not necessarily mean sacrificing experimental evaluation of treatment. Recent clinical research has demonstrated empirical evaluation of the single case with a high degree of experimental rigor.

Several authors have advocated empirical investigation of the single case to evaluate treatment (Bergin & Strupp, 1970, 1972; Chassan, 1967; Kazdin, in press d; Shapiro, 1966). The advantage of focusing upon the individual client is that it emphasizes therapeutic change in the individual client rather than average change across groups of clients. Recently, single-case experimentation has been used widely in behavior modification, particularly for treatment techniques derived from operant conditioning. Single-case applications have been used to evaluate behavioral treatments for diverse therapeutic problems, including delusions and hallucinations, avoidance behaviors, alcohol consumption, overeating, hyperactivity, autistic behaviors, and so on (see Hersen & Barlow, 1976; Kazdin, in press a; Leitenberg, 1976b). Although behavioral techniques have been used in the above applications, single-case methodology is not necessarily restricted to a specific type of treatment or model of behavior change.

Characteristics of Single-Case Experimental Methodology. Single-case experimental designs refer to several different methods of investigating treatment with one individual. Although the designs can be used with more than one individual and even with very large groups, they are uniquely suited for evaluating the individual client in treatment and will be discussed in that perspective here. The designs can address the usual questions that have occupied treatment research. Thus, single-case experiments can look at the effects of a treatment "package," analyze components of an effective treatment, construct an effective treatment by combining different components, and compare different treatments—all with an individual subject. Different designs are available and more or less suited to a particular question about treatment and to the constraints of the clinical situation. The present discussion can only highlight general characteristics of these designs. (For a more detailed discussion of specific designs, several sources may be consulted: Hersen & Barlow, 1976; Hartmann & Hall, 1976; Kazdin, in press d; Kazdin & Geesey, 1977; Leitenberg, 1973; Ulman & Sulzer-Azaroff, 1975.)

The general characteristics of single-case experimental designs are the observation of overt behavior, continuous assessment of behavior, the use of data to make decisions about treatment, and specific criteria for assessing the reliability and importance of therapeutic change. The objective study of overt behavior has been addressed earlier. Briefly, in single-case designs, problematic behavior is observed directly either in the situation of interest or in simulated circumstances where the behavior is sampled under laboratory conditions. Objective measures of overt behavior refer to direct observations of what the client does or does not do. The objectivity of the measurement strategy refers to the fact that observers can independently record the behavior reliably. Such observations, while not free from bias, have been shown to be much less amenable to assessment artifacts than are more global evaluative measures (cf. Kazdin, 1973b; Kent, O'Leary, Diament, & Dietz, 1974; Paul & Redfield, 1976; Schnelle, 1974). The objectivity derives from focusing upon observable behaviors so that the observations are based upon publicly available information. This focus upon overt behavior can be distinguished from global therapist ratings based upon impressionistic information about personality changes.

A second characteristic is the continuous measurement of behavior. Performance of the client is examined prior to treatment, usually on a daily basis. Assessment of the problem behavior or therapeutic focus continues through treatment. The importance of continuous assessment cannot be overemphasized. In the individual case, such assessment provides immediate information about whether treatment is having the desired effects. One needs to know while treatment is in effect if it is accomplishing or approaching the original treatment goal.

The advantages of continuous assessment apply equally to single-case or group research. In either type of research, continuous assessment of behavior helps break down the process-outcome distinction that has characterized traditional treatment research (cf. Bergin & Strupp, 1970; Kiesler, 1966, 1971; Paul, 1969a). The process of change constitutes an interim outcome measure and preview of the effects of continued treatment. Continuous measurement of change also reveals the course of change, which may be important in its own right. The process of change is not always as "therapeutic" as the final outcome. Some techniques make clients worse before making them better. For example, select techniques temporarily increase anxiety and arousal prior to eliminating avoidance behavior (Marks, 1975) or increase deviant behavior prior to its elimination (Kazdin, 1975a). Continuous assessment allows study of the course of change as well as its final outcome.

Another advantage of continuous assessment of behavior is that it may allow the therapist to make data-based decisions about treatment. If data can be obtained throughout the course of treatment, they can provide feedback to the therapist about client progress. The data can be used as an empirical basis for making treatment decisions. Treatment can be continued, intensified, or completely altered on the basis of the data.

The final characteristic of the single-case experimental approach to be discussed refers to the criteria for evaluating treatment. Single-case methodology has embraced both experimental and therapeutic criteria for evaluating treatment (Kazdin, in press b; Risley, 1970).

The experimental criterion refers to demonstrating that reliable changes in behavior have resulted from treatment. This criterion is satisfied differently for each experimental design. In general terms, the reliability of the findings is determined by assessing whether treatment is associated with change, whether the pattern of change makes implausible other threats to the internal validity of the demonstration, and whether the effects obtained would have been predicted from the data without the intervention.

The therapeutic criterion refers to evaluating the clinical importance of behavior change. This criterion evaluates the magnitude of performance and the importance of this change for the individual's day-to-day functioning. The clinical importance of the change has been assessed by determining whether treatment alters how the client is viewed by others in his or her everyday environment and whether treatment brings the client's behavior to within acceptable or normative levels of performance (Kazdin, in press b; Wolf, 1976). Acceptable or normative levels of performance are defined empirically by observing individuals who are functioning adequately in the natural environment.

Limitations of Single-Case Experimental Methodology. Although the single-case methodology offers important advantages for clinical research, it is advocated here as a supplement to traditional treatment research. Any research methodology has its own limitations and weaknesses. The single-case methodology, for example, is not particularly strong in revealing the client characteristics that may interact with specific treatments. Examination of subject variables requires group research that has characterized traditional psychotherapy evaluation. Also, the results of single-case demonstration provide no hint of the generality of the findings to other cases. Quite possibly the effects of treatment demonstrated with the individual case will not generalize to other individuals.

One answer to this problem is the replication of single-case experiments (Hersen & Barlow, 1976). The *direct replication* strategy tests the efficacy of a single method administered by the same therapist in the same setting on a particular problem with more than one client. If the treatment is demonstrably effective with all clients, the results are easily interpretable. Problems in interpretation arise, however, when the results are not that clear-cut, i.e., mixed. Sidman (1960) states that failure to replicate results with all subjects does not detract from the success achieved in some subjects. However, there is a danger in attributing the successes to the manipulation of the reinforcement and dismissing replicative failures as due to the inadequate use of otherwise effective reinforcers. In these instances it is possible that the observed changes in behavior are due to the influence of unobserved or uncontrolled factors that happened to covary with the treatment manipulation in the successful cases.

Hersen and Barlow (1976) summarize the problem of mixed replicative results:

> If one success is followed by two or three failures, then neither the reliability of the procedure nor the generality of the finding across clients has been established, and it is probably time to find out why. If two or three successes are mixed in with one or two failures, then the reliability of the procedure

will be established to some extent, but the investigator must decide when to begin investigating reasons for lack of client generality (p. 335).

In trying to find out the reasons for the mixed results, the investigator faces the same difficulty encountered in group methodology. Like technique-oriented group studies (e.g., Gelder et al., 1973), direct replication strategies require homogeneous clients. As we have pointed out, this is rarely the case. If the treatment is effective with all clients despite this heterogeneity, interpretation of the data is easy. But if the results are mixed, the investigator cannot know whether the method is of limited utility or whether any one of a number of causes of interclient variability was responsible for the inconsistent treatment outcome.

Interpretation of single-case experimental designs is uncomplicated when the target behaviors are stable during pretreatment baseline assessment and when target behavior during treatment does not overlap with baseline performance. However, such clear-cut treatment effects are not always obtained. Most treatments are not that powerful when applied separately, because clinical disorders are maintained by several interacting variables and hence not every determinant is controlled. Excessive variability of client behavior across different phases of the study makes it difficult to determine significant behavior change. Even when experimental conditions are reasonably well controlled and within-subject variability across successive phases of a single-case experiment is relatively minimal, researchers may not always agree as to whether or not the treatment intervention produced a significant change in that behavior (Jones, Weinrott, & Vaught, 1975).

Excessive variability in treatment outcome is not uncommon in clinical practice. In the tradition of operant research, most single-subject designs have been used under highly controlled conditions (e.g., the classroom or a hospital ward). As they are extended to less controlled conditions in clients' natural environments, the variability in the data can be expected to increase, and less than dramatic changes in behavior can be anticipated. To disregard outcomes of this nature, as Kazdin (1976c) observes, might be to overlook reliable effects that could have theoretical and/or clinical significance. Partly in response to problems of this nature, recent attention has been focused on the use of statistical analysis of single-case designs (Kazdin, 1976c).

Even if the data from direct replications can be unambiguously interpreted, the problem of generalizing the results from the individual case to a more general population of clients remains. The solution proposed is *systematic replication* (Hersen & Barlow, 1976). Systematic replication is defined as the attempt to replicate the findings from direct replication studies, varying the therapists who administer the procedures, the type of clients, the nature of the target behavior, the setting in which treatment occurs, or any combination thereof. But there are difficulties with this strategy. When is a systematic replication series finished? Or put differently, when can the investigator decide that the generality of a finding has been scientifically established? This question, of course, is not peculiar to single-subject methodology and embraces the more general concern of external validity in experimentation (Campbell & Stanley, 1963).

Single-case experimental designs have been hailed as the means of merging the roles of the scientist and the practitioner. However, the ethical, practical, and methodological difficulties inherent in establishing cause-effect relationships using single-subject methodology may not be significantly fewer than in between-group outcome research. If it is therapy that the client is receiving, many of the critical requirements of single-case experimental designs are difficult if not impossible to meet. In essence, all such designs necessitate baseline observations, holding certain conditions constant at different times, and intervening selectively in a limited manner at any one point. This clearly conflicts with the priority in any service-delivery setting, which is to treat the client's problems in as effective and efficient a manner as possible. Clinically relevant change, produced at the least possible cost (in terms of time, effort, money, and emotional stress), is the goal of clinical practice.

The practical problems are often insuperable, for what practitioner can meet the requirements of single-case experimental designs outlined above, e.g., continuous observation of overt behavior? In fact, few behavioral *practitioners* have reported using this methodology. The overwhelming majority of studies have been conducted by individuals who are primarily applied clinical researchers (e.g., Hersen & Barlow, 1976). In short, single-case experimental studies, conducted properly according to strict methodological and ethical requirements, will almost always be done as research qua research (cf. Franks & Wilson, 1977).

Recommendations
The limitations of single-case experimental designs do not in any way impugn their unique contribution to treatment evaluation. Indeed, the methodology outlined here does not seem to have received enough attention in the therapy literature outside of select applications in behavior modification. Therapy research would benefit greatly from increased use of single-case experimental methodology. There are several advantages of the single-case experimental approach. First, the approach provides an empirical and scientific basis for investigating treatment with individual clients. Second, the methodology allows investigation of problems that are not likely to be studied in between-group research. For example, treatment of relatively rare problems by definition cannot be studied in large-scale group investigations. However, these can be carefully studied and treated in each individual case using single-case experimental designs

(e.g., Barlow et al., 1973). Third, the single-case methodology allows the building of effective interventions by adding components to enhance behavior change in a cumulative fashion. In this manner single-subject methodology dovetails with the constructive strategy of treatment development discussed earlier. Conversely, the methodology allows analysis of treatment packages by withdrawing components of treatment to determine essential treatment elements—the single-subject equivalent of the dismantling strategy. Finally, different treatments can be compared for the individual client.

New therapy techniques are often developed from clinical practice. After a clinician believes he or she has an effective procedure, the technique may be evaluated in a between-group design either against a no-treatment control group or alternative treatments. The leap from clinical practice to between group research is great and may account for some of the unexciting results of many outcome studies and the unexciting results of empirically evaluated therapy in general. Between the clinical application or case study and large-scale between-group evaluation might fall single-case experimental research. The single-case methodology allows the careful subjecting of treatment to a rigorous test on a small scale. The constant feedback provided by continuous assessment of behavior allows the investigator to improvise treatment changes rapidly as needed to augment the effects of treatment. Repeated single-case application of treatment and demonstration of therapeutic efficacy would in many instances seem to be an appropriate screening device before techniques are subjected to between-group investigation. It is only relevant to compare different treatments or to evaluate an overall treatment package once empirically validated clinical research has suggested promise and the parameters that contribute to therapeutic change have been at least partially worked out. The lack of specificity of many treatments evaluated in group research comes from insufficiently objective information about important dimensions of therapy in clinical practice. Single-case experimental designs would seem to provide an important intermediate step in the overall evaluation of therapy techniques.

Finally, single-case experimental methodology are not necessarily incompatible with group designs. As Bandura (1976) notes:

> One can examine how each individual is affected by experimental procedures during induction or successive phases, and also compare statistically whether the individual demonstrations of the phenomenon occur more frequently among subjects who receive the procedures than among those who do not. Adding baseline comparison groups and quantitative evaluation of data in no way detracts from inspection of individual variability (pp. 150–151).

✳ *CHAPTER 5*

SUMMARY AND CONCLUSIONS

In the foregoing chapters we have surveyed the applications and efficacy of behavioral methods, provided a detailed critique of clinical comparative outcome studies, analyzed the conceptual and methodological issues arising from such an evaluation, and advocated alternative research evaluation strategies.

APPLICATION AND OUTCOME

The overview of outcome evidence on behavior therapy, while not exhaustive, serves to highlight several important issues. First, "behavior therapy" embraces a wide range of diverse methods that have differential efficacy. Behavior therapy is no longer restricted to imaginal systematic desensitization, aversion conditioning, and the token economy, as was once the case. Continuing research and refinement has resulted in more sophisticated and complex treatment techniques that are also more effective. Systematic desensitization, for example, once was the most effective behavioral treatment of anxiety-related disorders. However, subsequent research resulted in the development of in vivo methods, such as participant modeling, that are demonstrably superior to systematic desensitization. This research development has increased the efficacy of behavioral treatment of phobias and, even more important, of obsessive-compulsive disorders (Rachman & Hodgson, in press).

Second, these various behavioral methods have been applied to an extremely broad range of heterogenous disorders in psychiatric, medical, and educational domains. To characterize behavior therapy as applicable mainly to "monosymptomatic phobias" and "simple habits" is to perpetuate an unfortunate caricature. Behavior therapy, as Sloane et al.

(1975) emphasized, "is clearly a *generally* useful treatment" (p. 224). This general applicability of behavior therapy is all the more significant when it is remembered that traditional psychodynamic psychotherapy has always been largely limited to certain neurotic and personality disorders such as those studied by Sloane et al. (1975) and reviewed by Luborsky et al. (1975). (See also Candy et al., 1972; Garfield, 1975; Kernberg, 1973.) In much of the existing literature on the evaluation and outcome of therapy, behavior therapy is critically scrutinized for its overall relevance and applicability to clinical treatment. The implication is that existing psychotherapeutic methods are, in fact, relevant and broadly applicable. This misleading impression is convincingly contradicted by any realistic survey of the psychological treatment of the diverse disorders that drive people to community clinics, hospitals, and other treatment agencies.

Third, no single, overall assessment of "behavior therapy" is possible in view of this multiplicity of methods and diversity of relevant target disorders. A problem-by-problem analysis is necessary. Indeed, as techniques are refined and outcome research becomes more sophisticated, increasingly analytic and more specific statements will undoubtedly be made. "Behavior therapy," as some sort of monolithic entity, cannot be judged effective or not. The same applies to something called "psychotherapy." Only specific methods can be evaluated.

COMPARATIVE OUTCOME EVIDENCE

Behavioral researchers have had a tendency to overlook the evidence of comparative clinical outcome studies. In answer to the claim that few comparisons have been made between behavioral methods and alternative nonbehavioral methods (e.g., Stolz, Wienckowski, & Brown, 1975), Chapter 2 summarizes the findings of over seventy such studies. Unfortunately, the majority of these investigations are methodologically flawed and of little value in determining the relative efficacy of alternative methods. It is clear that comparisons of ill-defined treatment approaches applied to heterogeneous disorders using unsatisfactory global measures obfuscate rather than enlighten. As Durac (1977) has concluded, our thirst for this sort of study should be quenched; no further research of this kind is needed. Investigators who persist in this kind of outcome research will ultimately end up seeking many if not all of the solutions described by Durac.

IMPORTANT CONCEPTUAL AND METHODOLOGICAL ISSUES

Comparative outcome research has been plagued by the use of inadequate measurement of the effects of therapy. Global and subjective ratings deriving from highly questionable personality trait models have retarded advancement of knowledge about behavior change (Mischel, 1977). Objective behavioral measures must be increasingly included in *multiple* measures of the individual's psychological functioning. In addition, these multiple objective and subjective measures must reflect the specificity of behavior change. Related to the question of measurement of therapeutic outcome is the need for broader criteria in evaluating treatment effects. The importance or magnitude, durability, efficiency, cost-effectiveness, and client (consumer) satisfaction are all criteria of therapy evaluation that deserve future attention (see Kazdin & Wilson, in press).

Specificity of assessment, treatment, and evaluation is critical in the development of effective treatment methods. Accordingly, box-score counts of comparative studies in which different therapies are judged as better or worse than each other simply compound the difficulty in interpreting individual studies that are of limited value in the first place.

The implication in some of the behavioral literature is often that behavior therapy is the only form of psychological treatment that has been the focus of outcome research. Yet there is a relatively sizable body of outcome literature on some of the traditional psychotherapies (Bergin, 1971; Meltzoff & Kornreich, 1970). The critical problems rest more with the *quality* than the quantity of such research. The unfortunate reliance on traditional assessment methods and the telling lack of specificity and operationally defined treatments—methodological flaws that have marred some behavioral research—present major interpretive difficulties. Aside from a fundamental weakness in the measurement of therapeutic outcome, the research strategies used to evaluate the traditional psychotherapies have been too limited. Most of the research strategies described in Chapter 4 have rarely been applied to psychotherapy. Traditional research in this area has been characterized by a narrow dependence on inadequate, global comparative outcome studies and essentially process research on therapist-client variations. Powerful analytic methods such as the dismantling, constructive, and single-case experimental designs have found no favor among traditional psychotherapy researchers. Bergin and Strupp's (1970) call for new directions in research on the psychotherapies has yet to be heeded. Finally, in addition to the failure to develop suitable scientific evaluation strategies, traditional research on psychotherapy, as we have emphasized in the preceding chapters, has focused on a circumscribed range of behavior disorders, notably neurotic disturbances and personality disorders.

RECOMMENDED RESEARCH STRATEGIES

The recommendation that the sort of global comparative studies criticized above should be abandoned as an outcome research strategy is not new (e.g., Bergin & Strupp, 1970; Kiesler, 1966; Paul, 1967). For example, Bergin and Strupp (1970) advocated "the individual experimental case study and the experimental analogue approaches" as the type of research strategy that would elucidate the mechanisms of behavior change. However, they provided little in the way of specific illustration or information about how these approaches would be used.

In Chapter 4 the relative merits of laboratory-based treatment research and single-case experimental designs were discussed. Specifically, the unique roles these respective strategies can play in furthering the field were identified, as well as the way in which they might complement alternative methodologies. These alternative or complementary research strategies include group comparative outcome studies, suggestions for the proper conduct of which were outlined. Recognition of the shortcomings of traditional comparative research need not necessarily lead to a rejection of group experimental designs employing inferential statistics as Bergin and Strupp (1970) suggest. On the contrary, traditional statistical procedures appear to be invaluable in much of the outcome research that has been completed and should continue. Both group and single-case experimental designs have been demonstrably useful in evaluating behavior change methods.

BEHAVIOR THERAPY: A SCIENTIFIC REVOLUTION?

Recently Shapiro (1976) posed the question whether the behavior therapies represented a therapeutic breakthrough or the latest fad. His answer was that behavior therapy may be the latest fad. "Therapeutic claims for behavior therapy," he asserted, "are excessive and have outdistanced the controlled clinical evidence" (p. 158). While it would be difficult to dispute the statement that therapeutic claims have occasionally been hyperbolic, there is scant justification for judging behavior therapy a fad. The evidence for behavioral methods is often uneven and inconsistent. In some instances techniques are supported by only partially controlled research (e.g., the treatment of compulsive rituals); in other areas, mostly uncontrolled reports are available (e.g., drug addiction). But with some problems, such as anxiety and phobic disorders, enuresis, and others, the efficacy of behavioral treatment has been demonstrated unequivocally in well-controlled outcome studies.

The rigorous evaluation of behavioral methods according to the most stringent methodological standards is to be encouraged; in principle, the scientific basis of behavior therapy demands it. The same should be true for *any* psychologically-based treatment approach. It is not surprising that the evidence in favor of behavior therapy has been scrutinized frequently.

Behavior therapists themselves have been in the forefront of this ongoing evaluative effort in keeping with their own assumptions and scientific commitment. The precise specification and ready replicability of behavior techniques, the development of a variety of innovative objective and subjective outcome measures, and the delineation of specific treatment targets have aided greatly in this process. The same *cannot* be said of most nonbehavioral psychotherapies, particularly psychodynamic approaches. Predictably, rigorous outcome research on these psychotherapies has been relatively rare.

As a result of this lopsided experimental investigation of the psychotherapies, it is easy to adopt a double standard in evaluating relative efficacy of different approaches. Consider, for example, Shapiro's (1976) cautionary conclusion: "I would consider it premature to replace other more traditional (especially data-oriented) therapeutic techniques with behavior therapy until evidence of its effectiveness, in the form of controlled comparative studies, becomes available" (p. 158). Granted that better evidence of the efficacy of behavior therapy would be desirable, consider to what it is being compared. Where is the evidence— from any source—that supports traditional techniques? To what "data-oriented" techniques is Shapiro (1976) referring? As far as the psychotherapies are concerned, we know of *none* that approximate behavioral methods in terms of either the quantity or quality of supporting evidence.[a] (See also Franks and Wilson's [1977] analysis of Shapiro's [1976] paper.)

The analysis of the comparative outcome literature in Chapter 2 clearly shows that behavioral methods are as least as effective, and often more effective, than alternative approaches, particularly the verbal psychotherapies. Furthermore, even if it is only conceded that behavior therapy is not inferior to any other form of psychotherapy, it is still the treatment of choice in most instances by virtue of its greater efficiency (see Kazdin & Wilson, in press), not to mention its eminently greater applicability across a wide range of psychiatric, medical, and educational problems. The belief that traditional psychotherapy enjoys data-based empirical support against which behavior therapy has somehow to prove itself has assumed the status of a de facto truth. There might be reasons for preferring traditional psychotherapy over behavior therapy, but the notion that empirical considerations provide a justification is pure fiction.

In the faddish psychotherapies, as Sloane et al. (1975) point out, methods are never systematically studied. Instead, the authority figure(s) is too busy developing new techniques to conduct any empirical tests. In

---

[a] Bergin and Strupp (1970) engage in similarly wistful speculation in calling for "a *return* to empirical data" (emphasis added).

contrast to this highly subjective endeavor, behavioral procedures have been progressively tested, modified, and refined. For example, procedural and parametric modifications of techniques such as systematic desensitization, flooding, and participant modeling have all been systematically researched in well-controlled outcome research. As a result, more effective forms of these methods are being developed. Of equal importance is the fact that some techniques have been clearly shown to be ineffective in the treatment of specific problems (electrical aversion conditioning with alcoholism; covert sensitization with obesity; and systematic desensitization with chronic compulsive disorders). Yet each of these techniques has proved effective with other problems, (e.g., electrical aversion conditioning and covert sensitization with sexual deviance, and systematic desensitization with phobic disorders). This steady accumulation of progressively refined and discriminating evidence on different methods applied to specific disorders is the nature of scientific research. It is to be contrasted with the dramatic rise and then fall of therapeutic fads in which techniques are never systematically developed but invented and abandoned in an arbitrary fashion.

In all, the attempt to develop an empirically-based technology of behavior change has gone rather well in the less than two decades of serious research in behavior therapy. There have been setbacks and there have been false starts along the path to scientific respectability, which, as Skinner (1975) noted, is "steep and thorny." Yet progress has been made. In contrast to earlier conceptual cul-de-sacs, highly productive outcome questions are now being asked. And the appropriate research methodologies to provide the answers are being developed. Of course, the question "What treatment is effective for which individual with what problem?" is never "answered" in any ultimate sense (cf. Peterson, 1976). The great advantage of behavior therapy is that committed as it is to a scientific approach—its current imperfections notwithstanding—it will develop, progressively and indefinitely, continually being modified in response to applied research findings.

Therapy based upon psychological knowledge may still be an art in some respects. No longer, however, need it be the "art of applying a science which does not yet exist" (Meehl, 1960). The two decades since the publication of Wolpe's (1958) *Psychotherapy by Reciprocal Inhibition* have witnessed unprecedented research activity and the beginning of a science of therapeutic behavior change. More effective methods and more compelling empirical support are needed. But effective procedures have been developed, and their increasingly widespread rise promises to make what might be the first really significant contribution of psychological theory and practice to enhanced personal and social functioning.

REFERENCES

Abel, G.G., & Blanchard, E.B. The measurement and generation of sexual arousal in male sexual deviates. In M. Hersen, R.M. Eisler, & P.M. Miller (Eds.), *Progress in behavior modification,* Vol. 2. New York: Academic Press, 1976.

Agras, W.S., Chapin, H.N., & Oliveau, D.C. The natural history of phobia. *Archives of General Psychiatry,* 1972, **26,** 315–317.

Alevizos, P.N., & Callahan, E.J. Assessment of psychotic behavior. In A.R. Ciminero, K.S. Calhoun, & H.E. Adams (Eds.), *Handbook of behavioral assessment.* New York: John Wiley & Sons, 1977.

Alexander, A.B. Chronic asthma. In R.B. Williams & W.D. Gentry (Eds.), *Behavioral approaches to medical treatment.* Cambridge, Massachusetts: Ballinger, 1977.

Alexander, J.F., & Parsons, B.V. Short-term behavioral intervention with delinquent families: Impact on family process and recidivism. *Journal of Abnormal Psychology,* 1973, **81,** 219–225.

American Psychiatric Association, A Task Force Report, *Behavior Therapy in Psychiatry.* Washington, D.C.: American Psychiatric Association, 1973.

American Psychological Association, Committee on Ethical Standards in Psychological Research. *Ethical principles in the conduct of research with human participants.* Washington, D.C.: American Psychological Association, 1973.

Anderson, L.T., & Alpert, M. Operant analysis of hallucination frequency in a hospitalized schizophrenic. *Journal of Behavior Therapy and Experimental Psychiatry,* 1974, **5,** 13–18.

Anthony, W.A., Buell, G.J., Sharatt, S., & Althoff, M.D. Efficacy of psychiatric rehabilitation. *Psychological Bulletin,* 1972, **78,** 447–456.

Argyle, M., Bryant, B., & Trower, P. Social skills training and psychotherapy: A comparative study. *Psychological Medicine,* 1974, **4,** 435–443.

Armor, D.J., Polich, J.M., & Stambul, H.B. *Alcoholism and treatment.* Santa Monica, California: The Rand Corporation, 1976.

Ashby, W.A., & Wilson, G.T. Behavior therapy for obesity: Booster sessions and long-term maintenance of weight loss. *Behaviour Research and Therapy,* in press.

Atthowe, J.M., Jr. Behavior innovation and persistence. *American Psychologist,* 1973, **23,** 34–41.

Atthowe, J.M., Jr., & Krasner, L. Preliminary report on the application of contingent reinforcement procedures (token economy) on a "chronic" psychiatric ward. *Journal of Abnormal Psychology,* 1968. **73,** 37–43

Austin, N.K., Liberman, R.P., King, L.W., & DeRisi, W.J. A comparative evaluation of two day hospitals: Goal attainment scaling of behavior therapy vs. milieu therapy. *Journal of Nervous and Mental Disease,* 1976, **163,** 253–262.

Ayllon, T., & Haughton, E. Modification of symptomatic verbal behavior of mental patients. *Behaviour Research and Therapy,* 1964, **2,** 87–97.

Ayllon, T., & Kelly, K. Effects of reinforcement on standardized test performance. *Journal of Applied Behavior Analysis,* 1972, **5,** 477–484.

Ayllon, T., Layman, D., & Kandel, H.J. A behavioral-educational alternative to drug control of hyperactive children. *Journal of Applied Behavior Analysis,* 1975, **8,** 137–146.

Azrin, N.H. Improvements in the community-reinforcement approach to alcoholism. *Behaviour Research and Therapy,* 1976, **14,** 339–348.

Azrin, N.H. A strategy for applied research: Learning based but outcome oriented. *American Psychologist,* 1977, **32,** 140–149.

Azrin, N.H., & Armstrong, P.M. The "mini-meal"—a method for teaching eating skills to the profoundly retarded. *Mental Retardation,* 1973, **11,** 9–13.

Azrin, H.H., Flores, T., & Kaplan, S.J. Job-finding club: A group-assisted program for obtaining employment. *Behaviour Research and Therapy,* 1975, **13,** 17–27.

Azrin, N.H., & Foxx, R.M. *Toilet training in less than a day.* New York: Simon & Schuster, 1974.

Azrin, N.H., Kaplan, S.J., & Foxx, R.M. Autism reversal: Eliminating stereotyped self-stimulation of retarded individuals. *American Journal of Mental Deficiency,* 1973, **78,** 241–248.

Azrin, N.H., Naster, B.J., & Jones, R. Reciprocity counseling: A rapid learning-based procedure for marital counseling. *Behaviour Research and Therapy,* 1973, **11,** 365–382.

Azrin, N.H., & Powell, J. Behavioral engineering: The reduction of smoking behavior by a conditioning apparatus and procedure. *Journal of Applied Behavior Analysis,* 1968, **1,** 193–200.

Azrin, N.H., & Wesolowski, M.D. The use of positive practice to eliminate persistent floor sprawling by profoundly retarded persons. *Behavior Therapy,* 1975, **6,** 627–631.

Baekeland, F., Lundwall, L., & Kissin, B. Methods for the treatment of chronic alcoholism: A critical appraisal. In R.J. Gibbins, Y. Israel, H. Kalant, R.E. Popham, W. Schmidt, & R.G. Smart (Eds.), *Research advances in alcohol and drug problems,* Vol. 2. Toronto: Addiction Research Foundation, 1975.

Baer, D.M., Wolf, M.M., & Risley, T.R. Some current dimensions of applied behavior analysis. *Journal of Applied Behavior Analysis,* 1968, **1**, 91–97.

Balson, P.M. Encopresis: A case with symptom substitution. *Behavior Therapy,* 1973, **4**, 134–136.

Bancroft, J.H. A comparative study of aversion and desensitization in the treatment of homosexuality. In L.E. Burns & J.H. Worsely (Eds.), *Behaviour therapy in the 1970's.* Bristol, England: Wright, 1970.

Bancroft, J.H. *Deviant sexual behaviour.* Oxford: Oxford University Press, 1974.

Bandura, A. *Principles of behavior modification.* New York: Holt, Rinehart & Winston, 1969.

Bandura, A. Modeling theory. In W.S. Sahakian (Ed.), *Psychology of learning: Systems, models, and theories.* Chicago: Markham, 1970.

Bandura, A. Psychotherapy based upon modeling principles. In A.E. Bergin, & S.L. Garfield (Eds.), *Handbook of psychotherapy and behavior change: An empirical analysis.* New York: Wiley, 1971.

Bandura, A. Self-reinforcement: Theoretical and methodological considerations. *Behaviorism,* 1976, **4**, 135–155.

Bandura, A. On paradigms and recycled ideologies. Unpublished manuscript, Stanford University, 1977. (a)

Bandura, A. Self-efficacy: Toward a unifying theory of behavioral change. *Psychological Review,* 1977, **84**, 191–215. (b)

Bandura, A. *Social learning theory.* Englewood Cliffs, New Jersey: Prentice-Hall, 1977. (c)

Bandura, A., & Adams, N.E. Analysis of self-efficacy theory of behavior change. Unpublished manuscript, Stanford University, 1977.

Bandura, A., Adams, N.E., & Beyer, J. Cognitive processes mediating behavioral change. *Journal of Personality and Social Psychology,* 1977, **35**, 125–139.

Bandura, A., Blanchard, E.G., & Ritter, B. Relative efficacy of desensitization and modeling approaches for inducing behavioral, affective, and attitudinal changes. *Journal of Personality and Social Psychology,* 1969, **13**, 173–199.

Bandura, A., Jeffery, R.W., & Gajdos, E. Generalizing change through participant modeling with self-directed mastery. *Behaviour Research and Therapy.* 1975, **13**, 141–152.

Bandura, A., Jeffery, R.W., & Wright, C.L. Efficacy of participant modeling as a function of response induction aids. *Journal of Abnormal Psychology,* 1974, **83**, 56–64.

Barlow, D.H. Assessment of sexual behavior. In A.R. Ciminero, K.S. Calhoun, & H.E. Adams (Eds.), *Handbook of behavioral assessment.* New York: John Wiley & Sons, 1977.

Barlow, D.H., Agras, W.S., Leitenberg, H., & Wincze, J.F. An experimental analysis of the effectiveness of "shaping" in reducing maladaptive avoidance behavior: An analogue study. *Behaviour Research and Therapy,* 1970, **8**, 165–173.

Barlow, D.H., Reynolds, J., & Agras, W.S. Gender identity change in a transsexual. *Archives of General Psychiatry,* 1973, **29**, 569–576.

Barrett, C.L. Systematic desensitization versus implosive therapy. *Journal of Abnormal Psychology,* 1969, **74**, 587–592.

Bassett, J.E., Blanchard, E.B., & Koshland, E. Applied behavior analysis in a penal setting: Targeting "free world" behaviors. *Behavior Therapy,* 1975, **6,** 639–648.

Bateman, S. Application of Premack's generalization on reinforcement to modify occupational behavior in two severely retarded individuals. *American Journal of Mental Deficiency,* 1975, **79,** 604–610.

Beck, A.T. Cognitive therapy: Nature and relation to behavior therapy. *Behavior Therapy,* 1970, **1,** 184–200.

Beck, A.T. *Cognitive therapy and the emotional disorders.* New York: International Universities Press, 1976.

Bennett, P.S., & Maley, R.S. Modification of interactive behaviors in chronic mental patients. *Journal of Applied Behavior Analysis,* 1973, **6,** 609–620.

Bergin, A.E. The evaluation of therapeutic outcomes. In A.E. Bergin & S.L. Garfield (Eds.), *Handbook of psychotherapy and behavior change: An empirical analysis.* New York: Wiley, 1971.

Bergin, A.E., & Strupp, H.H. New directions in psychotherapy research. *Journal of Abnormal Psychology,* 1970, **76,** 13–26.

Bergin, A.E., & Strupp, H.H. (Eds.), *Changing frontiers in the science of psychotherapy.* Chicago: Aldine-Atherton, 1972.

Bergin, A.E., & Suinn, R.M. Individual psychotherapy and behavior therapy. In M.R. Rosenzweig & L.W. Porter (Eds.), *Annual review of psychology,* 1975, **26,** 509–556.

Berkowitz, B.P., & Graziano, A.M. Training parents as behavior therapists: A review. *Behaviour Research and Therapy,* 1972, **10,** 297–317.

Bernstein, D. Modification of smoking behavior: An evaluative review. *Psychological Bulletin,* 1969, **71,** 418–440.

Bernstein, D.A. Behavioral fear assessment: Anxiety or artifact? In H. Adams & I.P. Unikel (Eds.), *Issues and trends in behavior therapy.* Springfield, Illinois: Charles C Thomas, 1973.

Bernstein, D.A., & McAlister, A. The modification of smoking behavior: Progress and problems. *Addictive Behaviors,* 1976, **1,** 89–102.

Bernstein, D.A. & Nietzel, M.T. Procedural variation in behavioral avoidance tests. *Journal of Consulting and Clinical Psychology,* 1973, **41,** 165–174.

Bernstein, D.A., & Nietzel, M.T. Behavioral avoidance tests: The effects of demand characteristics and repeated measures of two types of subjects. *Behavior Therapy,* 1974, **5,** 183–192.

Bernstein, D.A., & Paul, G.L. Some comments on therapy analogue research with small animal "phobias." *Journal of Behavior Therapy and Experimental Psychiatry,* 1971, **2,** 225–237.

Best, D.L., Smith, S.C., Graves, D.J., & Williams, J.E. The modification of racial bias in preschool children. *Journal of Experimental Child Psychology,* 1975, **20,** 193–205.

Beutler, L.E. Cognitive vs. "other" psychotherapies: When is a cognitive therapy? Unpublished manuscript, Baylor College of Medicine, 1977.

Bieber, I., Dain, H.J., Dince, P.R., Drellich, M.G., Grand, H.G., Gundlach, R.H., Kremer, M.W., Rifkin, A.H., Wilbur, C.B., & Bieber, T.B. *Homosexuality: A psychoanalytic study.* New York: Basic Books, 1962.

Bijou, S.W., Peterson, R.F., & Ault, M.H. A method to integrate descriptive and experimental field studies at the level of data and empirical concepts. *Journal of Applied Behavior Analysis,* 1968, **1**, 175–191.

Birk, L., Huddleston, W., Miller, E., & Cohler, B. Avoidance conditioning for homosexuality. *Archives of General Psychiatry,* 1971, **25**, 314–323.

Birk, L. (Ed.), *Biofeedback: Behavioral medicine.* New York: Grune & Stratton, 1973.

Birky, H.J., Chambliss, J.E., & Wasden, R. A comparison of residents discharged from a token economy and two traditional psychiatric programs. *Behavior Therapy,* 1971, **2**, 46–51.

Birnbrauer, J.S. Mental retardation. In H. Leitenberg (Ed.), *Handbook of behavior modification and behavior therapy.* Englewood Cliffs, New Jersey: Prentice-Hall, 1976.

Blackwell, B. Treatment adherence. *British Journal of Psychiatry,* 1976, **129**, 513–531.

Blanchard, E.B. Behavioral medicine: A perspective. In R.B. Williams, Jr., & W.D. Gentry (Eds.), *Behavioral approaches to medical treatment.* Cambridge, Massachusetts: Ballinger, 1977.

Blanchard, E.B., & Epstein, L.H. The clinical usefulness of biofeedback. In M. Hersen, R.M. Eisler, & P.M. Miller (Eds.), *Progress in behavior modification,* Vol. 4. New York: Academic Press, 1977.

Blanchard, E.B., & Young, L.D. Self-control of cardiac functioning: A promise as yet unfulfilled. *Psychological Bulletin,* 1973, **79**, 145–163.

Blanchard, E.B., Young, L.D., & Haynes, M.R. A simple feedback system for the treatment of elevated blood pressure. *Behavior Therapy,* 1975, **6**, 241–245.

Borkovec, T.D. The role of expectancy and physiological feedback in fear research: A review with special reference to subject characteristics. *Behavior Therapy,* 1973, **4**, 491–505.

Borkovec, T.D. Investigations of fear and sleep disturbance: Methodological, measurement, and theoretical issues in therapy outcome research. In G.E. Schwartz & D. Shapiro (Eds.), *Consciousness and self-regulation: Advances in research.* New York: Plenum, 1977.

Borkovec, T.D., & Nau, S.D. Credibility of analogue therapy rationales. *Journal of Behavior Therapy and Experimental Psychiatry,* 1972, **3**, 257–260.

Borkovec, T.D., & O'Brien, G.T. Methodological and target behavior issues in analogue therapy outcome research. In M. Hersen, R.M. Eisler, & P.M. Miller (Eds.), *Progress in behavior modification,* Vol. 3. New York: Academic Press, 1976.

Borkovec, T.D., Stone, N.M., O'Brien, G.T., & Kaloupek, D.G. Evaluation of a clinically relevant target behavior for analogue outcome research. *Behavior Therapy,* 1974, **5**, 504–514.

Borkovec, T.D., Wall, R.L., & Stone, N.M. False physiological feedback and the maintenance of speech anxiety. *Journal of Abnormal Psychology,* 1974, **83**, 164–168.

Boudewyns, P.A. Implosive therapy and desensitization therapy with inpatients: A five-year follow-up. *Journal of Abnormal Psychology,* 1975, **84**, 159–160.

Boudewyns, P.A., & Wilson, A.E. Implosive therapy and desensitization therapy using free association in the treatment of inpatients. *Journal of Abnormal Psychology,* 1972, **79,** 259–268.

Brady, J.P. The place of behavior therapy in medical student and psychiatric resident training. *Journal of Nervous and Mental Disease,* 1973, **157,** 21–26.

Brady, J.P. Concluding remarks. In R.B. Williams & W.D. Gentry (Eds.), *Behavioral approaches to medical treatment.* Cambridge, Massachusetts: Ballinger, 1977.

Braukmann, C.J., & Fixsen, D.L. Behavior modification with delinquents. In M. Hersen, R.M. Eisler, & P.M. Miller (Eds.), *Progress in behavior modification,* Vol. 1. New York: Academic Press, 1975.

Breyer, N.L., & Allen, G.J. Effects of implementing a token economy on teacher attending behavior. *Journal of Applied Behavior Analysis,* 1975, **8,** 373–380.

Brigham, T.A., & Catania, A.C. (Eds.), *Handbook of applied behavior research: Social and instructional processes.* New York: Irvington Press/Halstead Press, in press.

Brigham, T.A., Graubard, P.S., & Stans, A. Analysis of the effects of sequential reinforcement contingencies on aspects of composition. *Journal of Applied Behavior Analysis,* 1972, **5,** 421–429.

Briscoe, R.V., Hoffman, D.B., & Bailey, J.S. Behavioral community psychology: Training a community board to problem solve. *Journal of Applied Behavior Analysis,* 1975, **8,** 157–168.

Brownell, K.D., & Barlow, D.H. The behavioral treatment of sexual deviation. In E. Foa & A. Goldstein (Eds.), *Handbook of behavioral interventions.* New York: Wiley, in press.

Bruch, H. Perils of behavior modification in the treatment of anorexia nervosa. *Journal of the American Medical Association,* 1974, **230,** 1419–1422.

Bucher, B., & Fabricatore, J. Use of patient-administered shock to suppress hallucinations. *Behavior Therapy,* 1970, **1,** 382–385.

Bucher, B., & Lovaas, O.I. Use of aversive stimulation in behavior modification. In M.R. Jones (Eds.), *Miami symposium on the prediction of behavior: Aversive stimulation.* Coral Gables, Florida: University of Miami Press, 1968.

Burchard, J.D., & Harig, P.T. Behavior modification and juvenile delinquency. In H. Leitenberg (Ed.), *Handbook of behavior modification and behavior therapy.* Englewood Cliffs, New Jersey: Prentice-Hall, 1976.

Bushell, D., Jr. The design of classroom contingencies. In F.S. Keller & E. Ribes-Inesta (Eds.), *Behavior modification: Applications to education.* New York: Academic Press, 1974.

Byassee, J.E. Essential hypertension. In R.B. Williams, Jr. & W.D. Gentry (Eds.), *Behavioral approaches to medical treatment.* Cambridge, Massachusetts: Ballinger, 1977.

Cahoon, D.D. Symptom substitution and the behavior therapies: A reappraisal. *Psychological Bulletin,* 1968, **69,** 149–156.

Callner, D.A. Behavioral treatment approaches to drug abuse: A critical review of the research. *Psychological Bulletin,* 1975, **82,** 143–164.

Cameron, D., & Spence, M. Recruitment of problem drinkers. *British Journal of Psychiatry,* 1976, **129,** 544–546.

Campbell, D.T., & Fiske, D. Convergent and discriminant validation by the multitrait-multimethod matrix. *Psychological Bulletin,* 1959, **56,** 81–105.

Campbell, D.T., & Stanley, J.C. Experimental and quasi-experimental designs for research and teaching. In N.L. Gage (Ed.), *Handbook of research on teaching.* Chicago: Rand McNally, 1963.

Candy, J., Balfour, F.H.G., Cawley, R.H., Hildebrand, H.P., Malan, D.H., Marks, I.M., & Wilson, J. A feasibility study for a controlled trial of formal psychotherapy. *Psychological Medicine,* 1972, **2,** 345–362.

Carlson, C.G., Hersen, M., & Eisler, R.M. Token economy programs in the treatment of hospitalized adult psychiatric patients. *Journal of Nervous and Mental Disease,* 1972, **155,** 192–204.

Cash, W.M., & Evans, I.M. Training pre-school children to modify their retarded siblings' behavior. *Journal of Behavior Therapy and Experimental Psychiatry,* 1975, **6,** 13–16.

Chadwick, B.A., & Day, R.C. Systematic reinforcement: Academic performance of underachieving students. *Journal of Applied Behavior Analysis,* 1971, **4,** 311–319.

Chassan, J.B. *Research design in clinical psychology and psychiatry.* New York: Appleton-Century-Crofts, 1967.

Chesser, E.S. Behaviour therapy: Recent trends and current practice. *British Journal of Psychiatry,* 1976, **129,** 289–307.

Christensen, D.E. Effects of combining methylphenidate and a classroom token system in modifying hyperactive behavior. *American Journal of Mental Deficiency,* 1975, **80,** 266–276.

Christensen, D.E., & Sprague, R.L. Reduction of hyperactive behavior by conditioning procedures alone and combined with methylphenidate (Ritalin). *Behaviour Research and Therapy,* 1973, **11,** 331–334.

Ciminero, A.R., Calhoun, K.S., & Adams, H.E. (Eds.), *Handbook of behavioral assessment.* New York: Wiley, 1977.

Clark, R.N., Burgess, R.L., & Hendee, J.C. The development of anti-litter behavior in a forest campground. *Journal of Applied Behavior Analysis,* 1972, **5,** 1–5.

Cochrane, R., & Sobol, M.P. Myth and methodology in behaviour therapy research. In M.P. Feldman & A. Broadhurst (Eds.), *Theoretical and empirical bases of the behaviour therapies.* London: Wiley, 1976.

Cohen, H.L., & Filipczak, J. *A new learning environment.* San Francisco: Jossey-Bass, 1971.

Cohen, M., Liebson, I.A., Faillace, L.A., & Allen, R.P. Moderate drinking by chronic alcoholics. *Journal of Nervous and Mental Disease,* 1971, **153,** 434–444.

Cooper, A., Furst, J.B., & Bridger, W.H. A brief commentary on the usefulness of studying fears of snakes. *Journal of Abnormal Psychology,* 1969, **74,** 413–414.

Cooper, J.E. A study of behaviour therapy in 30 psychiatric patients. *Lancet,* 1963, **i,** 411.

Cooper, J.E., Gelder, M.G., & Marks, I.M. Results of behaviour therapy in 77 psychiatric patients. *British Medical Journal,* 1965, **1,** 1222–1225.

Covi, L., Lipman, R., Derogatis, L., Smith, J., & Pattison, I. Drugs and group psychotherapy in neurotic depression. *American Journal of Psychiatry,* 1974, **131,** 191–198.

Craighead, W.E., Kazdin, A.E., & Mahoney, M.J. (Eds.), *Behavior modification: Principles, issues, and applications.* Boston: Houghton Mifflin, 1976.

Crighton, J., & Jehu, P. Treatment of examination anxiety by systematic desensitization or psychotherapy in groups. *Behaviour Research and Therapy,* 1969, **7,** 245–248.

Crowe, M.J., Marks, I.M., Agras, W.S., & Leitenberg, H. Time-limited desensitization, implosion and shaping for phobic patients: A crossover study. *Behavior Research and Therapy,* 1972, **10,** 319–328.

Datel, W.E., & Legters, L.J. The psychology of the army recruit. Paper presented at the American Medical Association. Chicago, June 1970.

Davidson, W.S., II, & Seidman, E. Studies of behavior modification and juvenile delinquency: A review, methodological critique, and social perspective. *Psychological Bulletin,* 1974, **81,** 998–1011.

Davison, G.C. Behavior modification techniques in institutional settings. In C.M. Franks (Ed.), *Behavior therapy: Appraisal and status.* New York: McGraw-Hill, 1969.

Davison, G.C., & Neale, J. *Abnormal psychology: An experimental approach,* 2nd Edition. New York: Wiley, in press.

Davison, G.C., & Wilson, G.T. Attitudes of behavior therapists toward homosexuality. *Behavior Therapy,* 1973, **4,** 686–696. (a)

Davison, G.C., & Wilson, G.T. Processes of fear reduction in systematic desensitization: Cognitive and social reinforcement factors in humans. *Behavior Therapy,* 1973, **4,** 1–21. (b)

DeLeon, G., & Mandell, W. A comparison of conditioning and psychotherapy in the treatment of functional enuresis. *Journal of Clinical Psychology,* 1966, **22,** 326–330.

DeLeon, G., & Sacks, S. Conditioning functional enuresis: A four-year follow-up. *Journal of Consulting and Clinical Psychology,* 1972, **39,** 299–300.

DeVries, D.L. Effects of environmental change and of participation on the behavior of mental patients. *Journal of Consulting and Clinical Psychology,* 1968, **32,** 532–536.

Dickinson, D.J. But what happens when you take that reinforcement away? *Psychology in the Schools,* 1974, **11,** 158–160.

DiLoreto, A. *Comparative psychotherapy.* Chicago: Aldine-Atherton, 1971.

DiScipio, W.J., & Trudeau, P.F. Symptom changes and self-esteem as correlates of positive conditioning of grooming in hospitalized psychotics. *Journal of Abnormal Psychology,* 1972. **80,** 244–248.

Doleys, D.M. Behavioral treatments for nocturnal enuresis in children: A review of the recent literature. *Psychological Bulletin,* 1977, **84,** 30–54.

Doty, D.W. Role playing and incentives in the modification of the social interaction of chronic psychiatric patients. *Journal of Consulting and Clinical Psychology,* 1975, **43,** 676–682.

Drabman, R.S. Behavior modification in the classroom. In W.E. Craighead, A.E. Kazdin, & M.J. Mahoney (Eds.), *Behavior modification: Principles, issues, and applications.* Boston: Houghton Mifflin, 1976.

Drabman, R., & Spitalnik, R. Training a retarded child as a behavioral teaching assistant. *Journal of Behavior Therapy and Experimental Psychiatry,* 1973, **4,** 269–272.

Durac, J. *A matter of taste.* London: Andre Deutsch, 1975.

Eastman, C. Behavioral formulations of depression. *Psychological Review,* 1976, **83,** 277–291.

Edlund, C.V. The effect on the test behavior of children, as reflected in the IQ scores, when reinforced after each correct response. *Journal of Applied Behavior Analysis,* 1972, **5,** 317–319.

Eitzen, D.S. The effects of behavior modification on the attitudes of delinquents. *Behaviour Research and Therapy,* 1975, **13,** 295–299.

Ellis, A. *Reason and emotion in psychotherapy.* New York: Lyle Stuart Press, 1962.

Ellis, A. *The essence of rational psychotherapy: A comprehensive approach to treatment.* New York: Institute for Rational Living, 1970.

Emmelkamp, P.M.G., & Wessels, H. Flooding in imagination vs. flooding *in vivo:* A comparison with agoraphobics. *Behaviour Research and Therapy,* 1975, **13,** 7–15.

Emrick, C.D. A review of psychologically oriented treatment of alcoholism: I. The use and interrelationships of outcome criteria and drinking behavior following treatment. *Quarterly Journal of Studies on Alcohol,* 1974, **35,** 523–549.

Emrick, C.D. A review of psychologically oriented treatment of alcoholism: II. The relative effectiveness of different treatment approaches and the effectiveness of treatment versus no treatment. *Journal of Studies on Alcohol,* 1975, **36,** 88–108.

Engel, B.T., & Bleecker, E.R. Application of operant conditioning techniques to the control of cardiac arrhythmias. In P.A. Obrist, A.H. Black, J. Brener, & L.V. DiCara (Eds.), *Cardiovascular psychophysiology.* Chicago: Aldine, 1974.

Everett, P.B., Hayward, S.C., & Meyers, A.W. The effects of a token reinforcement procedure on bus ridership. *Journal of Applied Behavior Analysis,* 1974, **7,** 1–9.

Eysenck, H.J. The effects of psychotherapy: An evaluation. *Journal of Consulting Psychology,* 1952, **16,** 319–324.

Eysenck, H.J. (Ed.), *Behaviour therapy and the neuroses.* Oxford: Pergamon Press, 1960.

Eysenck, H.J. Behaviour therapy, extinction, and relapse in neurosis. *British Journal of Psychiatry,* 1963, **109,** 12–18.

Eysenck, H.J. (Ed.), *Experiments in behaviour therapy.* Oxford: Pergamon Press, 1964.

Eysenck, H.J. Behavior therapy and its critics. *Journal of Behavior Therapy and Experimental Psychiatry,* 1970, **1,** 5–15.

Eysenck, H.J. A note on backward conditioning. *Behaviour Research and Therapy,* 1975, **13,** 201–202.

Eysenck, H.J. Behaviour therapy—dogma or applied science? In P. Feldman & A. Broadhurst (Eds.) *The experimental bases of behaviour therapy.* New York: Wiley, 1976. (a)

Eysenck, H.J. The learning theory model of neurosis—a new approach. *Behaviour Research and Therapy*, 1976, **14**, 251–268. (b)

Fairweather, G.W. *Social psychology in treating mental illness: An experimental approach.* New York: John Wiley & Sons, 1964.

Fairweather, G.W., Sanders, D.H., Cressler, D.L., & Maynard, H. *Community life for the mentally ill.* Chicago: Aldine, 1969.

Feldman, M.P., & MacCulloch, M.J. *Homosexual behavior: Therapy and assessment.* New York: Pergamon Press, 1971.

Fixsen, D.L., Phillips, E.L., Phillips, E.A., & Wolf, M.M. The teaching-family model of group home treatment. In W.E. Craighead, A.E. Kazdin, & M.J. Mahoney (Eds.), *Behavior modification: Principles, issues and applications.* Boston: Houghton Mifflin, 1976.

Fo, W.S.O., & O'Donnell, C.R. The buddy system: Relationship and contingency conditions in a community intervention program for youth with nonprofessionals as behavior change agents. *Journal of Consulting and Clinical Psychology*, 1974, **42**, 163–169.

Fo, W.S.O., & O'Donnell, C.R. The buddy system: Effect of community intervention on delinquent offenses. *Behavior Therapy*, 1975, **6**, 522–524.

Fordyce, W.E., Fowler, R.S., Lehmann, J.F., DeLateur, B.J., Sand, P.L., & Trieschmann, R.B. Operant conditioning in the treatment of chronic pain. *Archives of Physical Medicine and Rehabilitation*, 1973, **54**, 399–408.

Forehand, R., & Baumeister, A.A. Deceleration of aberrant behavior among retarded individuals. In M. Hersen, R.M. Eisler, & P.M. Miller (Eds.), *Progress in behavior modification*, Vol. 3. New York: Academic Press, 1976.

Foxx, R.M. The use of overcorrection to eliminate the public disrobing (stripping) of retarded women. *Behaviour Research and Therapy*, 1976, **14**, 53–61.

Foxx, R.M., & Azrin, N.H. *Toilet training the retarded: A rapid program for day and night time independent toileting.* Champaign, Illinois: Research Press, 1973.

Foxx, R.M., & Hake, D.F. Gasoline conservation: A procedure for measuring and reducing the driving of college students. *Journal of Applied Behavior Analysis*, 1977, **10**, 61–74.

Foxx, R.M., & Martin, E.D. Treatment of scavenging behavior (coprophagy and pica) by overcorrection. *Behaviour Research and Therapy*, 1975, **13**, 153–162.

Frank, J.D. *Persuasion and healing.* Baltimore: Johns Hopkins University Press, 1961.

Frankel, F., & Simmons, J.Q. Self-injurious behavior in schizophrenic and retarded children. *American Journal of Mental Deficiency*, 1976, **80**, 512–522.

Franks, C.M., & Wilson, G.T. *Annual review of behavior therapy: Theory and practice*, Vol. I. New York: Brunner/Mazel, 1973.

Franks, C.M., & Wilson, G.T. *Annual review of behavior therapy: Theory and practice*, Vol. II. New York: Brunner/Mazel, 1974.

Franks, C.M., & Wilson, G.T. *Annual review of behavior therapy: Theory and practice*, Vol. III. New York: Brunner/Mazel, 1975.

Franks, C.M., & Wilson, G.T. *Annual review of behavior therapy: Theory and practice*, Vol. IV. New York: Brunner/Mazel, 1976.

Franks, C.M., & Wilson, G.T. *Annual review of behavior therapy: Theory and practice,* Vol. V. New York: Brunner/Mazel, 1977.

Frisch, S.A., & Schumaker, J.B. Training generalized receptive propositions in retarded children. *Journal of Applied Behavior Analysis,* 1974, **7,** 611–621.

Galassi, M.D., & Galassi, J.P. The effects of role playing variations on the assessment of assertive behavior. *Behavior Therapy,* 1976, **7,** 343–347.

Gambrill, E.D. The use of behavioral methods in short-term detention settings. Paper presented at meeting of the Association for Advancement of Behavior Therapy, Chicago, November 1974.

Gardner, R.A. On box score methodology as illustrated by three reviews of overtraining reversal effects. *Psychological Bulletin,* 1966, **66,** 416–418.

Gardner, W.I. *Behavior modification in mental retardation.* Chicago: Aldine, 1971.

Garfield, S.L. Research on client variables in psychotherapy. In A.E. Bergin & S.L. Garfield (Eds.), *Handbook of psychotherapy and behavior change: An empirical analysis.* New York: John Wiley & Sons, 1971.

Garfield, S.L. Review of psychotherapy versus behavior therapy, by Sloane, R.B., et al. (1975). *Contemporary Psychology,* 1976, **21,** 328–329.

Gelder, M.G., Bancroft, J.H.J., Gath, D., Johnston, D.W., Mathews, A.M. & Shaw, P.M. Specific and non-specific factors in behavior therapy. *British Journal of Psychiatry,* 1973, **123,** 445–462.

Gelder, M.G., & Marks, I.M. Severe agoraphobia: A controlled prospective trial of behaviour therapy. *British Journal of Psychiatry,* 1966, **112,** 309–319.

Gelder, M.G., Marks, I.M., Wolff, H.H., & Clarke, M. Desensitization and psychotherapy in the treatment of phobic states: A controlled inquiry. *British Journal of Psychiatry,* 1967, **113,** 53–73.

Geller, E.S., Farris, J.C., & Post, D.S. Prompting a consumer behavior for pollution control. *Journal of Applied Behavior Analysis,* 1973, **6,** 367–376.

Geller, E.S., Wylie, R.G., & Farris, J.C. An attempt at applying prompting and reinforcement toward pollution control. *Proceedings of the 79th Annual Convention of the American Psychological Association,* 1971, **6,** 701–702.

Gentry, W.D. Noncompliance to medical regimen. In R.B. Williams, Jr. & W.D. Gentry (Eds.), *Behavioral approaches to medical treatment.* Cambridge, Massachusetts: Ballinger, 1977.

Gillan, P., & Rachman, S. An experimental investigation of desensitization in phobic patients. *British Journal of Psychiatry,* 1974, **124,** 392–401.

Gittelman-Klein, R., Klein, D.F., Abikoff, H., Katz, S., Gloisten, A.C., & Kates, W. Relative efficacy of methylphenidate and behavior modification in hyperkinetic children: An interim report. *Journal of Abnormal Psychology,* 1976, **4,** 361–379.

Gladstone, B.W., & Sherman, J.A. Developing generalized behavior-modification skills in high-school students working with retarded children. *Journal of Applied Behavior Analysis,* 1975, **8,** 169–180.

Glasgow, R.E., & Rosen, G.M. Behavioral bibliotherapy: A review of self-help behavior therapy manuals. *Psychological Bulletin,* in press.

Glass, G.V. Primary, secondary, and meta-analysis of research. *Educational Researcher,* 1976, **5,** 3–8.

Goldfried, M.R. Systematic desensitization as training in self-control. *Journal of Consulting and Clinical Psychology,* 1971, **37,** 228–234.

Goldfried, M.R., & Davison, G.C. *Clinical behavior therapy.* New York: Holt, Rinehart & Winston, 1976.

Goldfried, M.R., & Goldfried, A.P. Cognitive change methods. In F.H. Kanfer, & A.P. Goldstein (Eds.), *Helping people change: A textbook of methods.* New York: Pergamon Press, 1975.

Goldiamond, I., & Dyrud, J.E. Some applications and implications of behavior analysis for psychotherapy. In J.M. Shlien (Ed.), *Research in psychotherapy,* Vol. 3. Washington, D.C.: American Psychological Association, 1968.

Goldstein, A.P. *Psychotherapeutic attraction.* New York: Pergamon Press, 1971.

Goldstein, A.P., & Dean, S.J. (Eds.), *The investigation of psychotherapy: Commentaries and readings.* New York: John Wiley & Sons, 1966.

Goodwin, D.W., Guze, S.B., & Robins, E. Follow-up studies in obsessional neurosis. *Archives of General Psychiatry,* 1969, **20,** 182–187.

Götestam, K.G., Melin, L., & Öst, L. Behavioral techniques in the treatment of drug abuse: an evaluation review. *Addictive Behaviors,* 1976, **1,** 205–226.

Greenberg, D.J., Scott, S.B., Pisa, A., & Friesen, D.D. Beyond the token economy: A comparison of two contingency programs. *Journal of Consulting and Clinical Psychology,* 1975, **43,** 498–503.

Gripp, R.F., & Magaro, P.A. A token economy program evaluation with untreated control ward comparisons. *Behaviour Research and Therapy,* 1971, **9,** 137–149.

Gripp, R.F., & Magaro, P.A. The token economy program in the psychiatric hospital: A review and analysis. *Behaviour Research and Therapy,* 1974, **12,** 205–228.

Gurin, G., Veroff, J., & Feld, S. *Americans view their mental health.* New York: Basic Books, 1960.

Gurman, A.S., & Kniskern, D.P. Research on marital and family therapy: Progress, perspective and prospect. In S.L. Garfield & A.E. Bergin (Eds.), *Handbook of psychotherapy in behavior change: An empirical analysis,* 2nd Edition. New York: John Wiley & Sons, in press.

Hagen, R.L. Group therapy versus bibliotherapy in weight reduction. *Behavior Therapy,* 1974, **5,** 222–234.

Hall, R.V., Lund, D., & Jackson, D. Effects of teacher attention on study behavior. *Journal of Applied Behavior Analysis,* 1968, **1,** 1–12.

Hall, S.M., Hall, R.G., DeBoer, G., & O'Kulitch, P. Self and external management compared with psychotherapy in the control of obesity. *Behaviour Research and Therapy,* 1977, **15,** 89–96.

Hall, S.M., Hall, R.G., Hanson, R.W., & Borden, B.L. Permanence of two self-managed treatments of overweight. *Journal of Consulting and Clinical Psychology,* 1974, **42,** 781–786.

Hallam, R., Rachman, S., & Falkowski, W. Subjective, attitudinal, and physiological effects of electrical aversion therapy. *Behaviour Research and Therapy,* 1972, **10,** 1–13.

Hampe, E., Noble, H., Miller, L.C., & Barrett, C.L. Phobic children one and two years posttreatment. *Journal of Abnormal Psychology,* 1973, **82,** 446–453.

Hand, I., Lamontagne, Y., & Marks, I.M. Group exposure (flooding) in vivo for agoraphobics. *British Journal of Psychiatry,* 1974, **124,** 588–602.

Hanson, R.W., Borden, B.L., Hall, S.M., & Hall, R.G. Use of programmed instruction in teaching self-management skills to overweight adults. *Behavior Therapy,* 1976, **7,** 366–373.

Harmatz, M.G., & Lapuc, P. Behavior modification of overeating in a psychiatric population. *Journal of Consulting and Clinical Psychology,* 1968, **32,** 583–587.

Hartlage, L.C. Subprofessional therapists' use of reinforcement versus traditional psychotherapeutic techniques with schizophrenics. *Journal of Consulting and Clinical Psychology,* 1970, **34,** 181–183.

Hartman, W., & Fithian, M.A. *Treatment of sexual dysfunction.* Long Beach, California: Center for Marital and Sexual Studies, 1972.

Hartmann, D.P., & Atkinson, C. Having your cake and eating it too: A note on some apparent contradictions between therapeutic achievements and design requirements in N = 1 studies. *Behavior Therapy,* 1973, **4,** 589–591.

Hartmann, D.P., & Hall, R.V. The changing criterion design. *Journal of Applied Behavior Analysis,* 1976, **9,** 527–532.

Hauserman, N., Walen, S.R., & Behling, M. Reinforced racial integration in the first grade: A study in generalization. *Journal of Applied Behavior Analysis,* 1973, **6,** 193–200.

Heap, R.F., Boblitt, W.E., Moore, C.H., & Hord, J.E. Behavior-milieu therapy with chronic neuropsychiatric patients. *Journal of Abnormal Psychology,* 1970, **76,** 349–354.

Hedberg, A.G., & Campbell, L., III. A comparison of four behavioral treatments of alcoholism. *Journal of Behavior Therapy and Experimental Psychiatry,* 1974, **5,** 251–256.

Heller, K. Laboratory interview research as an analogue to treatment. In A.E. Bergin & S.L. Garfield (Eds.), *Handbook of psychotherapy and behavior change: An empirical analysis.* New York: John Wiley & Sons, 1971.

Heller, K., & Marlatt, G.A. Verbal conditioning, behavior therapy, and behavior change: Some problems of extrapolation. In C.M. Franks (Ed.), *Behavior therapy: Appraisal and status.* New York: McGraw-Hill, 1969.

Henderson, J.D., & Scoles, P.E. A community-based behavioral operant environment for psychotic men. *Behavior Therapy,* 1970, **1,** 245–251.

Hersen, M., & Barlow, D.H. *Single-case experimental designs: Strategies for studying behavior change.* New York: Pergamon Press, 1976.

Hersen, M., & Bellack, A.S. *Behavioral assessment: A practical handbook.* Oxford: Pergamon Press, 1976. (a)

Hersen, M., & Bellack, A.S. Social skills training for chronic psychiatric patients: Rationale, research findings, and future directions. *Comprehensive Psychiatry,* 1976, **17,** 559–580. (b)

Hersen, M., & Bellack, A.S. (Eds.), *Behavior therapy in the psychiatric setting.* Baltimore: Williams & Wilkins, in press.

Higgs, W.J. Effects of gross environmental change upon behavior of schizophrenics: A cautionary note. *Journal of Abnormal Psychology,* 1970, **76,** 421–422.

Hinde, R.A., & Stevenson-Hinde, J. (Eds.), *Constraints on learning: Limitations and predispositions.* London: Academic Press, 1973.

Hollingsworth, R., & Foreyt, J.P. Community adjustment of released token economy patients. *Journal of Behavior Therapy and Experimental Psychiatry,* 1975, **6**, 271–274.

Hoon, P.W., & Lindsley, O.R. A comparison of behavior and traditional therapy publication activity. *American Psychologist,* 1974, **29**, 694–697.

Horan, J.J., Hackett, G., Nicholas, W.C., Linberg, S.E., Stone, C.I., & Lukaski, H.C. Rapid smoking: A cautionary note. *Journal of Consulting and Clinical Psychology,* 1977, **45**, 341–343.

Horan, J.J., Linberg, S.E., & Hackett, G. Nicotine poisoning and rapid smoking. *Journal of Consulting and Clinical Psychology,* 1977, **45**, 344–347.

Hunt, G.H., & Azrin, N.H. The community-reinforcement approach to alcoholism. *Behaviour Research and Therapy,* 1973, **11**, 91–104.

Hunt, H.F. Behavior therapy for adults. In S. Arieti (Ed.), *American Handbook of psychiatry,* Vol. 5, 2nd Edition. New York: Basic Books, 1975.

Hunt, N.A., Barnett, L.W., & Branch, L.G. Relapse rates in addiction programs. *Journal of Clinical Psychology,* 1971, **27**, 455–456.

Hunt, W.A., & Matarazzo, J.D. Three years later: Recent developments in the experimental modification of smoking. *Journal of Abnormal Psychology,* 1973, **81**, 107–114.

Isaacs, W., Thomas, J., & Goldiamond, I. Application of operant conditioning to reinstate verbal behavior in psychotics. *Journal of Speech and Hearing Disorders,* 1960, **25**, 8–12.

Jackson, D.A., & Wallace, R.F. The modification and generalization of voice loudness in a fifteen-year-old retarded girl. *Journal of Applied Behavior Analysis,* 1974, **7**, 461–471.

Jacob, R.G., Kraemer, H.C., & Agras, W.S. Relaxation therapy in the treatment of hypertension: A review. *Archives of General Psychiatry,* 1977, in press.

Jacobson, N.S. Problem-solving and contingency contracting in the treatment of marital discord. *Journal of Consulting and Clinical Psychology,* 1977, **45**, 92–100.

Jacobson, N.S., & Baucom, D.H. Design and assessment of nonspecific control groups in behavior modification research. *Behavior Therapy,* 1977, **8**, 709–719.

Jacobson, N.S., & Martin, B. Behavioral marriage therapy: Current status. *Psychological Bulletin,* 1976, **83**, 540–556.

Jeffery, R.W., Wing, R.R., & Stunkard, A.J. Behavioral treatment of obesity: The state of the art. *Behavior Therapy,* in press.

Jeffrey, D.B. Treatment evaluation issues in research on addictive behaviors. *Addictive Behaviors,* 1975, **1**, 23–36.

Jehu, D., Morgan, R., Turner, R., & Jones, A. A controlled trial of the treatment of nocturnal enuresis in residential homes for children. *Behaviour Research and Therapy,* 1977, **15**, 1–16.

Jenkins, W.O., Witherspoon, A.D., DeVine, M.D., deValera, E.K., Muller, J.B., Barton, M.C., & McKee, J.M. The post-prison analysis of criminal behavior and longitudinal follow-up evaluation of institutional treatment. A report on the Experimental Manpower Laboratory for Corrections, February 1974.

Jesness, C.F. Comparative effectiveness of behavior modification and transactional analysis programs for delinquents. *Journal of Consulting and Clinical Psychology,* 1975, **43,** 758–779.

Jesness, C.F., & DeRisi, W.J. Some variations in techniques of contingency management in a school for delinquents. In J.S. Stumphauzer (Ed.), *Behavior therapy with delinquents.* Springfield, Illinois: Charles C Thomas, 1973.

Jones, R.R., Weinrott, M., & Vaught, R.S. Visual vs. statistical inference in operant research. Paper presented at the Annual Convention of the American Psychological Association, Chicago, September 1975.

Jones, R.T., & Kazdin, A.E. Programming response maintenance after withdrawing token reinforcement. *Behavior Therapy,* 1975, **6,** 153–164.

Jordan, H.A., & Levitz, L.S. Behavior modification in a self-help group. *Journal of the American Dietary Association,* 1973, **62,** 27–29.

Kale, R.J., Kaye, J.H., Whelan, P.A., & Hopkins, B.L. The effects of reinforcement on the modification, maintenance, and generalization of social responses of mental patients. *Journal of Applied Behavior Analysis,* 1968, **1,** 307–314.

Kanfer, F.H. Verbal conditioning: A review of its current status. In T.R. Dixon & D.L. Horton (Eds.), *Verbal behavior and general behavior theory.* Englewood Cliffs, New Jersey: Prentice-Hall, 1968.

Kaplan, H. *The new sex therapy.* New York: Brunner/Mazel, 1974.

Karacki, L., & Levinson, R.B. A token economy in a correctional institution for youthful offenders. *Howard Journal of Penology and Crime Prevention,* 1970, **13,** 20–30.

Karen, R.L., Eisner, M., & Endres, R.W. Behavior modification in a sheltered workshop for severely retarded students. *American Journal of Mental Deficiency,* 1974, **79,** 338–347.

Katz, R.C., & Zlutnick, S. *Behavioral therapy and health care: Principles and applications.* New York: Pergamon Press, 1974.

Kaufman, K.F., & O'Leary, K.D. Reward, cost and self-evaluation procedures for disruptive adolescents in a psychiatric hospital. *Journal of Applied Behavior Analysis,* 1972, **5,** 293–309.

Kazdin, A.E. The effect of response cost in suppressing behavior in a prepsychotic retardate. *Journal of Behavior Therapy and Experimental Psychiatry,* 1971, **2,** 137–140.

Kazdin, A.E. Covert modeling and the reduction of avoidance behavior. *Journal of Abnormal Psychology,* 1973, **81,** 87–95. (a)

Kazdin, A.E. Role of instructions and reinforcement in behavior changes in token reinforcement programs. *Journal of Educational Psychology,* 1973, **64,** 63–71. (b)

Kazdin, A.E. Covert modeling, model similarity, and reduction of avoidance behavior. *Behavior Therapy,* 1974, **5,** 325–340. (a)

Kazdin, A.E. The effect of model identity and fear-relevant similarity on covert modeling. *Behavior Therapy,* 1974, **5,** 624–635. (b)

Kazdin, A.E. *Behavior modification in applied settings.* Homewood, Illinois: Dorsey, 1975. (a)

Kazdin, A.E. Covert modeling, imagery assessment, and assertive behavior. *Journal of Consulting and Clinical Psychology,* 1975, **43,** 716–724. (b)

Kazdin, A.E. The impact of applied behavior analysis on diverse areas of research. *Journal of Applied Behavior Analysis,* 1975, **8,** 213–229. (c)

Kazdin, A.E. Recent advances in token economy research. In M. Hersen, R.M. Eisler, & P.M. Miller (Eds.), *Progress in behavior modification,* Vol. 1. New York: Academic Press, 1975. (d)

Kazdin, A.E. Implementing token programs: The use of staff and patients for maximizing change. In R.L. Patterson (Ed.), *Maintaining effective token economies.* Springfield, Illinois: Charles C Thomas, 1976. (a)

Kazdin, A.E. The modification of "schizophrenic" behavior. In P.A. Magaro (Ed.), *The construction of madness: Emerging conceptions and interventions into the psychotic process.* New York: Pergamon Press, 1976. (b)

Kazdin, A.E. Statistical analyses for single-case experimental designs. In M. Hersen & D.H. Barlow, *Single-case experimental designs: Strategies for studying behavior change.* New York: Pergamon, 1976. (c)

Kazdin, A.E. Artifact, bias, and complexity of assessment: The ABC's of reliability. *Journal of Applied Behavior Analysis,* 1977, **10,** 141–150. (a)

Kazdin, A.E. Extensions of reinforcement techniques to socially and environmentally relevant behaviors. In M. Hersen, R.M. Eisler, & P.M. Miller (Eds.), *Progress in behavior modification,* Vol. 4. New York: Academic Press, 1977. (b)

Kazdin, A.E. Research issues in covert conditioning. *Cognitive Therapy and Research,* 1977, **1,** 45–58. (c)

Kazdin, A.E. *The token economy: A review and evaluation.* New York: Plenum Press, 1977. (d)

Kazdin, A.E. Evaluating the generality of findings in analogue therapy research. Unpublished manuscript, Center for Advanced Study in the Behavioral Sciences, Stanford, California, 1977. (e)

Kazdin, A.E. The application of operant techniques in treatment, rehabilitation, and education. In S.L. Garfield & A.E. Bergin (Eds.), *Handbook of psychotherapy and behavior change,* 2nd edition. New York: John Wiley & Sons, in press. (a)

Kazdin, A.E. Assessing the clinical or applied significance of behavior change through social validation. *Behavior Modification,* in press. (b)

Kazdin, A.E. Behavior modification in mental retardation. In J.T. Neisworth & R.M. Smith (Eds.), *Retardation: Issues, assessment, and intervention.* New York: McGraw-Hill, in press. (c)

Kazdin, A.E. Methodology of applied behavior analysis. In T. Brigham & A.C. Catania (Eds.), *Handbook of applied behavior research: Social and instructional processes.* New York: Irvington Press/Halstead Press, in press. (d)

Kazdin, A.E. *History of behavior modification: Experimental foundations of contemporary research.* Baltimore: University Park Press, in press. (e)

Kazdin, A.E. *Research design in clinical psychology.* Philadelphia: J.B. Lippincott, in preparation. (f)

Kazdin, A.E., & Bootzin, R.R. The token economy: An evaluative review. *Journal of Applied Behavior Analysis,* 1972, **5,** 343–372.

Kazdin, A.E., & Erickson, L.M. Developing responsiveness to instructions in severely and profoundly retarded residents. *Journal of Behavior Therapy and Experimental Psychiatry,* 1975, **6,** 17–21.

Kazdin, A.E., & Geesey, S. Simultaneous-treatment design comparisons of the effects of earning reinforcers for one's peers versus for oneself. *Behavior Therapy,* 1977, **8,** 689–693.

Kazdin, A.E., & Polster, R. Intermittent token reinforcement and response maintenance in extinction. *Behavior Therapy,* 1973, **4,** 386–391.

Kazdin, A.E., & Wilcoxon, L.A. Systematic desensitization and nonspecific treatment effects: A methodological evaluation. *Psychological Bulletin,* 1976, **83,** 729–758.

Kazdin, A.E., & Wilson, G.T. Criteria for evaluating psychotherapy. *Archives of General Psychiatry,* in press.

Keeley, S.M., Shemberg, K.M., & Carbonell, J. Operant clinical intervention: Behavior management or beyond? Where are the data? *Behavior Therapy,* 1976, **7,** 292–305.

Keilitz, I., Tucker, D.J., & Horner, R.D. Increasing mentally retarded adolescents' verbalizations about current events. *Journal of Applied Behavior Analysis,* 1973, **6,** 621–630.

Keller, F.S. "Good-bye teacher. . . ." *Journal of Applied Behavior Analysis,* 1968, **1,** 79–89.

Kelley, K.M., & Henderson, J.D. A community-based operant learning environment II: Systems and procedures. In R.D. Rubin, H. Fensterheim, A.A. Lazarus, & C.M. Franks (Eds.), *Advances in behavior therapy.* New York: Academic Press, 1971.

Kennedy, R.E. Behavior modification in prisons. In W.E. Craighead, A.E. Kazdin, & M.J. Mahoney (Eds.), *Behavior modification: Principles, issues, and applications.* Boston: Houghton Mifflin, 1976.

Kent, R.N., & Foster, S.L. Direct observational procedures: Methodological issues in naturalistic settings. In A.R. Ciminero, K.S. Calhoun, & H.E. Adams (Eds.), *Handbook of behavioral assessment.* New York: John Wiley & Sons, 1977.

Kent, R.N., & O'Leary, K.D. A controlled evaluation of behavior modification with conduct problem children. *Journal of Consulting and Clinical Psychology,* 1976, **44,** 586–596.

Kent, R., & O'Leary, K.D. Treatment of conduct problem children: B.A. and/or Ph.D. therapists. *Behavior Therapy,* 1977, **8,** 653–658.

Kent, R.N., O'Leary, K.D., Diament, C., & Dietz, A. Expectation biases in observational evaluation of therapeutic change. *Journal of Consulting and Clinical Psychology,* 1974, **42,** 774–780.

Kernberg, O.F. "Summary and conclusions of 'Psychotherapy and psychoanalysis, final report of the Menninger Foundation's psychotherapy research project.' " *International Journal of Psychiatry,* 1973, **11,** 62–77.

Kiesler, D.J. Some myths of psychotherapy research and the search for a paradigm. *Psychological Bulletin,* 1966, **65,** 110–136.

Kiesler, D.J. Experimental designs in psychotherapy research. In A.E. Bergin &

S.L. Garfield (Eds.), *Handbook of psychotherapy and behavior change: An empirical analysis*. New York: John Wiley & Sons, 1971.

Kimble, G. *Conditioning and learning*. New York: Appleton-Century-Crofts, 1961.

King, G.F., Armitage, S.G., & Tilton, J.R. A therapeutic approach to schizophrenics of extreme pathology: An operant-interpersonal method. *Journal of Abnormal and Social Psychology*, 1960, **61**, 276–286.

Kingsley, R.G., & Wilson, G.T. Behavior therapy for obesity: A comparative investigation of long-term efficacy. *Journal of Consulting and Clinical Psychology*, 1977, **45**, 288–298.

Klein, N.C., Alexander, J.F. & Parsons, B.V. Impact of family systems intervention on recidivism and sibling delinquency: A model of primary prevention and program evaluation. *Journal of Consulting and Clinical Psychology*, 1977, **45**, 469–474.

Klein, R.D., Hapkiewicz, W.G., & Roden, A.H. (Eds.), *Behavior modification in educational settings*. Springfield, Illinois: Charles C Thomas, 1973.

Knapczyk, D.R., & Yoppi, J.O. Development of cooperative and competitive play responses in developmentally disabled children. *American Journal of Mental Deficiency*, 1975, **80**, 245–255.

Knapp, T.J., & Peterson, L.W. Behavior management in medical and nursing practice. In W.E. Craighead, A.E. Kazdin, & M.J. Mahoney (Eds.), *Behavior modification: Principles, issues, and applications*. Boston: Houghton Mifflin, 1976.

Koch, S. Psychology and emerging conceptions of knowledge as unitary. In T. Wann (Ed.), *Behaviorism and phenomenology*. Chicago: University of Chicago Press, 1964.

Kockott, G., Dittmar, F., & Nusselt, L. Systematic desensitization of erectile impotence: A controlled study. *Archives of Sexual Behavior*, 1975, **4**, 493–500.

Kohlenberg, R., & Phillips, T. Reinforcement and rate of litter depositing. *Journal of Applied Behavior Analysis*, 1973, **6**, 391–396.

Kohlenberg, R., Phillips, T., & Proctor, W. A behavioral analysis of peaking in residential electrical energy consumers. *Journal of Applied Behavior Analysis*, 1976, **9**, 13–18.

Kringlen, E. Obsessional neurotics: A long-term follow-up. *British Journal of Psychiatry*, 1965, **111**, 709–722.

Lana, R.E. Pretest sensitization. In R. Rosenthal & R.L. Rosnow (Eds.), *Artifact in behavioral research*. New York: Academic Press, 1969.

Lang, P.J. The mechanics of desensitization and the laboratory study of fear. In C.M. Franks (Ed.), *Behavior therapy: Appraisal and status*. New York: McGraw-Hill, 1969.

Lang, P.J., Lazovik, A.D., & Reynolds, D.J. Desensitization, suggestibility, and pseudotherapy. *Journal of Abnormal Psychology*, 1965, **70**, 395–402.

Lang, P.J., Melamed, B.G., & Hart, J. A psychophysiological analysis of fear modification using an automated desensitization procedure. *Journal of Abnormal Psychology*, 1970, **76**, 220–234.

Lavigueur, H. The use of siblings as an adjunct to the behavioral treatment of children in the home with parents as therapists. *Behavior Therapy,* 1976, **7,** 602–613.

Lazarus, A.A. New methods of psychotherapy: A case study. *South African Medical Journal,* 1958, **32,** 660–664.

Lazarus, A.A. Group therapy of phobic disorders by systematic desensitization. *Journal of Abnormal and Social Psychology,* 1961, **63,** 504–510.

Lazarus, A.A. The results of behaviour therapy in 126 cases of severe neurosis. *Behaviour Research and Therapy,* 1963, **1,** 65–78.

Lazarus, A.A. Broad spectrum behavior therapy and the treatment of agoraphobia. *Behaviour Research and Therapy,* 1966, **4,** 95–97.

Lazarus, A.A. Broad-spectrum behavior therapy. *Newsletter of the Association for Advancement of Behavior Therapy,* 1969, **4,** 5–6.

Lazarus, A.A. *Behavior therapy and beyond.* New York: McGraw-Hill, 1971.

Lazarus, A.A. *Multimodal behavior therapy.* New York: Springer, 1976.

Lazarus, A.A. Has behavior therapy outlived its usefulness? *American Psychologist,* 1977, **32,** 550–554.

Lazarus, A.A., & Davison, G.C. Clinical innovation in research and practice. In A.E. Bergin & S.L. Garfield (Eds.), *Handbook of psychotherapy and behavior change: An empirical analysis.* New York: John Wiley & Sons, 1971.

Leitenberg, H. The use of single case methodology in psychotherapy research. *Journal of Abnormal Psychology,* 1973, **82,** 87–101.

Leitenberg, H. Behavioral approaches to treatment of neuroses. In H. Leitenberg (Ed.), *Handbook of behavior modification and behavior therapy.* Englewood Cliffs, New Jersey: Prentice-Hall, 1976. (a)

Leitenberg, H. (Ed.), *Handbook of behavior modification and behavior therapy.* Englewood Cliffs, New Jersey: Prentice-Hall, 1976. (b)

Leitenberg, H., Agras, W.S., Barlow, D.H., & Oliveau, D.C. Contribution of selective positive reinforcement and therapeutic instructions to systematic desensitization. *Journal of Abnormal Psychology,* 1969, **74,** 113–118.

Leitenberg, H., & Callahan, E. Reinforced practice and the reduction of different kinds of fears in adults and children. *Behaviour Research and Therapy,* 1973, **11,** 19–30.

Leitenberg, H., Wincze, J., Butz, R., Callahan, E., & Agras, W. Comparsion of the effect of instructions and reinforcement in the treatment of a neurotic avoidance response: A single case experiment. *Journal of Behavior Therapy and Experimental Psychiatry,* 1970, **1,** 53–58.

Leon, G.R. Current directions in the treatment of obesity. *Psychological Bulletin,* 1976, **83,** 557–578.

Levis, D.J., & Carrera, R. Effects of 10 hours of implosive therapy in the treatment of outpatients. *Journal of Abnormal Psychology,* 1967, **72,** 504–508.

Levitz, L.S., & Stunkard, A.J. A therapeutic coalition for obesity: Behavior modification and patient self-help. *American Journal of Psychiatry,* 1974, **131,** 423–427.

Levy, R., & Meyer, V. Ritual prevention in obsessional patients. *Proceedings of the Royal Society of Medicine,* 1971, **64,** 1115–1118.

Libb, J.W., & Clements, C.B. Token reinforcement in an exercise program for hospitalized geriatric patients. *Perceptual and Motor Skills,* 1969, **28,** 957–958.

Liberman, R.P. Reinforcement of social interaction in a group of chronic mental patients. In R.D. Rubin, H. Fensterheim, J. D. Henderson, & L.P. Ullmann (Eds.), *Advances in behavior therapy.* New York: Academic Press, 1972.

Liberman, R.P. Applying behavioral techniques in a community mental health center. In R.D. Rubin, J.P. Brady, & J.D. Henderson (Eds.), *Advances in behavior therapy,* Vol. 4. New York: Academic Press, 1973.

Liberman, R.P., Fearn, C.H., DeRisi, W., Roberts, J., & Carmona, M. The credit-incentive system: Motivating the participation of patients in a day hospital. *British Journal of Social and Clinical Psychology,* 1977, **16,** 85–94.

Liberman, R.P., Levine, J., Wheeler, E., Sanders, N., & Wallace, C.J. Marital therapy in groups: A comparative evaluation of behavioral and interactional formats. *Acta Psychiatrica Scandinavica,* 1976, Supplementum 266.

Liberman, R.P., Teigen, J., Patterson, R., & Baker, V. Reducing delusional speech in chronic, paranoid schizophrenics. *Journal of Applied Behavior Analysis,* 1973, **6,** 57–64.

Lichtenstein, E. Modification of smoking behavior: Good designs—ineffective treatments. *Journal of Consulting and Clinical Psychology,* 1971, **36,** 163–166.

Lichtenstein, E., Harris, D.E., Birchler, G.R., Wahl, J.H., & Schmahl, D.P. Comparison of rapid smoking, warm smoky air, and attention placebo in the modification of smoking behavior. *Journal of Consulting and Clinical Psychology,* 1973, **40,** 92–98.

Lick, J., & Bootzin, R. Expectancy factors in the treatment of fear: Methodological and theoretical issues. *Psychological Bulletin,* 1975, **82,** 917–931.

Litman, G.K. Behavioral modification techniques in the treatment of alcoholism: A review and critique. In R.J. Gibbins, Y. Israel, H. Kalant, R.E. Popham, W. Schmidt, & R.G. Smart (Eds.), *Research advances in alcohol and drug problems,* Vol. III, New York: John Wiley & Sons, 1976.

Lovaas, O.I., Berberich, J.P., Perloff, B.F., & Schaeffer, B. Acquisition of imitative speech in schizophrenic children. *Science,* 1966, **51,** 705–707.

Lovaas, O.I., & Bucher, B.D. (Eds.), *Perspectives in behavior modification with deviant children.* Englewood Cliffs, New Jersey: Prentice-Hall, 1974.

Lovaas, O.I., Koegel, R., Simmons, J.Q., & Long, J.S. Some generalization and follow-up measures on autistic children in behavior therapy. *Journal of Applied Behavior Analysis,* 1973, **6,** 131–166.

Lovaas, O.I., & Newsom, C.D. Behavior modification with psychotic children. In H. Leitenberg (Ed.), *Handbook of behavior modification and behavior therapy.* Englewood Cliffs, New Jersey: Prentice-Hall, 1976.

Lovaas, O.I., Schaeffer, B., & Simmons, J.Q. Building social behavior in autistic children by use of electric shock. *Journal of Experimental Research in Personality,* 1965, **1,** 99–109.

Luborsky, L., Singer, B., & Luborsky, L. Comparative studies of psychotherapies: Is it true that everyone has won and all must have prizes? *Archives of General Psychiatry,* 1975, **32,** 995–1008.

Lutzker, J.R. Social reinforcement control of exhibitionism in a profoundly mentally retarded adult. *Mental Retardation,* 1974, **12,** 46–47.

Lutzker, J.R., & Sherman, J. Producing generative sentence usage by imitation and reinforcement procedures. *Journal of Applied Behavior Analysis,* 1974, **7,** 447–460.

MacDonald, M.L. Reversal of disengagement: Inducing social interaction in the institutionalized elderly. *Gerontologist,* in press.

MacDonald, M.L., & Butler, A.K. Reversal of helplessness: Producing walking behavior in nursing home wheelchair residents using behavior modification procedures. *Journal of Gerontology,* 1974, **29,** 97–101.

MacDonough, T. A critique of the first Feldman and MacCulloch avoidance conditioning treatment for homosexuals. *Behavior Therapy,* 1972, **3,** 104–111.

Mahoney, M.J. *Cognition and behavior modification.* Cambridge, Massachusetts: Ballinger, 1974. (a)

Mahoney, M.J. Self-reward and self-monitoring techniques for weight control. *Behavior Therapy,* 1974, **5,** 48–57. (b)

Mahoney, M.J., & Arnkoff, D. Cognitive and self-control therapies. In S.L. Garfield & A.E. Bergin (Eds.), *Handbook of psychotherapy and behavior change: An empirical analysis,* 2nd edition. New York: John Wiley & Sons, in press.

Mahoney, M.J., Kazdin, A.E., & Lesswing, N.J. Behavior modification: Delusion or deliverance. In C.M. Franks & G.T. Wilson (Eds.), *Annual review of behavior therapy theory and research,* Vol. 2. New York: Brunner/Mazel, 1974.

Maley, R.F., Feldman, G.L., & Ruskin, R.S. Evaluation of patient improvement in a token economy treatment program. *Journal of Abnormal Psychology,* 1973, **82,** 141–144.

Maloney, K.B., & Hopkins, B.L. The modification of sentence structure and its relationship to subjective judgments of creativity in writing. *Journal of Applied Behavior Analysis,* 1973, **6,** 425–433.

Mandelker, A.V., Brigham, T.A., & Bushell, D. The effects of token procedures on a teacher's social contacts with her students. *Journal of Applied Behavior Analysis,* 1970, **3,** 169–174.

Marcia, J.E., Rubin, B.M., & Efran, J.S. Systematic desensitization: Expectancy change or counterconditioning. *Journal of Abnormal Psychology,* 1969, **74,** 382–387.

Marholin, D., II, & Gray, D. Effects of group response cost procedures on cash shortages in a small business. *Journal of Applied Behavior Analysis,* 1976, **9,** 25–30.

Marholin, D., II, Siegel, L.J., & Phillips, D. Treatment and transfer: A search for empirical procedures. In M. Hersen, R.M. Eisler, & P.M. Miller (Eds.), *Progress in behavior modification,* Vol. 3. New York: Academic Press, 1976.

Marks, I.M. *Fears and phobias.* New York: Academic Press, 1969.

Marks, I.M. Phobic disorders four years after treatment: A prospective follow-up. *British Journal of Psychiatry,* 1971, **118,** 683–688.

Marks, I.M. Behavioral treatment of phobic and obsessive-compulsive disorders: A critical appraisal. In M. Hersen, R.M. Eisler, & P.M. Miller (Eds.), *Progress in behavior modification,* Vol. 1. New York: Academic Press, 1975.

Marks, I.M. Management of sexual disorders. In H. Leitenberg (Ed.), *Handbook of behavior modification and behavior therapy.* Englewood Cliffs, New Jersey: Prentice-Hall, 1976. (a)

Marks, I.M. The current status of behavioral psychotherapy: Theory and practice. *American Journal of Psychiatry,* 1976, **133**, 253–261. (b)

Marks, I.M. Behavioural psychotherapy of neurotic disorders. In S.L. Garfield & A.E. Bergin (Eds.), *Handbook of psychotherapy and behavior change: An empirical basis,* 2nd edition. New York: John Wiley & Sons, in press.

Marks, I.M., Boulougouris, J.C., & Marset, P. Flooding versus desensitization in the treatment of phobic patients: A crossover study. *British Journal of Psychiatry,* 1971, **119**, 353–375.

Marks, I.M., & Gelder, M.G. A controlled retrospective study of behaviour therapy in phobic patients. *British Journal of Psychiatry,* 1965, **111**, 561–573.

Marks, I.M., & Gelder, M. Transvestism and fetishism: Clinical and psychological changes during faradic aversion. *British Journal of Psychiatry,* 1967, **113**, 711–739.

Marks, I.M., Rachman, S., & Hodgson, R. Treatment of chronic obsessive-compulsive neurosis by in-vivo exposure. *British Journal of Psychiatry,* 1975, **127**, 349–364.

Marks, J., Sonoda, B., & Schalock, R. Reinforcement vs. relationship therapy for schizophrenics. *Journal of Abnormal Psychology,* 1968, **73**, 397–402.

Marlatt, G.A. Craving for alcohol, loss of control, and relapse: A cognitive-behavioral analysis. Paper presented at NATO International Conference on Behavioral Approaches to Alcoholism, Bergen, Norway, August 1977.

Marlatt, G.A., & Nathan, P.E. (Eds.), *Behavioral assessment and treatment of alcoholism.* New Brunswick, New Jersey: Center for Alcohol Studies, in press.

Marmor, J. Foreward. In R.B. Sloane et al. (1975), *Psychotherapy versus behavior therapy.* Cambridge, Massachusetts: Harvard University Press, 1975.

Masters, W.H., & Johnson, V.E. *Human sexual inadequacy.* Boston: Little-Brown, 1970.

Mathews, A.M., Bancroft, J., Whitehead, A., Hackmann, A., Julier, D., Bancroft, J., Gath, D., & Shaw, P. The behavioural treatment of sexual inadequacy: A comparative study. *Behaviour Research and Therapy,* 1976, **14**, 427–436.

Mathews, A.M., Johnston, D.W., Lancashire, M., Munby, M., Shaw, P.M., & Gelder, M.G. Imaginal flooding and exposure to real phobic situations: Treatment outcome with agoraphobic patients. *British Journal of Psychiatry,* 1976, **129**, 362–371.

McClannahan, L.E., & Risley, T.R. A store for nursing home residents. *Nursing Homes,* 1973, **22**, 10–11.

McConaghy, N.A. A controlled trial of imipramine, amphetamine, pad-and-bell conditioning and random wakening in the treatment of nocturnal enuresis. *Medical Journal of Australia,* 1969, **2**, 237–239.

McConaghy, N.A., & Barr, R.F. Classical, avoidance and backward conditioning treatments of homosexuality. *British Journal of Psychiatry,* 1973, **122**, 151–162.

McConahey, O.L. A token system for retarded women: Behavior modification, drug therapy, and their combination. In T. Thompson & J. Grabowski (Eds.), *Behavior modification of the mentally retarded*. New York: Oxford University Press, 1972.

McConahey, O.L., & Thompson, T. Concurrent behavior modification and chlorpromazine therapy in a population of institutionalized mentally retarded women. *Proceedings of the 79th Annual Convention of the American Psychological Association*, 1971, **6**, 761–762.

McConahey, O.L., Thompson, T., & Zimmerman, R. A token system for retarded women: Behavior therapy, drug administration, and their combination. In T. Thompson & J. Grabowski (Eds.), *Behavior modification of the mentally retarded*, 2nd edition. New York: Oxford University Press, 1977.

McFall, R.M., & Marston, A.R. An experimental investigation of behavior rehearsal in assertive training. *Journal of Abnormal Psychology*, 1970, **76**, 295–303.

McFall, R.M., & Twentyman, C.T. Four experiments on the relative contributions of rehearsal, modeling, and coaching to assertion training. *Journal of Abnormal Psychology*, 1973, **81**, 199–218.

McGlynn, F.D., & Walls, R. Credibility ratings for desensitization and pseudotherapy among moderately and mildly snake-avoidant college students. *Journal of Clinical Psychology*, 1976, **32**, 140–145.

McReynolds, W.T. Systematic desensitization, insight-oriented psychotherapy and relaxation therapy in a psychiatric population. Unpublished doctoral dissertation. University of Texas at Austin, 1969.

McReynolds, W.T., & Coleman, J. Token economy: Patient and staff changes. *Behaviour Research and Therapy*, 1972, **10**, 29–34.

McReynolds, W.T., & Paulsen, B.K. Stimulus control as the behavioral basis of weight loss procedures. In G.J. Williams, S. Martin, & J. Foreyt (Eds.), *Obesity: Behavioral approaches to dietary management*. New York: Brunner/Mazel, 1976.

McReynolds, W.T., & Tori, C. Further assessment of attention-placebo effects and demand characteristics in studies of systematic desensitization. *Journal of Consulting and Clinical Psychology*, 1972, **38**, 261–269.

Meehl, P.E. The cognitive activity of the clinician. *American Psychologist*, 1960, **15**, 19–27.

Meichenbaum, D.H. The effects of instruction and reinforcement on thinking and language behaviour of schizophrenics. *Behaviour Research and Therapy*, 1969, **7**, 101–114.

Meichenbaum, D.H. Cognitive modification of test anxious college students. *Journal of Consulting and Clinical Psychology*, 1972, **39**, 370–380.

Meichenbaum, D.H. *Cognitive behavior modification*. Morristown, New Jersey: General Learning Press, 1974.

Meichenbaum, D.H. *Cognitive behavior modification*. New York: Plenum Press, 1977.

Meichenbaum, D., Gilmore, J., & Fedoravicius, A. Group insight versus group desensitization in treating speech anxiety. *Journal of Clinical and Consulting Psychology*, 1971, **36**, 410–421.

Meltzoff, J., & Kornreich, M. *Research in psychotherapy.* New York: Atherton, 1970.

Meyer, V. Modification of expectations in cases with obsessional rituals. *Behaviour Research and Therapy,* 1966, **4,** 273–280.

Meyer, V., & Crisp, A. H. Some problems in behavior therapy. *British Journal of Psychiatry,* 1966, **112,** 367–381.

Milan, M.A., & McKee, J.M. Behavior modification: Principles and applications in corrections. In D. Glaser (Ed.), *Handbook of criminology.* Chicago: Rand McNally, 1974.

Milan, M.A., Wood, L.F., Williams, R.L., Rogers, J.G., Hampton, L.R., & McKee, J.M. *Applied behavior analysis and the Important Adult Felon Project I: The cellblock token economy.* Elmore, Alabama: Rehabilitation Research Foundation, 1974.

Milby, J.B., Pendergrass, P.E., & Clarke, C.J. Token economy versus control ward: A comparison of staff and patient attitudes toward ward environment. *Behavior Therapy,* 1975, **6,** 22–29.

Miller, G.A., Galanter, E., & Pribram, K.H. *Plans and the structure of behavior.* New York: Holt, Rinehart and Winston, 1960.

Miller, L.C., Barrett, C.L., Hampe, E., & Noble, H. Comparison of reciprocal inhibition, psychotherapy, and waiting list control for phobic children. *Journal of Abnormal Psychology,* 1972, **79,** 269–279.

Miller, P.M. A behavioral intervention program for chronic public drunkenness offenders. *Archives of General Psychiatry,* 1975, **32,** 915–918.

Miller, P.M., Hersen, M., Eisler, R., & Hemphill, D. Effects of faradic aversion therapy on drinking by alcoholics. *Behaviour Research and Therapy,* 1973, **11,** 491–498.

Miller, W.R., & Caddy, G.R. Abstinence and controlled drinking in the treatment of problem drinkers. *Journal of Studies on Alcohol,* in press.

Mills, H.L., Agras, W.S., Barlow, D.H., & Mills, J.R. Compulsive rituals treated by response prevention. *Archives of General Psychiatry,* 1973, **28,** 524–529.

Minkin, N., Braukmann, C.J., Minkin, B.L., Timbers, G.D., Timbers, B.J., Fixsen, D.L., Phillips, E.L., & Wolf, M.M. The social validation and training of conversational skills. *Journal of Applied Behavior Analysis,* 1976, **9,** 127–139.

Mischel, W. *Personality and assessment.* New York: Wiley, 1968.

Mischel, W. *Introduction to personality.* New York: Holt, Rinehart and Winston, 1971.

Mischel, W. Toward a cognitive social learning reconceptualization of personality. *Psychological Review,* 1973, **80,** 252–283.

Mischel, W. On the future of personality measurement. *American Psychologist,* 1977, **32,** 246–254.

Moore, N. Behaviour therapy in bronchial asthma: A controlled study. *Journal of Psychosomatic Research,* 1965, **9,** 257–276.

Morganstern, K. P. Implosive therapy and flooding procedures: A critical review. *Psychological Bulletin,* 1972, **79,** 318–334.

Morris, R.J., & Suckerman, K.R. The importance of the therapeutic relationship in systematic desensitization. *Journal of Consulting and Clinical Psychology,* 1974, **42,** 147. (a)

Morris, R.J., & Suckerman, K.R. Therapist warmth as a factor in automated systematic desensitization. *Journal of Consulting and Clinical Psychology,* 1974, **42**, 244–250. (b)

Moser, A.J. Covert punishment of hallucinatory behavior in a psychotic male. *Journal of Behavior Therapy and Experimental Psychiatry,* 1974, **5**, 297–301.

Mowrer, O.H. On the dual nature of learning—a reinterpretation of "conditioning" and "problem solving." *Harvard Educational Review,* 1947, **17**, 102–148.

Mowrer, O.H. *Learning theory and behavior.* New York: Wiley, 1960.

Munjack, D., Cristol, A., Goldstein, A., Phillips, D., Goldberg, A., Whipple, K., Staples, F., & Kanno, P. Behavioural treatment of orgasmic dysfunction: A controlled study. *British Journal of Psychiatry,* 1976, **129**, 497–502.

Nathan, P.E., & Briddell, D.W. Behavioral assessment and treatment of alcoholism. In B. Kissin, & H. Begleiter, (Eds.), *The biology of alcoholism,* Vol. V. New York: Plenum Press, 1977.

Nau, D.S., Caputo, L.A., & Borkovec, T.D. The relationship between credibility of therapy and simulated therapeutic effects. *Journal of Behavior Therapy and Experimental Psychiatry,* 1974, **5**, 129–134.

Nelson, C.M., Worell, J., & Polsgrove, L. Behaviorally disordered peers as contingency managers. *Behavior Therapy,* 1973, **4**, 270–276.

Ney, P.G., Palvesky, A.E., & Markely, J. Relative effectiveness of operant conditioning and play therapy in childhood schizophrenia. *Journal of Autism and Childhood Schizophrenia,* 1971, **1**, 337–349.

Nietzel, M.T., Winett, R.A., MacDonald, M.L., & Davidson, W.S. *Behavioral approaches to community psychology.* New York: Pergamon Press, 1977.

Nisbett, R. Hunger, obesity, and the ventromedial hypothalamus. *Psychological Review,* 1972, **79,** 433–470.

Nordquist, V.M. The modification of a child's enuresis: Some response-response relationships. *Journal of Applied Behavior Analysis,* 1971, **4**, 241–247.

Novick, J. Symptomatic treatment of acquired and persistent enuresis. *Journal of Abnormal Psychology,* 1966, **77**, 363–368.

Nydegger, R.V. The elimination of hallucinatory and delusional behavior by verbal conditioning and assertive training: A case study. *Journal of Behavior and Experimental Psychiatry,* 1972, **3**, 225–227.

Obler, M. Systematic desensitization in sexual disorders. *Journal of Behavior Therapy and Experimental Psychiatry,* 1973, **4**, 93–101.

O'Brien, F., Azrin, N.H., & Henson, K. Increased communications of chronic mental patients by reinforcement and response priming. *Journal of Applied Behavior Analysis,* 1969, **2**, 23–29.

O'Connor, R.D. Relative efficacy of modeling, shaping, and the combined procedures for modification of social withdrawal. *Journal of Abnormal Psychology,* 1972, **79**, 327–334.

O'Leary, K.D., & Borkovec, T.D. Placebo groups: Unrealistic and unethical controls in psychotherapy research. Unpublished manuscript, 1977.

O'Leary, K.D., & Drabman, R. Token reinforcement programs in the classroom: A review. *Psychological Bulletin,* 1971, **75**, 379–398.

O'Leary, K.D., & Wilson, G.T. *Behavior therapy: Application and outcome.* Englewood Cliffs, New Jersey: Prentice-Hall, 1975.

O'Leary, S.G., & O'Leary, K.D. Behavior modification in the school. In H. Leitenberg (Ed.), *Handbook of behavior modification and behavior therapy.* Englewood Cliffs, New Jersey: Prentice-Hall, 1976.

Olson, R.P., & Greenberg, D.J. Effects of contingency-contracting and decision-making groups with chronic mental patients. *Journal of Consulting and Clinical Psychology,* 1972, **38**, 376–383.

Orlinsky, D.O., & Howard, K.I. *Varieties of psychotherapeutic experience.* New York: Teachers College Press, 1975.

Orne, M.T. Demand characteristics and the concept of quasi-controls. In R. Rosenthal & R.L. Rosnow (Eds.), *Artifact in behavioral research.* New York: Academic Press, 1969.

Öst, L., & Götestam, K. Behavioral and pharmacological treatments for obesity: An experimental comparison. *Addictive Behaviors,* 1976, **1**, 331–338.

Parloff, M.B. Therapist-patient relationships and outcome of psychotherapy. *Journal of Consulting Psychology,* 1961, **25**, 29–38.

Parrino, J.J., George, L., & Daniels, A.C. Token control of pill-taking behavior in a psychiatric ward. *Journal of Behavior Therapy and Experimental Psychiatry,* 1971, **2**, 181–185.

Patterson, G.R. Behavioral intervention procedures in the classroom and in the home. In A.E. Bergin, & S.L. Garfield (Eds.), *Handbook of psychotherapy and behavior change: An empirical analysis.* New York: John Wiley & Sons, 1971.

Patterson, G.R. Interventions for boys with conduct problems: Multiple settings, treatments, and criteria. *Journal of Consulting and Clinical Psychology,* 1974, **42**, 471–481.

Patterson, G.R. A performance theory for coercive family interaction. In R. Cairns (Ed.), *Social interaction: Methods, analysis, and illustration.* Society Research Child Development Monograph, in press.

Patterson, G.R., Cobb, J.A., & Ray, R.S. A social engineering technology for retraining families of aggressive boys. In H.E. Adams & I.P. Unikel (Eds.), *Issues and trends in behavior therapy.* Springfield, Illinois: Charles C Thomas, 1973.

Patterson, G.R., & Hops, H. Coercion, a game for two: Intervention techniques for marital conflict. In R.E. Ulrich & P. Mountjoy (Eds.), *The experimental analysis of social behavior.* New York: Appleton-Century-Crofts, 1972.

Patterson, G.R., & Reid, J.B. Intervention for families of aggressive boys: A replication study. *Behaviour Research and Therapy,* 1973, **11**, 1–12.

Patterson, R., & Teigen, J. Conditioning and post-hospital generalization of non-delusional responses in a chronic psychotic patient. *Journal of Applied Behavior Analysis,* 1973, **6**, 65–70.

Patterson, V., Levene, H., & Breger, L. Treatment and training outcomes with two time-limited therapies. *Archives of General Psychiatry,* 1971, **25**, 161–167.

Pattison, E.M. A conceptual approach to alcoholism treatment goals. *Addictive Behaviors,* 1976, **1**, 177–192.

Paul, G.L. *Insight versus desensitization in psychotherapy.* Stanford, California: Stanford University Press, 1966.

Paul, G.L. Insight vs. desensitization in psychotherapy two years after termination. *Journal of Consulting Psychology,* 1967, **31,** 333–348. (a)

Paul, G.L. Outcome research in psychotherapy. *Journal of Consulting Psychology,* 1967, **31,** 109–118. (b)

Paul, G.L. Behavior modification research: Design and tactics. In C.M. Franks (Ed.), *Behavior therapy: Appraisal and status.* New York: McGraw-Hill, 1969. (a)

Paul, G.L. Outcome of systematic desensitization. II: Controlled investigations of individual treatment, technique variations, and current status. In C.M. Franks (Ed.), *Behavior therapy: Appraisal and status.* New York: McGraw-Hill, 1969. (b)

Paul, G.L., & Shannon, D.T. Treatment of anxiety through systematic desensitization in therapy groups. *Journal of Abnormal Psychology,* 1966, **71,** 124–135.

Pedalino, E., & Gamboa, V.U. Behavior modification and absenteeism: Intervention in one industrial setting. *Journal of Applied Psychology,* 1974, **59,** 694–698.

Penick, S.B., Filion, R., Fox, S., & Stunkard, A.J. Behavior modification in the treatment of obesity. *Psychosomatic Medicine,* 1971, **33,** 49–55.

Peterson, D.R. *The clinical study of social behavior.* New York: Appleton-Century-Crofts, 1968.

Peterson, D.R. Is psychology a profession? *American Psychologist,* 1976, **31,** 572–581.

Pomerleau, O.F., Pertschuk, M., Adkins, D., & Brady, J.P. *Comparison of behavioral and traditional treatment for problem drinking.* Paper presented at the Annual Meeting of the Association for Advancement of Behavior Therapy, New York, December 1976.

Poser, E.G. The effect of therapist's training on group therapeutic outcome. *Journal of Consulting Psychology,* 1966, **30,** 283–289.

Quilitch, H.R. Purposeful activity increased on a geriatric ward through programmed recreation. *Journal of the American Geriatrics Society,* 1974, **22,** 226–229.

Rachlin, H. Self-control. *Behaviorism,* 1974, **2,** 94–107.

Rachman, S. Introduction to behaviour therapy. *Behaviour Research and Therapy,* 1963, **1,** 4–15.

Rachman, S. *The effects of psychotherapy.* New York: Pergamon Press, 1971.

Rachman, S. Clinical applications of observational learning, imitation and modeling. *Behavior Therapy,* 1972, **3,** 379–397.

Rachman, S. The modification of obsessions: A new formulation. *Behaviour Research and Therapy,* 1976, **14,** 437–444. (a)

Rachman, S. Observational learning and therapeutic modelling. In M.P. Feldman & A. Broadhurst (Eds.), *Theoretical and empirical bases of the behaviour therapies.* London: John Wiley & Sons, 1976. (b)

Rachman, S., & Hodgson, R. Synchrony and desynchrony in fear and avoidance: I. *Behaviour Research and Therapy,* 1974, **12,** 311–318.

Rachman, S., & Hodgson, R. *Obsessions and compulsions.* Englewood Cliffs, New Jersey: Prentice-Hall, in press.

Rachman, S., & Teasdale, J. *Aversion therapy and behaviour disorders: An analysis.* Coral Gables, Florida: University of Miami Press, 1969.

Ramp, E., & Semb, G. (Eds.), *Behaviour analysis: Areas of research and application.* Englewood Cliffs, New Jersey: Prentice-Hall, 1975.

Redfield, J., & Paul, G.L. Bias in behavioral observation as a function of observer familiarity with subjects and typicality of behavior. *Journal of Consulting and Clinical Psychology,* 1976, **44,** 156.

Rekers, G.A., & Lovaas, O.I. Behavioral treatment of deviant sex-role behaviors in a male child. *Journal of Applied Behavior Analysis,* 1974, **7,** 173–190.

Rickard, H.C., Dignam, P.J., & Horner, R.F. Verbal manipulation in a psychotherapeutic relationship. *Journal of Clinical Psychology,* 1960, **16,** 364–367.

Rimland, B. *Infantile autism.* New York: Appleton-Century-Crofts, 1964.

Rimland, B. Comparative effects of treatment on child's behavior (Drugs, therapies, schooling, and several non-treatment events). Institute for Child Behavior Research, Publication 34, May 1977.

Rioch, M.M., Elkes, E., Flint, A.A., Usdansky, B.C., Newman, R.G., & Silber, E. National Institute of Mental Health pilot study in training mental health counselors. *American Journal of Orthopsychiatry,* 1963, **33,** 678–689.

Risley, T.R. Behavior modification: An experimental-therapeutic endeavor. In L.A. Hamerlynck, P.O. Davidson, & L.E. Acker (Eds.), *Behavior modification and ideal mental health services.* Calgary, Alberta, Canada: University of Calgary Press, 1970.

Ritchie, R.J. A token economy system for changing controlling behavior in the chronic pain patients. *Journal of Behavior Therapy and Experimental Psychiatry,* 1976, **7,** 341–343.

Rooth, F.G., & Marks, I.M. Persistent exhibitionism: Short-term response to self-regulation and relaxation treatment. *Archives of Sexual Behavior,* 1974, **3,** 227–248.

Röper, G., Rachman, S., & Marks, I.M. Passive and participant modelling in exposure treatment of obsessive-compulsive neurotics. *Behaviour Research and Therapy,* 1975, **13,** 271–279.

Rosen, G.M. The development and use of nonprescription behavior therapies. *American Psychologist,* 1976, **31,** 139–141.

Rosen, G.M., Glasgow, R.E., & Barrera, M. Jr. A controlled study to assess the clinical efficacy of totally self-administered systematic desensitization. *Journal of Consulting and Clinical Psychology,* 1976, **44,** 208–217.

Rosenthal, D., & Frank, J.D. Psychotherapy and the placebo effect. *Psychological Bulletin,* 1956, **53,** 294–302.

Rosenthal, T.L., & Bandura, A. Psychological modeling: Theory and practice. In S.L. Garfield & A.E. Bergin (Eds.), *Handbook of psychotherapy and behavior change,* 2nd edition. New York: John Wiley & Sons, in press.

Rugh, J.D., & Schwitzgebel, R.L. Instrumentation for behavioral assessment. In A.R. Ciminero, K.S. Calhoun, & H.E. Adams (Eds.), *Handbook of behavioral assessment.* New York: John Wiley & Sons, 1977.

Rush, A.J., Beck, A.T., Kovacs, M., & Hollon, S. Comparative efficacy of cognitive therapy and pharmacotherapy in the treatment of depressed outpatients. *Cognitive Therapy and Research,* 1977, **1,** 17–37.

Rutner, I.T., & Bugle, C. An experimental procedure for modification of psychotic behavior. *Journal of Consulting and Clinical Psychology*, 1969, **33**, 651–653.

Ryan, B.A. *Keller's Personalized System of Instruction: An appraisal*. Washington, D.C.: American Psychological Association, 1972.

Rybolt, G.A. Token reinforcement therapy with chronic psychiatric patients: A three-year evaluation. *Journal of Behavior Therapy and Experimental Psychiatry*, 1975, **6**, 188–191.

Sachs, D.A. Behavioral techniques in a residential nursing home facility. *Journal of Behavior Therapy and Experimental Psychiatry*, 1975, **6**, 123–127.

Sajwaj, T., Twardosz, S., & Burke, M. Side effects of extinction procedures in a remedial preschool. *Journal of Applied Behavior Analysis*, 1972, **5**, 163–175.

Saudargas, R.A. Setting criterion rates of teacher praise: Effects of video-tape feedback in a behavior analysis followthrough classroom. In G. Semb (Ed.), *Behavior analysis and education*. Lawrence, Kansas: Follow-Through Project, Department of Human Development, 1972.

Schaefer, H.H., & Martin, P.L. Behavioral therapy for "apathy" of hospitalized schizophrenics. *Psychological Reports*, 1966, **19**, 1147–1158.

Schnelle, J.F. A brief report on invalidity of parent evaluations of behavior change. *Journal of Applied Behavior Analysis*, 1974, **7**, 341–343.

Schwartz, J., & Bellack, A.S. A comparison of a token economy with standard inpatient treatment. *Journal of Consulting and Clinical Psychology*, 1975, **43**, 107–108.

Schwartz, J.L., & Dubitzky, M. *Psychosocial factors involved in cigarette smoking and cessation*. Berkeley, California: Institute for Health Research, 1968.

Schwitzgebel, R.L., & Schwitzgebel, R.K. *Psychotechnology: Electronic control of mind and behavior*. New York: Holt, Rinehart & Winston, 1973.

Scott, R.W., Blanchard, E.B., Edmundson, E.D., & Young, L.D. A shaping procedure for heart-rate control in chronic tachycardia. *Perceptual and Motor Skills*, 1973, **37**, 327–338.

Seaver, W.B., & Patterson, A.H. Decreasing fuel oil consumption through feedback and social commendation. *Journal of Applied Behavior Analysis*, 1976, **9**, 147–152.

Seligman, M.E.P. Phobias and preparedness. *Behavior Therapy*, 1971, **2**, 307–320.

Seligman, M.E.P., Klein, D.C., & Miller, W.R. Depression. In H. Leitenberg (Ed.), *Handbook of behavior modification and behavior therapy*. Englewood Cliffs, New Jersey: Prentice-Hall, 1976.

Shafto, F., & Sulzbacher, S. Comparing treatment tactics with a hyperactive preschool child: Stimulant medication and programmed teacher intervention. *Journal of Applied Behavior Analysis*, 1977, **10**, 13–20.

Shapiro, A.K. The behavior therapies: Therapeutic breakthrough or latest fad? *American Journal of Psychiatry*, 1976, **133**, 154–159.

Shapiro, D., & Schwartz, G.E. Biofeedback and visceral learning: Clinical applications. *Seminars in Psychiatry*, 1972, **4**, 171–184.

Shapiro, D., & Surwit, R.S. Learned control of physiological function and disease. In H. Leitenberg (Ed.), *Handbook of behavior modification and behavior therapy*. Englewood Cliffs, New Jersey: Prentice-Hall, 1976.

Shapiro, M.B. The single case in clinical-psychological research. *Journal of Genetic Psychology,* 1966, **74**, 3–23.

Shean, J.D., & Zeidberg, Z. Token reinforcement therapy: A comparison of matched groups. *Journal of Behavior Therapy and Experimental Psychiatry,* 1971, **2**, 95–105.

Sherman, A.R., Mulac, A., & McCann, M.S. Synergistic effect of self-relaxation and rehearsal feedback in the treatment of subjective and behavioral dimensions of speech anxiety. *Journal of Consulting and Clinical Psychology,* 1974, **42**, 819–827.

Sherman, J.A. Use of reinforcement and imitation to reinstate verbal behavior in mute psychotics. *Journal of Abnormal Psychology,* 1965, **70**, 155–164.

Shlien, J.M. (Ed.), *Research in psychotherapy,* Vol. 3. Washington, D.C.: American Psychological Association, 1968.

Sidman, M. *Tactics of scientific research.* New York: Basic Books, 1960.

Singerman, K., Borkovec, T.D., & Baron, R.S. Failure of a "misattribution therapy" manipulation with a clinically relevant target behavior. *Behavior Therapy,* 1976, **7**, 306–313.

Skinner, B.F. *Science and human behavior.* New York: Free Press, 1953.

Skinner, B.F. *Beyond freedom and dignity.* New York: Alfred A. Knopf, 1971.

Skinner, B.F. The steep and thorny way to a science of behavior. *American Psychologist,* 1975, **30**, 42–49.

Slade, P.D. The effects of systematic desensitization on auditory hallucinations. *Behaviour Research and Therapy,* 1972, **10**, 85–91.

Sloane, R.B., Staples, F.R., Cristol, A.H., Yorkston, N.J., & Whipple, K. *Psychotherapy versus behavior therapy.* Cambridge, Massachusetts: Harvard University Press, 1975.

Smith, M.L., & Glass, G.V. Meta-analysis of psychotherapy outcome studies. *American Psychologist,* 1977, **32**, 752–760.

Smolev, S.R. Use of operant techniques for the modification of self-injurious behavior. *American Journal of Mental Deficiency,* 1971, **76**, 295–305.

Sobell, L.C., & Sobell, M.B. Outpatient alcoholics give valid self-reports. *Journal of Nervous and Mental Disease,* 1975, **161**, 32–42.

Sobell, M.B., & Sobell, L.C. Second year treatment outcome of alcoholics treated by individualized behavior therapy: Results. *Behaviour Research and Therapy,* 1976, **14**, 195–216.

Solomon, R.W., & Wahler, R.G. Peer reinforcement control of classroom problem behavior. *Journal of Applied Behavior Analysis,* 1973, **6**, 49–56.

Stahl, J.R., & Leitenberg, H. Behavioral treatment of the chronic mental hospital patient. In H. Leitenberg (Ed.), *Handbook of behavior modification and behavior therapy.* Englewood Cliffs, New Jersey: Prentice-Hall, 1976.

Steinmark, S.W., & Borkovec, T.D. Active and placebo treatment effects on moderate insomnia under counterdemand and positive demand instructions. *Journal of Abnormal Psychology,* 1974, **83**, 157–163.

Stern, R., & Marks, I.M. Brief and prolonged flooding. *Archives of General Psychiatry,* 1973, **28**, 270–276.

Stokes, T.F., & Baer, D.M. An implicit technology of generalization. *Journal of Applied Behavior Analysis,* in press.

Stokes, T.F., Baer, D.M., & Jackson, R.L. Programming the generalization of a greeting response in four retarded children. *Journal of Applied Behavior Analysis,* 1974, **7,** 599–610.

Stolz, S.B., Wienckowski, L.A., & Brown, B.S. Behavior modification: A perspective on critical issues. *American Psychologist,* 1975, **30,** 1027–1048.

Strupp, H.H. A psychodynamicist looks at modern behavior therapy. Paper presented at the 10th annual meeting of the Association for Advancement of Behavior Therapy, New York, December 1976.

Strupp, H.H., & Hadley, S.W. A tripartite model of mental health and therapeutic outcomes. *American Psychologist,* 1977, **32,** 187–196.

Strupp, H.H., & Luborsky, L. (Eds.). *Research in psychotherapy,* Vol. 2. Washington, D.C.: American Psychological Association, 1962.

Stuart, R.B. Notes on the ethics of behavior research and intervention. In L.A. Hamerlynck, L.C. Handy, & E.J. Mash (Eds.), *Behavior change: Methodology, concepts, and practice.* Champaign, Illinois: Research Press, 1973.

Stuart, R.B., & Davis, B. *Slim chance in a fat world: Behavioral control of obesity.* Champaign, Illinois: Research Press, 1972.

Stumphauzer, J.S. (Ed.), *Behavior therapy with delinquents.* Springfield, Illinois: Charles C Thomas, 1973.

Stunkard, A.J. New therapies for the eating disorders. *Archives of General Psychiatry,* 1972, **26,** 391–398.

Stunkard, A.J. Obesity and the social environment: Current status, future prospects. Paper presented at the Bicentennial Conference on Food and Nutrition in Health and Disease, Philadelphia, Pennsylvania, December 1976. (a)

Stunkard, A.J. *The pain of obesity.* Palo Alto, California: Bull Publishing Co., 1976. (b)

Stunkard, A.J., & Mahoney, M.J. Behavioral treatment of the eating disorders. In H. Leitenberg (Ed.), *Handbook of behavior modification and behavior therapy.* Englewood Cliffs, New Jersey: Prentice-Hall, 1976.

Subotnik, L. Spontaneous remission: Fact or artifact? *Psychological Bulletin,* 1972, **77,** 32–48.

Sulzer-Azaroff, B., & Mayer, G.R. *Applying behavior-analysis procedures with children and youth.* New York: Holt, Rinehart & Winston, 1977.

Taylor, C.B., Farquhar, J.W., Nelson, E., & Agras, S. The effects of relaxation therapy upon high blood pressure. *Archives of General Psychiatry,* 1977, **34,** 339–345.

Teasdale, J.D., Walsh, P.A., Lancashire, M., & Mathews, A.M. Group exposure for agoraphobics: A replication study. *British Journal of Psychiatry,* 1977, **130,** 186–193.

Tharp, R.G., & Wetzel, R.J. *Behavior modification in the natural environment.* New York: Academic Press, 1969.

Thase, M.E., & Moss, M.K. The relative efficacy of covert modeling procedures and guided participant modeling on the reduction of avoidance behavior. *Journal of Behavior Therapy and Experimental Psychiatry,* 1976, **7,** 7–12.

Thompson, T., & Grabowski, J. (Eds.), *Behavior modification of the mentally retarded,* 2nd edition. New York: Oxford University Press, 1977.

Thoresen, C.E. (Ed.), *Behavior modification in education: The seventy-second yearbook of the national society for the study of education.* Chicago, Illinois: University of Chicago Press, 1973.

Thoresen, C.E., & Mahoney, M.M. *Behavioral self-control.* New York: Holt, Rinehart & Winston, 1974.

Thorne, F.C. Rules of evidence in the evaluation of the effect of psychotherapy. *Journal of Clinical Psychology,* 1952, **8**, 38–41.

Townsend, R.E., House, J.F., & Addario, D. A comparison of biofeedback-mediated relaxation and group therapy in the treatment of chronic anxiety. *American Journal of Psychiatry,* 1975, **132**, 598–601.

Tracey, D.A., Briddell, D.W., & Wilson, G.T. Generalization of verbal conditioning to verbal and nonverbal behavior: Group therapy with chronic psychiatric patients. *Journal of Applied Behavior Analysis,* 1974, **7**, 391–402.

Truax, C.B. Reinforcement and non-reinforcement in Rogerian psychotherapy. *Journal of Abnormal Psychology,* 1966, **71**, 1–9.

Truax, C.B., & Mitchell, K.M. Research on certain therapist interpersonal skills in relation to process and outcome. In A.E. Bergin & S.L. Garfield (Eds.), *Handbook of psychotherapy and behavior change: An empirical analysis.* New York: John Wiley & Sons, 1971.

Trudel, G., Boisvert, J., Maruca, F., & Leroux, P. Unprogrammed reinforcement of patients' behaviors in wards with and without token economy. *Journal of Behavior Therapy and Experimental Psychiatry,* 1974, **5**, 147–149.

Turkewitz, H., O'Leary, K.D., & Ironsmith, M. Generalizati on and maintenance of appropriate behavior through self-control. *Journal of Consulting and Clinical Psychology,* 1975, **43**, 577–583.

Tuso, M.A., & Geller, E.S. Behavior analysis applied to environmental/ecological problems: A review. *Journal of Applied Behavior Analysis,* 1976, **9**, 526.

Twardosz, S., & Baer, D.M. Training two severely retarded adolescents to ask questions. *Journal of Applied Behavior Analysis,* 1973, **6**, 655–661.

Ullmann, L.P. *Institution and outcome: A comparative study of psychiatric hospitals.* London: Pergamon Press, 1967.

Ullmann, L.P., & Krasner, L. *Case studies in behavior modification.* New York: Holt, Rinehart & Winston, 1965.

Ullmann, L.P., & Krasner, L. *A psychological approach to abnormal behavior,* 2nd edition. Englewood Cliffs, New Jersey: Prentice-Hall, 1975.

Ulman, J.D., & Sulzer-Azaroff, B. Multielement baseline design in educational research. In E. Ramp & G. Semb (Eds.), *Behavior analysis: Areas of research and application.* Englewood Cliffs, New Jersey: Prentice-Hall, 1975.

Ulrich, R., Stachnik, T., & Mabry, J. (Eds.), *Control of human behavior: Behavior modification in education,* Vol. 3. Glenview, Illinois: Scott, Foresman and Company, 1974.

Valins, S., & Ray, A. Effects of cognitive desensitization on avoidance behavior. *Journal of Personality and Social Psychology,* 1967, **7**, 345–350.

Vogler, R.E., Compton, J.V., & Weissbach, T.A. Integrated behavior change techniques for alcoholics. *Journal of Consulting and Clinical Psychology,* 1975, **43**, 233–243.

Vogler, R.E., Ferstl, R., Kraemer, S., & Brengelmann, J.C. Electrical aversion conditioning of alcoholics: One year follow-up. *Journal of Behavior Therapy and Experimental Psychiatry,* 1975, **6**, 171–173.

Vogler, R.E., Lunde, S.E., Johnson, G.R., & Martin, P.L. Electrical aversion conditioning with alcoholics. *Journal of Consulting and Clinical Psychology,* 1970, **34**, 302–307.

Vogler, R.E., Lunde, S.E., & Martin, P.L. Electrical aversion conditioning with chronic alcoholics: Follow-up and suggestions for research. *Journal of Consulting and Clinical Psychology,* 1971, **36**, 450.

Wahler, R.G. Some structural aspects of deviant child behavior. *Journal of Applied Behavior Analysis,* 1975, **8**, 27–42.

Wahler, R.G., Sperling, K.A., Thomas, M.R., Teeter, N.C., & Luper, H.L. The modification of childhood stuttering: Some response-response relationships. *Journal of Experimental Child Psychology,* 1970, **9**, 411–428.

Walker, H.M., & Hops, H. The use of group and individual reinforcement contingencies in the modification of social withdrawal. In L.A. Hamerlynck, L.C. Handy, & E.J. Mash (Eds.), *Behavior change: Methodology, concepts, and practice.* Champaign, Illinois: Research Press, 1973.

Walker, H.M., Hops, H., & Johnson, S.M. Generalization and maintenance of classroom treatment effects. *Behavior Therapy,* 1975, **6**, 188–200.

Wallace, C.J. Assessment of psychotic behavior. In M. Hersen & A.S. Bellack (Eds.), *Behavioral assessment: A practical handbook.* Oxford: Pergamon Press, 1976.

Wallace, C.J., & Davis, J.R. Effects of information and reinforcement on the conversational behavior of chronic psychiatric patient dyads. *Journal of Consulting and Clinical Psychology,* 1974, **42**, 656–662.

Wallerstein, R.S. *Hospital treatment of alcoholism: A comparative experimental study.* New York: Basic Books, 1957.

Watson, J.B., & Rayner, R. Conditioned emotional reactions. *Journal of Experimental Psychology,* 1920, **3**, 1–14.

Watson, J.P., & Marks, I.M. Relevant and irrelevant fear in flooding—A crossover study of phobic patients. *Behavior Therapy,* 1971, **2**, 275–293.

Weber, S.J., & Cook, T.D. Subject effects in laboratory research: An examination of subject roles, demand characteristics, and valid inference. *Psychological Bulletin,* 1972, **77**, 273–295.

Webster, D.R., & Azrin, N.H. Required relaxation: A method of inhibiting agitative-disruptive behavior of retardates. *Behaviour Research and Therapy,* 1973, **11**, 67–78.

Weimer, W.B., & Palermo, D.S. (Eds.), *Cognition and the symbolic processes.* New York: Halstead Press, 1975.

Weiss, R.L., Birchler, G.R., & Vincent, J.P. Contractual models for negotiation training in marital dyads. *Journal of Marriage and the Family,* 1974, **36**, 321–331.

Weiss, R.L., Hops, H., & Patterson, G.R. A framework for conceptualizing marital conflict, a technology for altering it, some data for evaluating it. In L.A. Hamerlynck, L.C. Handy, & E.J. Mash (Eds.), *Behavior change: Methodology, concepts, and practice.* Champaign, Illinois: Research Press, 1973.

Weitzman, B. Behavior therapy and psychotherapy. *Psychological Review,* 1967, **74**, 300–317.

Welch, M.W., & Gist, J.W. *The open token economy system: A handbook for a behavioral approach to rehabilitation.* Springfield, Illinois: Charles C Thomas, 1974.

Werry, J.S., & Cohrssen, J. Enuresis: An etiologic and therapeutic study. *Journal of Pediatrics,* 1965, **67,** 423–431.

Wheeler, A.J., & Sulzer, B. Operant training and generalization of a verbal response form in a speech-deficient child. *Journal of Applied Behavior Analysis,* 1970, **3,** 139–147.

Whitman, T.L., Zakaras, M., & Chardos, S. Effects of reinforcement and guidance procedures on instruction-following behavior of severely retarded children. *Journal of Applied Behavior Analysis,* 1971, **4,** 283–290.

Wiens, A.N., Montague, J.R., Manaugh, T.S., & English, C.J. Pharmacological aversive counter-conditioning to alcohol in a private hospital: One-year follow-up. *Journal of Studies on Alcohol,* 1976, **37,** 1320–1324.

Wilkins, W. Desensitization: Social and cognitive factors underlying the effectiveness of Wolpe's procedure. *Psychological Bulletin,* 1971, **76,** 311–317.

Williams, M.T., Turner, S.M., Watts, J.G., Bellack, A.S., & Hersen, M. Group social skills training for chronic psychiatric patients. *European Journal of Behavioural Analysis and Modification,* in press.

Williams, R.B., Jr., & Gentry, W.D. (Eds.), *Behavioral approaches to medical treatment.* Cambridge, Massachusetts: Ballinger, 1977.

Wilson, G.T. Booze, beliefs, and behavior: Cognitive factors in alcohol use and abuse. Paper presented at NATO International Conference on Behavioral Approaches to Alcoholism, Bergen, Norway, August 1977.

Wilson, G.T. Aversion therapy for alcoholism: Issues, ethics, and evidence. In G.A. Marlatt & P.E. Nathan (Eds.), *Behavioral assessment and treatment of alcoholism.* New Brunswick, New Jersey: Center for Alcohol Studies, in press (a)

Wilson, G.T. Cognitive behavior therapy: Paradigm shift or passing phase? In J.P. Foreyt & D. Rathjen (Eds.), *Cognitive behavior therapy: Research and application,* New York: Plenum, in press. (b)

Wilson, G.T. On the much discussed nature of the term "behavior therapy." *Behavior Therapy,* in press. (c)

Wilson, G.T. Toward specifying the "nonspecifics" in behavior therapy: A social learning analysis. In M.J. Mahoney (Ed.), *Cognition and clinical science.* New York: Plenum, in press. (d)

Wilson, G.T., & Davison, G.C. Processes of fear reduction in systematic desensitization: Animal studies. *Psychological Bulletin,* 1971, **76,** 1–14.

Wilson, G.T., & Davison, G.C. Behavior therapy and homosexuality: A critical perspective. *Behavior Therapy,* 1974, **5,** 16–28.

Wilson, G.T., & Evans, I.M. Adult behavior therapy and the therapist-client relationship. In C.M. Franks & G.T. Wilson (Eds.), *Annual review of behavior therapy: Theory and practice,* Vol. IV. New York: Brunner/Mazel, 1976.

Wilson, G.T., & Evans, I.M. The therapist-client relationship in behavior therapy. In A.S. Gurman & A.M. Razin (Eds.), *The therapist's contribution to effective psychotherapy: An empirical approach.* New York: Pergamon, in press.

Wilson, G.T., Leaf, R.C., & Nathan, P.E. The aversive control of excessive alcohol consumption by chronic alcoholics in the laboratory setting. *Journal of Applied Behavior Analysis,* 1975, **8,** 13–26.

Wilson, G.T., & Tracey, D.A. An experimental analysis of aversive imagery versus electrical aversive conditioning in the treatment of chronic alcoholics. *Behaviour Research and Therapy,* 1976, **14,** 41–51.

Wincze, J.P., Leitenberg, H., & Agras, W.S. The effects of token reinforcement and feedback on the delusional verbal behavior of chronic paranoid schizophrenics. *Journal of Applied Behavior Analysis,* 1972, **5,** 247–262.

Wolf, M.M. Social validity: The case for subjective measurement or how applied behavior analysis is finding its heart. Paper presented at the American Psychological Association, Washington, D.C., September 1976.

Wolf, M.M., Giles, D.K., & Hall, R.V. Experiments with token reinforcement in a remedial classroom. *Behaviour·Research and Therapy,* 1968, **6,** 51–64.

Wollersheim, P. Effectiveness of group therapy based upon learning principles in the treatment of overweight women. *Journal of Abnormal Psychology,* 1970, **76,** 462–474.

Wolpe, J. *Psychotherapy by reciprocal inhibition.* Stanford, California: Stanford University Press, 1958.

Wolpe, J. Foreword. In Sloane, R.B., et al. *Psychotherapy versus behavior therapy.* Cambridge, Massachusetts: Harvard University Press, 1975.

Wolpe, J. Behavior therapy and its malcontents—II. Multimodal eclecticism, cognitive exclusivism and "exposure" empiricism. *Journal of Behavior Therapy and Experimental Psychiatry,* 1976, **7,** 109–116.

Wolpe, J. Inadequate behavior analysis: The Achilles heel of outcome research in behavior therapy. *Journal of Behavior Therapy and Experimental Psychiatry,* 1977, **8,** 1–4.

Wolpe, J., & Lazarus, A.A. *Behavior therapy techniques.* New York: Pergamon Press, 1966.

Wulbert, M., & Dries, R. The relative efficacy of methylphenidate (Ritalin) and behavior-modification techniques in the treatment of a hyperactive child. *Journal of Applied Behavior Analysis,* 1977, **10,** 21–31.

Yates, A.J. *Theory and practice in behavior therapy,* 2nd edition. New York: Wiley, 1975.

Yen, S., & McIntire, R.W. (Eds.), *Teaching behavior modification.* Kalamazoo, Michigan: Behaviordelia, 1976.

Zifferblatt, S.M. Increasing patient compliance through the applied analysis of behavior. *Preventive Medicine,* 1975, **4,** 173–182.

Zitrin, C.M., Klein, D.F., & Woerner, M.G. Behavior therapy, supportive psychotherapy, imipramine and phobias. Unpublished paper, Long Island Jewish-Hillside Medical Center, Hillside Division, Glen Oaks, New York, 1976.

Author Index

Subject Index

About the Authors

Alan E. Kazdin

Alan E. Kazdin currently is Professor of Psychology at the Pennsylvania State University. He received his Ph.D. at Northwestern University (1970). He has been at Pennsylvania State University since 1971 except for a leave of absence as a Fellow at the Center for Advanced Study in the Behavioral Sciences, Stanford, California (1976–1977). Kazdin is President-Elect of the Association for Advancement of Behavior Therapy. He has been an Associate Editor of the *Journal of Applied Behavior Analysis* and presently is an Associate Editor of *Behavior Therapy*. He serves on the editorial boards of the *Journal of Consulting and Clinical Psychology, Behavior Modification,* the *Journal of Behavior Therapy and Experimental Psychiatry,* and *Cognitive Research and Therapy*. He has authored *Behavior Modification in Applied Settings* and *The Token Economy: A Review and Evaluation* and has coauthored (with W. E. Craighead and M. J. Mahoney) *Behavior Modification: Principles, Issues, and Applications.*

G. Terence Wilson

G. Terence Wilson is Professor of Psychology at the Graduate School of Applied and Professional Psychology, Rutgers University. He holds graduate degrees from the University of Witwatersrand (Johannesburg) and the State University of New York at Stony Brook and was a Fellow at the Center for Advanced Study in the Behavioral Sciences, Stanford, California (1976–1977). He has served on the editorial boards of several journals including the *Journal of Consulting and Clinical Psychology, Behavior Therapy,* and *Cognitive Therapy and Research,* and is an Associate Editor of the *Journal of Applied Behavior Analysis.* He is a coauthor (with K. D. O'Leary) of *Behavior Therapy: Application and Outcome* and edits (with Cyril M. Franks) the *Annual Review of Behavior Therapy: Theory and Practice.*

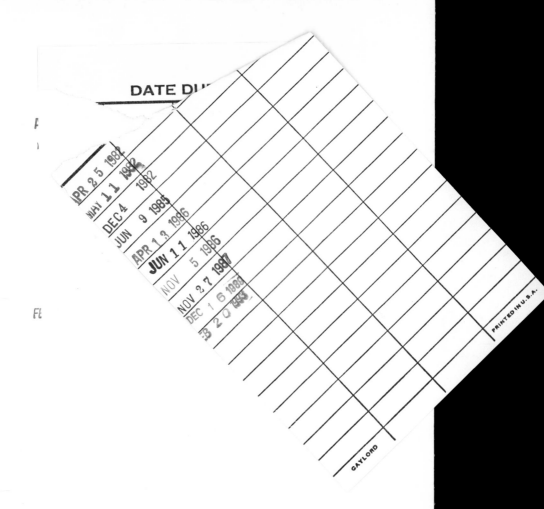